SITUATED LITERACIES

'One of the most scholarly and at the same time readable and wise collections of insights available, this book provides a base line and an inspiration from which new studies can be conducted.'

Brian V. Street, *King's College London, UK*

Literacies are situated. All uses of written language can be seen as located in particular times and places. Equally, all literate activity is indicative of broader social practices.

Situated Literacies is a rich and varied collection of key writings from leading, international scholars in the field of literacy. Each contribution, written in a clear, accessible style, makes the link between literacies in specific contexts and broader social practices.

Detailed ethnographic studies of a wide variety of specific situations, all involving real texts and lived practices, are balanced with general claims about the nature of literacy. Contributors address a coherent set of issues:

- the visual and material aspects of literacy
- concepts of time and space in relation to literacy
- the functions of literacies in shaping and sustaining identities in communities of practice
- the relationship between texts and the practices associated with their use
- the role of discourse analysis in literacy studies.

Together these studies, along with a foreword by Denny Taylor, make a timely and important contribution to understanding the ways in which literary practices are part of broader social processes and suggest directions for the further development of literacy studies. *Situated Literacies* is essential reading for anyone involved in literacy education.

Contributors: David Barton, James Paul Gee, Mary Hamilton, Roz Ivanič, Kathryn Jones, Janet Maybin, Fiona Ormerod, Simon Pardoe, Kathy Pitt, Renata de Pourbaix, Karin Tusting, Anita Wilson.

David Barton, Mary Hamilton and **Roz Ivanič** are all based at Lancaster University. David Barton is the *Literacies* series editor and has previously collaborated with Mary Hamilton on *Local Literacies* (1998). Roz Ivanič is the co-author of *The Politics of Writing* (1997).

LITERACIES

Series Editor: David Barton

Lancaster University

Literacy practices are changing rapidly in contemporary society in response to broad social, economic and technological changes: in education, the workplace, the media and in everyday life. This series reflects the burgeoning research and scholarship in the field of literacy studies and its increasingly interdisciplinary nature. The series aims to provide a home for books on reading and writing which consider literacy as a social practice and which situate it within broader institutional contexts. The books develop and draw together work in this field; they aim to be accessible, interdisciplinary and international in scope, and to cover a wide range of social and institutional contexts.

Titles in the series:

SITUATED LITERACIES
Reading and writing in context
Edited by David Barton, Mary Hamilton and Roz Ivanič

GLOBAL LITERACIES AND THE WORLD WIDE WEB
Edited by Gail E. Hawisher and Cynthia L. Selfe

MULTILITERACIES
Literacy learning and the design of social futures
Edited by Bill Cope and Mary Kalantzis

Editorial Board:

SITUATED LITERACIES

Reading and writing in context

Edited by
David Barton, Mary Hamilton and Roz Ivanič

London and New York

First published 2000
by Routledge
2 Park Square, Milton Park, Abingdon, Oxon, OX14 4RN

Simultaneously published in the USA and Canada
by Routledge
270 Madison Ave, New York NY 10016

Routledge is an imprint of the Taylor & Francis Group

Transferred to Digital Printing 2005

Typeset in Baskerville by
Keystroke, Jacaranda Lodge, Wolverhampton

British Library Cataloguing in Publication Data
A catalogue record for this book is available from the British Library

Library of Congress Cataloging in Publication Data
Situated literacies / edited by David Barton, Mary Hamilton and Roz Ivanič.
p. cm. – (Literacies)
Includes bibliographical references.
1. Literacy–Social aspects. 2. Discourse analysis. I. Barton,
David, 1949– . II. Hamilton, Mary, 1949– . III. Ivanič, Roz.
IV. Series.
LC149.S52 1999
302.2'244—dc21 99-12658
CIP

ISBN 0-415-20670-7 (hbk)
ISBN 0-415-20671-5 (pbk)

CONTENTS

FIGURES

TABLES

CONTRIBUTORS

David Barton is Professor of Language and Literacy in the Department of Linguistics, Lancaster University. He is author of *Literacy: An Introduction to the Ecology of Written Language* (1994), co-author of *Local Literacies* (1998) and an editor of *Sustaining Local Literacies* (1994) and *Writing in the Community* (1991).

James Paul Gee is Tashia Morgridge Professor of Reading in the Department of Curriculum and Instruction at the University of Wisconsin at Madison. He is the author of *Social Linguistics and Literacies* (1990, second edition 1996), *The Social Mind* (1992), with Glynda Hull and Colin Lankshear, *The New Work Order* (1996) and *Introduction to Discourse Analysis* (1999).

Mary Hamilton is Senior Research Fellow in the Department of Educational Research, Lancaster University. She has written a number of recent articles on the history and policy of adult basic education, and is co-author of *Local Literacies* (1998) and co-editor of *Worlds of Literacy* (1994).

Roz Ivanič is Senior Lecturer in the Department of Linguistics at Lancaster University. Her interests include writing as a social practice, issues of access to higher education, and alternative forms of knowledge and learning. Her publications include *Writing and Identity* (1998) and, with Romy Clark, *The Politics of Writing* (1997).

Kathryn Jones is currently based at Lancaster University. Her main interests are multilingualism, literacy and language policy. In addition to her work on the literacy practices of Welsh users, her recent research includes a project on language issues in education for the Tanzanian Ministry of Education and Culture and a project on language and gender for the Equal Opportunities Commission.

Janet Maybin is Lecturer in the School of Education at the Open University, Milton Keynes, England. Trained as a social anthropologist, she has published articles about children's informal language practices, and edited books about socially oriented research into language and literacy.

Fiona Ormerod is a Research Associate at Lancaster University. She is interested in child language and literacy development, particularly in the relationship between home and school practices, and the interaction of different semiotic modes in literacy learning.

Simon Pardoe is an Honorary Research Fellow at Lancaster University, and tutor at Lancaster Farms Young Offenders' Institution. He was previously a Senior Lecturer in Business Studies, and the Advisory Lecturer for Learning Materials, within further education in Inner London.

Kathy Pitt is currently working on a critical discourse analysis of family literacy materials at Lancaster University. She has travelled widely and done many kinds of different work, including over ten years of teaching adults in a variety of institutions.

Renata de Pourbaix teaches at the School of Linguistics and Applied Language Studies, Carleton University, Canada. Her research interests focus on the interface between new technologies and communication choices. She is currently exploring university language learners' discourse practices within virtual communities.

Karin Tusting is based at Lancaster University. She is researching the role of texts in the construction and maintenance of Catholic identity. Her interests lie in developing the study of language as social practice through combining literacy studies and critical discourse analysis. Her background is in Linguistics and French, and she is currently co-editing *New Approaches to Text Analysis* (1999) with Robert Crawshaw.

Anita Wilson is based at Lancaster University. She relies on the cooperation and good nature of members of the prison community in order to research the relevance and significance of various literacies in the day to day life of men in prison.

FOREWORD

At a meeting of the Literacy Research Group at Lancaster University, David Barton says that the generation of theory is more than an academic exercise. David is a matter of fact sort of man, but on this occasion there is an intensity about the way in which he speaks. 'If the *Guardian* keeps having titles like "Two Million Illiterates in Britain"' he says, 'then New Literacy Studies has failed and I have wasted my time.' It's a tense moment and nobody speaks. David is opening a two day conference and he quickly recovers his momentum. 'If we talk about broader cultural practices can we study them without participating in those practices?' he asks. Roz Ivanič picks up on his question and talks about power relationships and social responsibility. She raises the issue of symmetry and asks who benefits when we study literacy, but all I can think about is the statement that David has just made. Has he wasted his time? Have I? Have we?

In the United Kingdom the headlines announce 'LABOUR BACKS ELITE PUPILS', and there is talk of 'streaming', 'tracking', 'whole class teaching', and 'rote learning'. At home in the United States the headlines are equally inflammatory. Giant caps fill the front page. 'KIDS WHO CAN'T LEARN'. 'WHY ANDY COULDN'T READ'. As we sit at tables around the room at the Lancaster conference, the governments of both countries are taking control of the ways in which children are taught to read, with mandatory phonics in the UK and official definitions of 'reading' and 'reading research' in the USA. I write down what Roz has just said. Like her I believe it is imperative that we ask who benefits from our studies of literacy, and that we care about issues of symmetry, power relationships and social responsibility.

I look around the room at the researchers who are gathered there. The group has been working together for a long time. Most of them I don't know and I can't figure out who are the students and who are the professors. I think to myself that this is the way it ought to be, given what Roz just said. Janet Maybin is talking. She raises questions about the use of 'literacies'. She focuses on the levels of abstraction inherent in the term, and she compares it with the use of 'literacy practices'. Janet goes on to talk about the early drafts of the articles which appear in this book. She poses the question: 'What are our responsibilities to the participants in our studies?' Other members of the literacy research group enter the conversation. Mary Hamilton asks, 'Who defines a literacy event?' She explains, 'What's a literacy event for one person is not necessarily a literacy event for another'. The discussion continues and Mary punctuates the conversation with more questions. 'If the participants in the research don't consider a particular social practice a literacy event then should we?' Then she asks 'Whose literacies?'

Jim Gee is participating in the conversation. He critiques constructivism and explores the deep paradoxes of progressive education. He speaks of 'cutting edge pedagogies' which 'completely obscure the epistemological foundations of the discourse'. He refers to Lisa Delpit and talks of cultural capital. 'You have to know what's going on to participate', he says. I smile, because that's Ray McDermott's question, and I have already asked it this morning at the conference. I've read the research of David and Roz and I'm familiar with the genre of their written texts, but as I listen to them talk I become aware of the deeply contextualised history of their oral discourse. When Jim or I participate in the conversation we speak as outsiders, sometimes we extend the conversation but we also interrupt it. Jim is still talking. He says, 'a child has or doesn't have cultural capital'. Later David, reflecting on literacy practices that change lives, states that 'cultural capital is more complex than you've got it or you haven't got it'. It's this sort of point and counterpoint which occurs throughout the day and which pushes our thinking.

Kathryn Jones is sitting next to Jim. She's conducting an ethnographic study in Wales, documenting the literacy practices of Welsh farmers. She is also analysing the bureaucratic texts that frame their lives now that the Ministry of Agriculture in the United Kingdom is subject to the agricultural rules and regulations of the wider European community. She speaks of the official records that must be kept to identify livestock and track their movement. Kathryn explains that these documents are 'part of a whole chain of abstract legal texts' and she talks about the official 'assumption of fraud' with which I am very familiar. These are the toxic texts of which I wrote when I was working with homeless men and women in the USA, and as I make the connection between Dewi of whom Kathryn speaks, and Cindy, Sam, Laurie and Kathryn of whom I wrote in *Toxic Literacies.* I muse on the relationships between the literacy practices which occur in different settings.

The conversation continues. Fiona Ormerod and Roz Ivanič speak of the physicality of texts and of their longitudinal study of eight to eleven year olds and the texts that they construct. They have a child's 'project' with them and they talk about the importance of viewing the project as a text which is a material object with distinct physical features. They discuss the ways in which texts themselves reveal physically and textually the tools that were used to create them, and the decisions that were made in their construction. Kathy Pitt then discusses her study of family literacy, raising questions about school based programmes where reading is defined as decoding and the text is autonomous. She speaks of the colonisation of family literacy and of the ways in which literacy as social practice offers the possibility of more democratic approaches. Again I make connections, and when I leave I give a copy of *Many Families Many Literacies* to Kathy so that she can also see the relationships between the work that she is doing in the UK and the work researchers are doing in the USA.

Karin Tusting is the next to speak. Her research focuses on how time affects literacy practices. She speaks of the complexities and multiplicities of time in social life and of time always being relative to the observer. 'Writing is enduring', Karin says, 'experienced in different times'. Then she adds, 'Inscribing makes it permanent'. Kathryn picks up on what Karin is saying and she talks about texts and time and materiality, giving specific examples from her research in a Welsh farming community. Then Simon Pardoe takes us back to the questions that Roz raised about symmetry at the beginning of the conversation. Simon talks about symmetry as a methodological principle for researching literacy and students' writing. He speaks of examining texts from both the tutor's and the student's point of view, and of the need to consider sociological explanations with respect to truth and error. Anita Wilson follows, taking us into third-space theory, borderland discourse, and the inbetween literacies of prisons. Then, as if responding to Mary's question about whose literacies, Anita questions the purposes of her research. 'It's not just for my benefit,' she says. As she speaks I can again see the connections between her research and my own work with men and women who have been imprisoned, but I also recognise other relationships. Like me, Anita is also engaged in exploring the relationships between research and advocacy. Finally, Renata de Pourbaix discusses her research on computer conferencing as an emergent form of literacy. She speaks of the students she is studying as 'an emergent academic community'. She raises questions of both time and space in the literacy practices of her virtual community, and Roz joins in the discussion by talking about literacy practices that transcend both time and space. Then David jumps in and talks about the ways in which research fixes time – which in retrospect seems to be an apt place to end the meeting.

A year has passed since I was in Lancaster, and a lot has happened in that time. David and Mary have published their book *Local Literacies*, Roz has published *Identity and Writing*, and I have published *Beginning to Read and the Spin Doctors of Science*. In the UK children sit each day and do their phonics, and in the USA there are cities in which every child in a particular grade is supposed to be working on the same page, in the same way, at the same time, on any given day. 'What happens is controlled by politicians and publishers', a superintendent of schools complains. 'We're drowning', a principal tells me. In her school the pedagogical practices her teachers have been developing for the past ten years have been replaced by a highly controlled basal series. Reading has become controlled by a whole chain of legal abstract texts. 'We need freedom to be professionals', a teacher says, as she tells me there is no time for author studies, guided reading, writers' workshops or research projects. '*We know* what helps kids become good readers and writers', another teacher says, 'It's overwhelmingly depressing'.

At Hofstra University, teachers come in on a daily basis and tell us of the restrictions that are being placed on the ways in which they work with their students. The Reading Excellence Act, which defines 'reading' and 'reading research', was amended by the teachers who organised to oppose the bill, but the damage had already been done through the media blitz that can be traced to right wing think tanks and basal producers. 'Propaganda is to democracy what violence is to totalitariasm', Noam Chomsky writes in *Manufacturing Consent.* 'The techniques have been honed to a high art, far beyond anything that Orwell dreamed of'. The bill has passsed and the US has been given an official definition of how kids learn to read. Reading has been redefined based on mechanical models of cognitive research, with the brain a granary, a library, or a computer. No questions are asked about power relationships in literacy, no thought is given to symmetry, and nobody is asking 'whose literacies?'

Is the Literacy Research Group at Lancaster University wasting their time with their studies of situated literacies? How could anyone think so? As the official discourse narrows the possibilities of school based literacies, it is imperative that we continue to develop resistance theories. The dominant autonomous theories of reading in school – we can't even call them theories of literacy because reading is treated separately and writing is often ignored – tell us nothing of the literacy practices that are constitutive of the everyday lives of the children that we teach. We interrupt their learning. In *Mind and Nature* Gregory Bateson calls this 'breaking the patterns that connect'. Sharing literacy practices in use provides us with the insights we need to support the literacies of children whose learning is denied in school. It provides us with the opportunity to ensure that school literacies are culturally relevant, and that they draw upon the literacies of the children's families and communities.

In many ways my visit to Lancaster brought me home. Not geographically as some might expect, but philosophically, theoretically, epistemologically. I am comfortable with the ways of thinking and knowing of the New Literacy Studies Research Group. Each research study in *Situated Literacies* pushes my thinking and expands my conceptions of literacy practices. As I write, the doctoral students with whom I work at Hofstra are using the frameworks established by the Lancaster Research Group to conduct studies of literacy practices in their own communities. For many students this is the first time they have had the opportunity to study literacy outside of a school setting. The experience is changing their understanding of the literacies that are a part of everyday life, and they are rethinking the literacies that occur in school settings. Following in the footsteps of the Lancaster New Literacy Studies group, we have formed our own research group, and based upon the research that has taken place at Lancaster University we are planning a study of the literacy practices – the local literacies – in an urban New York community. *Situated Literacies* adds new dimensions to our studies. In every way, it is an important book that challenges the unjustifiable generalisations about literacy derived from positivistic science.

Denny Taylor
Hofstra University
7 November 1998

INTRODUCTION

Exploring situated literacies

Literacies are situated. All uses of written language can be seen as located in particular times and places. Equally, all literate activity is indicative of broader social practices. This volume is concerned with making the links between literacies in specific contexts and broader social structuring. By examining the fine detail of specific grounded examples, each study reported here contributes to understanding the ways in which literacy practices are part of broader social processes.

The common starting point of these studies is the framework which has become known as the new literacy studies (as in Gee 1996; Street 1995; Barton 1994); the common approach is that literacy is seen as a social practice. Each study is concerned with exploring what this means and expanding our understanding of literacy. This is done by making connections between empirical data and social theory. Different areas of social theory are drawn upon, including theories of globalisation, media and visual design, social semiotics, bureaucracies and power relations, time, cultural identity and scientific knowledge. Many of the papers start from the detailed analysis of particular literacy events; others start from texts of various sorts. Several papers link the analysis of practices with the analysis of texts, drawing specifically on critical discourse analysis to illuminate the connection between texts and practices. The papers are based upon real texts and lived practices and locate literacy in time, space and discourse. The overall aim of the volume is to explore the commonalities in these different studies and to develop literacy studies further.

One result of the focus on literacy as a social practice is that literacies are positioned in relation to the social institutions and power relations which sustain them. Education is one such institution and half of the papers are concerned with educational settings as diverse as conventional schooling, work-place literacy programmes, college courses and family literacy programmes. The other papers focus on a range of different social institutions, including prison, the church and the media. Methodological implications and issues concerning reflexivity are pursued by several of the papers.

Most of the authors of these chapters are members of the Literacy Research Group at Lancaster University and many have worked together for several years, developing a distinct approach to the study of literacy. The idea of this book evolved from activities associated with a theme year entitled 'Expanding the New Literacy Studies'. As part of this we invited three other literacy researchers to join us in a seminar at Lancaster and to comment on our work. They were Jim Gee from the University of Wisconsin, Denny Taylor from Hofstra University and Janet Maybin from the Open University. Jim Gee and Janet Maybin have contributed chapters to this book, and Denny Taylor provided the Foreword.

The first chapter, 'Literacy practices', by David Barton and Mary Hamilton introduces the concept of 'literacy practices' as central to a social view of literacy, and expands on six propositions about the nature of literacy from this perspective. It presents a view of literacy as multiple, patterned by power relationships, purposeful, historically situated, and changing over time. The six propositions which are spelt out in detail in this chapter acted as a starting-point for the development of the other papers in the book, and provide the orienting theory for reading them.

The second chapter, 'Expanding the new literacy studies: using photographs to explore literacy as social practice', develops from the first by reporting on a research project which has prompted a need to refine the terms we use to describe and account for literacy practices. Mary Hamilton discusses the distinction between 'literacy events' and 'literacy practices', and identifies key elements in literacy events from the work of other social theorists and her own empirical work. She then discusses the role of visual data in social research, and in particular the sorts of information that can be derived from studying media images of social phenomena. The main part of her paper consists of an analysis of 400 media images of literacy, subdivided into interactions between people and texts, literacy in the environment, writing on the body and reproductions of documents. She uses the key elements of literacy events which she identified at the start of the chapter to distinguish among these four categories, and to show how 'literacy practices' cannot be tied to 'literacy events' in a simple way. She demonstrates how the frozen moment of time captured by photographs draws attention to the complexity of literacy practices. This is revealing both about the nature of literacy and about the representation of literacy in the media.

'Time' is an aspect of literacy practices which, being invisible, is often overlooked. In Chapter 3, 'The new literacy studies and time: an exploration', Karin Tusting presents a complex view of time, drawing on the work of several social theorists, particularly Adam (1990). She applies Adam's multifaceted conception of time to each of the six propositions about literacy presented in Chapter 1, showing how this perspective can contribute a more insightful understanding of aspects of socially situated literacy practices. She then demonstrates the sorts of insights that can be gained from a focus on time, drawing on her own research into the literacy practices of a Catholic community. She shows how aspects of time are inscribed in the literacy events associated with children's First Holy Communion, and how the literacy practices associated with the weekly parish newsletter are used to synchronise community activities on many levels.

In Chapter 4, 'There is no escape from third-space theory: Borderland Discourse and the "in-between" literacies of prisons', Anita Wilson argues that it is misleading to make a binary distinction between 'inside' prison and 'outside', but rather it is important to recognise a 'third space': a culture which is neither one nor the other, but built out of elements of both. She applies this important insight to examples of literacy practices she has observed in a variety of incarcerative settings. She argues that it is important to recognise the influence of both a discourse of 'Literacy as autonomous' and a discourse of 'literacies as sociocultural constructs' in the creation of literacies in this 'third space'. She points to similarities and differences between specific prisons in the way in which the 'third space' is configured in terms of literacy practices, showing how its maintenance is essential to the construction of identity for those who live within it.

In the next chapter, 'Becoming just another alphanumeric code: farmers' encounters with the literacy and discourse practices of agricultural bureaucracy at the livestock auction', Kathryn Jones examines the literacy practices of bilingual Welsh hill farmers, using detailed ethnographic methods to investigate their participation in a regular livestock auction. The chapter brings together the detail of locally situated literacy practices with their broader significance as part of national and European Union control of agricultural production. Drawing on social theory she demonstrates how globalisation and disembedding, two characteristics of contemporary society, are realised through people's participation in bureaucratic literacy practices.

In Chapter 6, 'Texts in practices: interpreting the physical characteristics of texts', Fiona Ormerod and Roz Ivanič describe one aspect of their longitudinal research with children in years 4 to 6 of primary school. The research is concerned with changes over time in the literacy practices and products associated with the children's independent project work at home and at school. A multi-modal textual analysis focuses on the linguistic, visual and physical features of the projects whilst interviews with the children provide information about the events, process, thoughts and feelings surrounding their work. This chapter draws on social semiotic theory to focus particularly on the materiality of the texts: the ways in which the physical characteristics of the texts contribute to an understanding of the children's literacy practices.

In Chapter 7, 'Family literacy: a pedagogy for the future?', Kathy Pitt turns to another area of educational practice. She examines the government's vision for family literacy projects in Britain; these are educational initiatives which teach parents and their children in an integrated programme. Using critical discourse analysis she examines the view of family literacy education portrayed in a set of Basic Skills Agency training videos. Although drawing on traditions of both adult education and school education, the predominant setting for family literacy education portrayed in these videos is the school; a narrow range of texts is featured in the videos, and a limited set of school-based literacy practices. She argues that this narrow conception of literacy fails to provide a foundation for adults and children to participate in the contemporary world of changing literacy demands in work and public domains.

Renata de Pourbaix follows a group of college students who are second language learners encountering computer-mediated conferencing for the first time. Her chapter, 'Emergent literacy practices in an electronic community', discusses issues that arise when a new discourse community is established using an unfamiliar medium of communication. She identifies the situation as an intersection of academic, informational and technological literacies and traces the students' changing practices as they negotiate a set of conventions to govern this new, virtual space. She looks at the ways in which participants moderate one another's behaviour, developing shared expectations and standards; how multiple identities are revealed through the elaboration of electronic signatures and increasingly complex patterns of message posting practices. Finally, she speculates about the educational effects of this process, showing how participants' understanding and awareness of the three intersecting literacies grow as they gain control of the medium of communication.

In Chapter 9, 'Respect and the pursuit of "symmetry"' *in researching literacy and student writing,* Simon Pardoe examines the writing practices of environmental science students and tutors' responses to them. The central argument of this chapter is a methodological one: that qualitative, ethnographic research does not just offer detail to complement the powerful generalisations of large scale quantitative studies, but offers a different kind of insight, one that fundamentally challenges the assumptions underlying such studies, based on notions of respect and relativism. The author draws on theories from the sociology of scientific knowledge and the public understanding of science. In particular he demonstrates how the principle of *symmetry* could be a valuable one for literacy studies in researching the diversity of practices and writers' accounts of them. The principle of symmetry asserts that we should be equally interested in the social and discursive processes involved in producing knowledge claims, whether these are currently accepted as 'fact' or rejected as 'error'. The texts produced by student scientists must be linked to the conventional practices, established professional knowledges, evidence, information and beliefs that both students and tutors are drawing on and which shape their understandings and evaluations of what they are doing.

In 'Researching literacy practices: learning from activities with teachers and students' David Barton describes a methodology for researching literacy practices which can be incorporated into courses which aim to challenge the idea of literacy as an autonomous skill and introduce students to the theoretical perspective of literacy as situated practice. The methodology uses observation, interview, photographic and other means of recording data from everyday situations. He locates this work within theories of learning which emphasise the importance of critical reflexivity for understanding and therefore make the crucial links between research, teaching and learning. The chapter gives details of how this approach has been implemented in a variety of educational situations, including cross-cultural investigations. As well as learning about specific practices (including their own) students come to understand what is meant by a social theory of literacy and their research can contribute to knowledge about literacy practices more generally.

The next two chapters act as commentaries on New Literacy Studies (NLS) as represented by the research reported in the earlier chapters. In Chapter 11, 'The new literacy studies: from "socially situated" to the work of the social', Jim Gee starts by considering the NLS as one of a number of movements, centred in a wide variety of different disciplines, which over the last few decades have taken a 'social turn' away from a focus on individuals and 'private' minds to a focus on knowledge, words and deeds in their local, social, cultural and political contexts. After a brief overview of fourteen of these movements, he discusses how this turn to the social and cultural has become less politically progressive than some people had hoped and thought would be the case. In particular, he shows how high-tech, global, 'new capitalism' has recruited themes of socially situated and distributed knowledge and meaning in the service both of profit and of new forms of hegemonic control of workers. He closes with a reconsideration of the NLS that seeks to highlight the political through a renewed introduction of humans as active agents in the construction, negotiation over, and transformation of their social worlds. He also argues that this viewpoint renders the sorts of research carried out by the Lancaster group crucial for further progress and renewal in the New Literacy Studies.

In the next chapter, 'The new literacy studies: context, intertextuality and discourse', Janet Maybin asks what is distinctive about research within the NLS and what kinds of insights research within this framework can provide. Looking at work within the field of literacy, we can see a continuing cross-fertilisation of ideas and research practices from the different movements, as notions of how to document and analyse literacy in social practice have been developed during the 1980s and 1990s. Building on Heath's definition of a 'literacy event', subsequent work in the field has developed a more complex treatment of social and cultural context, and more sophisticated notions of the role of discourse in shaping the function and meaning of reading and writing activities. The studies in this book have grown out of, and are part of, this continuing exploration and theorisation of the social and cultural aspects of people's literacy activities. In this chapter she draws together and discusses some emerging patterns in the researchers' documentation and analysis of literacy events and the social relationships, values, attitudes and feelings involved. She focuses in particular on the treatment of *context*, *intertextuality*, and *discourse*, which reveal the pivotal role of literacy practices in articulating the links between individual people's everyday experience, and broader social institutions and structures.

In the final chapter, 'New literacy studies at the interchange', Karin Tusting, Roz Ivanič and Anita Wilson discuss particular themes identified in earlier chapters which make links between the chapters and which suggest directions for the further development of literacy studies. Some of these are themes, such as *symmetry* or *time*, which were identified in particular chapters and which could be usefully pursued more broadly. Other themes, such as ways of theorising the relation of texts and practices, arise in many chapters; here the discussion is integrated and pointers are given for developing new analytical frameworks for future studies of situated literacies.

References

Adam, B. (1990) *Time and Social Theory*, Cambridge: Polity Press.

Barton, D. (1994) *Literacy: An Introduction to the Ecology of Written Language*, Oxford: Blackwell.

Gee, J. (1996) *Social Linguistics and Literacies: Ideology in Discourses*, 2nd edn, London: Falmer Press.

Street, B. (1995) *Social Literacies*, London: Longman.

1

LITERACY PRACTICES[1]

David Barton and Mary Hamilton

A social theory of literacy: practices and events

In this chapter we provide a framework in terms of a theory of literacy. It is a brief overview of a social theory of literacy. This can be seen as the starting-point or orienting theory, which the detailed studies in this book then expand upon, react to and develop. We define what is meant by literacy practices and literacy events and explain some of the tenets of a social theory of literacy. This is pursued in Barton and Hamilton (1998), where a further example of situated literacies not covered in this book can be found.

We present here the theory of literacy as social practice in the form of a set of six propositions about the nature of literacy, as in Figure 1.1. The starting-point of this approach is the assertion that *literacy is a social practice*, and the propositions are an elaboration of this. The discussion is a development on that in Barton (1994, pp. 34–52), where contemporary approaches to literacy are discussed within the framework of the metaphor of ecology. The notion of *literacy practices* offers a powerful way of conceptualising the link between the activities of reading and writing and the social structures in which they are embedded and which they help shape. When we talk about practices, then, this is not just the superficial choice of a word but the possibilities that this perspective offers for new theoretical understandings about literacy.

Our interest is in social practices in which literacy has a role; hence the basic unit of a social theory of literacy is that of *literacy practices*. Literacy practices are the general cultural ways of utilising written language which people draw upon in their lives. In the simplest sense literacy practices are what people do with literacy. However practices are not observable units of behaviour since they also involve values, attitudes, feelings and social relationships (see Street 1993, p. 12). This includes people's awareness of literacy, constructions of literacy and discourses of literacy, how people talk about and make sense of literacy. These are processes internal to the individual; at the same time, practices are the social processes which

- *Literacy is best understood as a set of social practices; these can be inferred from events which are mediated by written texts.*
- *There are different literacies associated with different domains of life.*
- *Literacy practices are patterned by social institutions and power relationships, and some literacies are more dominant, visible and influential than others.*
- *Literacy practices are purposeful and embedded in broader social goals and cultural practices.*
- *Literacy is historically situated.*
- *Literacy practices change and new ones are frequently acquired through processes of informal learning and sense making.*

Figure 1.1 Literacy as social practice

connect people with one another, and they include shared cognitions represented in ideologies and social identities. Practices are shaped by social rules which regulate the use and distribution of texts, prescribing who may produce and have access to them. They straddle the distinction between individual and social worlds, and literacy practices are more usefully understood as existing in the relations between people, within groups and communities, rather than as a set of properties residing in individuals.

To avoid confusion, it is worth emphasising that this usage is different from situations where the word *practice* is used to mean learning to do something by repetition. It is also different from the way the term is used in recent international surveys of literacy, to refer to 'common or typical activities or tasks' (OECD/Statistics Canada 1996). The notion of practices as we have defined it above – cultural ways of utilising literacy – is a more abstract one that cannot wholly be contained in observable activities and tasks.

Turning to another basic concept, *literacy events* are activities where literacy has a role. Usually there is a written text, or texts, central to the activity and there may be talk around the text. Events are observable episodes which arise from practices and are shaped by them. The notion of events stresses the situated nature of literacy, that it always exists in a social context. It is parallel to ideas developed in sociolinguistics and also, as Jay Lemke has pointed out, to Bahktin's assertion that the starting point for the analysis of spoken language should be 'the social event of verbal interaction', rather than the formal linguistic properties of texts in isolation (Lemke 1995).

Many literacy events in life are regular, repeated activities, and these can often be a useful starting-point for research into literacy. Some events are linked into routine sequences and these may be part of the formal procedures and expectations of social institutions like work-places, schools and welfare agencies. Some events are structured by the more informal expectations and pressures of the home or peer group. Texts are a crucial part of literacy events and the study of literacy is partly a study of texts and how they are produced and used. These three components, practices, events and texts, provide the first proposition of a social theory of literacy, that: *literacy is best understood as a set of social practices; these are observable in events which are mediated by written texts.* The local literacies study was concerned with identifying the events and texts of everyday life and describing people's associated practices. Our prime interest there was to analyse events in order to learn about practices. As with the definition of practices, we take a straightforward view of events at this point, as being activities which involve written texts; discussion throughout this book returns to the definitions of these terms. An example of an everyday literacy event, taken from the local literacies study, is that of cooking a pudding; it is described in Figure 1.2.

This work complements other studies, primarily in Linguistics, which focus on the analysis of texts. The study of everyday literacy practices points attention to the texts of everyday life, the texts of personal life; these are distinct from other texts which are more usually studied such as educational texts, mass media texts and other published texts. Work in the field of literacy studies adds the perspective of practices to studies of texts, encompassing what people do with texts and what these activities mean to them. In our own work, practices remain central and we are led to examine how texts fit into the practices of people's lives, rather than the other way round. Nevertheless, we see the full study of written language, as exemplified in the chapters in this book, as being the analysis of both texts and practices.

Once one begins to think in terms of literacy events there are certain things about the nature of reading and writing which become apparent. For instance, in many literacy events there is a mixture of written and spoken language. Many studies of literacy practices have print literacy and written texts as their starting point but it is clear that in literacy events people use written language in an integrated way as part of a range of semiotic systems; these semiotic systems include mathematical systems, musical notation, maps and other non-text based images. The cookery text has numeracy mixed with print literacy and the recipes come from books, magazines, television and orally from friends and relatives. By identifying

When baking a lemon pie in her kitchen, Rita follows a recipe. She uses it to check the amounts of the ingredients. She estimates the approximate amounts, using teacups and spoons chosen specially for this purpose. The recipe is hand written on a piece of note-paper; it was written out from a book by a friend more than ten years ago. The first time she read the recipe carefully at each stage, but now she only looks at it once or twice. The piece of paper is marked and greasy by having been near the cooking surface on many occasions. It is kept in an envelope with other hand-written recipes and ones cut out of magazines and newspapers. The envelope and some cookery books are on a shelf in the kitchen. The books range in age and condition and include some by Robert Carrier. Sometimes she sits and reads them for pleasure.

Rita does not always go through the same set of activities in making the pie. Sometimes she makes double the amount described in the recipe if more people will be eating it. Sometimes she cooks the pie with her daughter Hayley helping her where necessary. Sometimes she enjoys cooking it, at other times it is more of a chore, when time is limited or she has other things she would rather do. Rita has passed the recipe on to several friends who have enjoyed the pie.

Rita does not always follow recipes exactly, but will add herbs and spices to taste; sometimes she makes up recipes; at one point she describes making a vegetable and pasta dish similar to one she had had as a take-away meal. She exchanges recipes with other people, although she does not lend her books.

Figure 1.2 Cooking literacy

literacy as one of a range of communicative resources available to members of a community, we can examine some of the ways in which it is located in relation to other mass media and new technologies. This is especially pertinent at a time of rapidly changing technologies.

Looking at different literacy events it is clear that literacy is not the same in all contexts; rather, there are different *literacies*. The notion of different literacies has several senses: for example, practices which involve different media or symbolic systems, such as a film or computer, can be regarded as different literacies, as in *film literacy* and *computer literacy*. Another sense is that practices in different cultures and languages can be regarded as different literacies. While accepting these senses of the term, the main way in which we use the notion here is to say that literacies are coherent configurations of literacy practices; often these sets of practices are identifiable and named, as in *academic literacy* or *work-place literacy* and they are associated with particular aspects of cultural life.

This means that, within a given culture, *there are different literacies associated with different domains of life.* Contemporary life can be analysed in a simple way into domains of activity, such as home, school, work-place. It is a useful starting-point to examine the distinct practices in these domains, and then to compare, for example, home and school, or school and work-place. We begin with the home domain and everyday life. The home is often identified as a primary domain in people's literacy lives, for example by James Gee (1990), and central to people's developing sense of social identity. Work is another identifiable domain, where relationships and resources are often structured quite differently from in the home. We might expect the practices associated with cooking, for example, to be quite different in the home and in the work-place – supported, learned and carried out in different ways. The division of labour is different in institutional kitchens, the scale of the operations, the clothing people wear when cooking, the health and safety precautions they are required to take, and so on. Such practices contribute to the idea that people participate in distinct *discourse communities*, in different domains of life. These communities are groups of people held together by their characteristic ways of talking, acting, valuing, interpreting and using written language. (See discussion in Swales 1990, pp. 23–7.)

Domains, and the discourse communities associated with them, are not clear-cut, however: there are questions of the permeability of boundaries, of leakages and movement between boundaries, and of overlap between domains. Home and community, for instance, are often treated as being the same domain; nevertheless they are distinct in many ways, including the dimension of public and private behaviour. An important part of the local literacies study was to clarify the domain being studied and to tease apart notions of home, household, neighbourhood and community. Another aspect is the extent to which this domain is a distinct one with its own practices, and the extent to which the practices that exist in the home originate there, or home practices are exported to other domains. In particular, the private home context appears to be infiltrated by practices from many different public domains.

Domains are structured, patterned contexts within which literacy is used and learned. Activities within these domains are not accidental or randomly varying: there are particular configurations of literacy practices and there are regular ways in which people act in many literacy events in particular contexts. Various institutions support and structure activities in particular domains of life. These include family, religion and education, which are all social institutions. Some of these institutions are more formally structured than others, with explicit rules for procedures, documentation and legal penalties for infringement, whilst others are regulated by the pressure of social conventions and attitudes. Particular literacies have been created by and are structured and sustained by these institutions. Part of this study aims to highlight the ways in which institutions support particular literacy practices.

Socially powerful institutions, such as education, tend to support dominant literacy practices. These dominant practices can be seen as part of whole discourse formations, institutionalised configurations of power and knowledge which are embodied in social relationships. Other vernacular literacies which exist in people's everyday lives are less visible and less supported. This means that *literacy practices are patterned by social institutions and power relationships, and some literacies are more dominant, visible and influential than others.* One can contrast dominant literacies and vernacular literacies; many of the studies in this book are concerned more with documenting the vernacular literacies which exist, and with exploring their relationship to more dominant literacies.

People are active in what they do and *literacy practices are purposeful and embedded in broader social goals and cultural practices.* Whilst some reading and writing is carried out as an end in itself, typically literacy is a means to some other end. Any study of literacy practices must therefore situate reading and writing activities in these broader contexts and motivations for use. In the cooking example, for instance, the aim is to bake a lemon pie, and the reading of a recipe is incidental to this aim. The recipe is incorporated into a broader set of domestic social practices associated with providing food and caring for children, and it reflects broader social relationships and gendered divisions of labour.

Classic studies of literacies in the home, such as those by Heath (1983) and Taylor and Dorsey-Gaines (1988), have offered classifications of the functions and uses of literacy for individuals. This approach can be revealing in providing an overview of the range of literacy practices in a community and, in doing so, links back to Richard Hoggart's classic work from 1957, *The Uses of Literacy.* In practice, however, it is often difficult to identify discrete functions, what is counted as a function is inconsistent, and they overlap a great deal (as discussed in Barton 1994, pp. 152–4; see also Clark and Ivanič 1997, Chapter 5). In the current study we move beyond this approach, to examine how literacy activities are supported, sustained, learned and impeded in people's lives and relationships, and the social meanings they have. It is very clear from our local literacies work that a particular type of text, such as diary or letter, cannot be used as a basis for assigning functions, as reading or writing any vernacular text can serve many functions; people appropriate texts for their own ends. Just as a text does not have autonomous meanings which are independent of its social context of use, a text also does not have a set of functions independent of the social meanings with which it is imbued.

A first step in reconceptualising literacy is to accept the multiple functions literacy may serve in a given activity, where it can replace spoken language, enable communication, solve a practical problem or act as a memory aid – in some cases, all at the same time. It is also possible to explore the further work which literacy can do in an activity, and the social meanings it takes on. For instance, there are ways in which literacy acts as *evidence*, as *display*, as *threat*, and as *ritual*. Texts can have multiple roles in an activity and literacy can act in different ways for the different participants in a literacy event; people can be incorporated into the literacy practices of others without reading or writing a single word. The acts of reading and writing are not the only ways in which texts are assigned meaning (as in Barton and Hamilton 1998, Chapter 14).

It is important to shift from a conception of literacy located in individuals to examine ways in which people in groups utilise literacy. In this way literacy becomes a community resource, realised in social relationships rather than a property of individuals. This is true at various levels; at the detailed micro level it can refer to the fact that in particular literacy events there are often several participants taking on different roles and creating something more than their individual practices. At a broader macro level it can mean the ways in which whole communities use literacy. There are social rules about who can produce and use particular literacies and we wish to examine this social regulation of texts. Shifting away from literacy as an individual attribute is one of the most important implications of a practice account of literacy, and one of the ways in which it differs most from more traditional accounts. The ways in which literacy acts as a resource for different sorts of groups are a central theme of Barton and Hamilton (1998), which describes some of the ways in which families, local communities and organisations regulate and are regulated by literacy practices.

Literacy practices are culturally constructed, and, like all cultural phenomena, they have their roots in the past. To understand contemporary literacy it is necessary to document the ways in which *literacy is historically situated*: literacy practices are as fluid, dynamic and changing as the lives and societies of which they are a part. We need a historical approach for an understanding of the ideology, culture and traditions on which current practices are based. The influences of one hundred years of compulsory schooling in Britain, or several centuries of organised religion, can be identified in the same way as influences from the past decade can be identified. These influences are located partly in the literacy practices themselves, complemented by family memories which go back to the beginning of the century and earlier. There is also a broader context of a cultural history of three thousand years of literacy in the world, and the ways in which this shapes contemporary practices.

A person's practices can also be located in their own history of literacy. In order to understand this we need to take a life history approach, observing the history within a person's life. There are several dimensions to this: people use literacy to make changes in their lives; literacy changes people and people find themselves in the contemporary world of changing literacy practices. The literacy practices an individual engages with change across their lifetime, as a result of changing demands, available resources, as well as the possibilities and their interests.

Related to the constructed nature of literacy, any theory of literacy implies a theory of learning. *Literacy practices change and new ones are frequently acquired through processes of informal learning and sense making* as well as formal education and training. This learning takes place in particular social contexts and part of this learning is the internalisation of social processes. It is therefore important to understand the nature of informal and vernacular learning strategies and the nature of situated cognition, linking with the work of researchers influenced by Lev Vygotsky, such as Sylvia Scribner, Jean Lave and colleagues (Scribner 1984; Lave and Wenger, 1991). For this it is necessary to draw upon people's insights into how they learn, their theories about literacy and education, the vernacular strategies they use to learn new literacies. We start out from the position that people's understanding of literacy is an important aspect of their learning, and that people's theories guide their actions. It is here that a study of literacy practices has its most immediate links with education.

Note

1 This chapter is adapted from pages 6–13 of D. Barton and M. Hamilton, *Local Literacies: Reading and Writing in One Community*, Routledge, 1998, with permission of the publishers.

References

Barton, D. (1994) *Literacy: An Introduction to the Ecology of Written Language*, Oxford: Blackwell.

Barton, D. and Hamilton, M. (1998) *Local Literacies: Reading and Writing in One Community*, London: Routledge.

Clark, R. and Ivanič, R. (1997) *The Politics of Writing*, London: Routledge.

Gee, J. P. (1990) *Social Linguistics and Literacies: Ideology in Discourses*, London: Falmer Press.

Heath, S. (1983) *Ways with Words: Language, Life and Work in Communities and Classrooms*, Cambridge: Cambridge University Press.

Hoggart, R. (1957) *The Uses of Literacy: Aspects of Working-Class Life*, London: Chatto.

Lave, J. and Wenger, E. (1991) *Situated Learning: Legitimate Peripheral Participation*, Cambridge: Cambridge University Press.

Lemke, J. (1995) *Textual Politics: Discourse and Social Dynamics*, London: Taylor and Francis.

OECD/Statistics Canada (1996) *Literacy, Economy and Society*, Ontario: OECD.

Scribner, S. (1984) 'Studying working intelligence', in B. Rogoff and J. Lave (eds) *Everyday Cognition: Its Development in Social Context*, Cambridge, MA: Harvard University Press.

Street, B. (ed.) (1993) *Cross-cultural Approaches to Literacy*, Cambridge: Cambridge University Press.

Swales, J. (1990) *Genre Analysis: English in Academic and Research Settings*, Cambridge: Cambridge University Press.

Taylor, D. and Dorsey-Gaines, C. (1988) *Growing Up Literate: Learning from Inner-city Families*, London: Heinemann.

2

EXPANDING THE NEW LITERACY STUDIES

Using photographs to explore literacy as social practice[1]

Mary Hamilton

Introduction: literacy practices and events

This chapter shows how visual data can be used to focus and extend knowledge of literacy as social practice in two ways, by

(a) identifying the elements of literacy practices more closely and, through this,
(b) challenging and elaborating the underlying concepts of *practice* and *event.*

A theory of literacy as social practice as put forward by Street (1984), Gee (1992) and Barton and Hamilton (1998) emphasises the social relationships and institutions within which literacy is embedded. This is in contrast to traditional approaches to literacy which construe it as a set of cognitive skills possessed (or lacked) by individuals. Literacy events have been identified as constituents of literacy practices. According to Shirley Heath a literacy event is 'any occasion in which a piece of writing is integral to the nature of participants' interactions and their interpretative processes' (Heath 1982, p. 93).

Brian Street explains that he employs 'literacy practices' as a broader concept 'pitched at a higher level of abstraction and referring to both behaviour and conceptualisations related to the use of reading and/or writing. "Literacy practices" incorporate not only "literacy events" as empirical occasions to which literacy is integral, but also "folk models" of those events and the ideological preconceptions that underpin them' (1993, pp. 12–13).

Empirical research into literacy practices collects (among other kinds of evidence) observable data about literacy events: who is using written texts, where and how. Photographs are particularly appropriate for documenting these aspects of literacy since they are able to capture moments in which interactions around texts take place. The photographs can then be used directly as a source of such data – either photographs taken as part of the research, or an existing corpus of images such as those in newspapers.

In taking our own photographs or in noticing existing photographs taken by others, we came with a particular idea of what would count as a typical literacy event: we looked for images of people interacting directly with written texts. The prototypical literacy event we began with is exemplified in Figure 2.1. This is an ethnographic image showing *activities in the job centre* which include a range of interactions involving people and texts, such as people reading displays of job vacancies, newspapers, or filling in application and registration forms. Another example is a newspaper image of *two Muscovites discussing a ballot paper*, with one woman helping another to cast her vote for the first time, explaining how she should fill in her ballot paper.

These prototypical images contain four elements which were the starting points for the analysis offered in this paper: participants, settings, artefacts and activities (see Table 2.1). These elements are very close to those that Theo van Leeuwen identifies as constituents of social practices more

Table 2.1 Basic elements of literacy events and practices

Elements visible within literacy events (These may be captured in photographs)	*Non-visible constituents of literacy practices (These may only be inferred from photographs)*
Participants: the people who can be seen to be interacting with the written texts	The hidden participants – other people, or groups of people involved in the social relationships of producing, interpreting, circulating and otherwise regulating written texts
Settings: the immediate physical circumstances in which the interaction takes place	The domain of practice within which the event takes place and takes its sense and social purpose
Artefacts: the material tools and accessories that are involved in the interaction (including the texts)	All the other resources brought to the literacy practice including non-material values, understandings, ways of thinking, feeling, skills and knowledge
Activities: the actions performed by participants in the literacy event	Structured routines and pathways that facilitate or regulate actions; rules of appropriacy and eligibility – who does/doesn't, can/can't engage in particular activities

generally: participants, activities, performance indicators (how to do it right); appropriate times and places; tools needed; dress; eligibility criteria for the participants (who is allowed to act) (see van Leeuwen 1993, p. 204). They also relate to discussions of social practice offered by James Paul Gee (Gee 1992, p. 123) and Anthony Giddens (Giddens 1984); to Pierre Bourdieu's notion of *habitus* and to the work of theorists such as Jurgen Habermas and Erving Goffman who have emphasised the importance of face to face interaction in social practice, focusing on people as actors in the everyday 'lifeworld'. Those who work in the sociolinguistic tradition of Dell Hymes (see Duranti 1988) have also used such elements in their attempts to characterise the nature of context.

It is important to stress again, however, that in terms of the definitions offered in Table 2.1, visible literacy events are just the tip of an iceberg: literacy practices can only be *inferred* from observable evidence because they include invisible resources, such as knowledge and feelings; they embody social purposes and values; and they are part of a constantly changing context, both spatial and temporal. It is only some visual traces of literacy practices that are captured in still photographs – observable, but frozen moments of a dynamic process. Even aspects of literacy practices that seem clearly visible in events are in fact defined only in relation to cultural knowledge that the viewer brings. It might therefore be more precise to say that *all* elements of practices are inferred from the images, but some with more direct visual cues than others.

Events are local activities, whereas practices are more global patterns. The relationship between them is described differently by different disciplines where people are working to understand the social construction of technologies and how cultural systems operate (as in LaTour 1993; Silverstone and Hirsch, 1994; Myers 1996). Of particular interest to a theory of literacy as social practice, are the ideas of Dorothy Smith who has noted the special role of written texts in social practices, how they solidify fleeting local actions and interactions across time and space and are implicated in what she calls 'the relations of ruling' (Smith, 1993). Bruno LaTour refers to a 'thread of practices and instruments, of documents and translations' which 'allow us to pass with continuity from the local to the global' (LaTour 1993, p. 121). In the research described here, we are engaged in tracing the threads of literacy practices through contemporary social life, using visual evidence of them.

The uses of visual data in social research

The use of visual data has a long history in some disciplines, for example visual anthropology, while it has been largely ignored in others (see Prosser 1995, 1997). Specifically, photos can be used in a number of ways, many of which are listed in Hodge and Jones (1996). These include using photographs as an interview stimulus and more generally as a catalyst for further research. They can be part of a systematic record of evidence. They may function as a reflective tool for developing theory; to create visual narratives of particular aspects of cultures, as data themselves or to set a context for other data collection. They can be used to explore image making within communities of interest to the researcher – for example creating photo stories with members of those communities, discussing existing images such as family albums, wedding pictures, holiday snaps.

In the ethnographic research into literacy carried out by members of the Literacy Research Group, we began by taking our own photographs and encouraged others to do so, using visual images as an additional source of data and as a reflective tool for developing theory through observation and discussion (Barton *et al.* 1993; Hamilton and Davies 1993; Hodge and Jones 1996). Some of us[1] are now analysing newspaper photographs and other media images of literacy, which changes the nature of the research considerably (Hamilton and Rimmershaw 1996, and see Chapter 7, this volume).

Researching media images of literacy

Mass produced images of literacy practices are of interest to us because of our long-standing concern with the ways that literacy and those with literacy difficulties are portrayed (through both words and pictures) in the media and through the publicity of government agencies such as the Basic Skills Agency. The public image of those with literacy difficulties is often a negative one but we were not sure how this negativity was achieved or how to go about constructing alternative, 'positive' images. The central issue is one of public discourses of literacy and how to critique them.

Stories about literacy standards and education appear regularly in the press. Such stories and especially the headlines that advertise them are overwhelmingly concerned with failure in literacy amongst both adults and children. It would be more accurate to assume, that where the key word 'literacy' occurs in the newspaper, it is really signifying a concern with 'illiteracy'. A selection of headlines gives the flavour, as in Table 2.2.

However, it is not in the context of these literacy stories that most of the visual images of literacy practices occur. In general, they are elsewhere in the newspaper – within stories about daily political, domestic and sporting events, disputes with neighbours and bureaucracies. Their occurrence, of course, varies with the type of stories regularly carried in a particular paper. The pictures we have collected do include ones that are part of stories about education, and some stories are directly concerned with an aspect of common literacy practices (e.g. reading popular magazines or having a legal writ served on you). However, nowhere is the word 'literacy' itself used in these stories – it appears to have a very constrained meaning.

Table 2.2 Literacy hits the headlines

Children's reading ability plummets	*Guardian*	29.6.90
A fifth of 10-year-olds 'have trouble writing'	*Guardian*	5.7.90
Kids who can't read	*D. Mirror*	23.4.91
Prince hits at school 'illiteracy'	*Guardian*	23.4.91
Schools fail to teach basics of reading	*D. Telegraph*	23.4.91
Seven-year-olds' reading shows decline in study	*Guardian*	14.2.92
Literacy skills lacked by six million adults	*D. Telegraph*	16.6.93
The dangers of illiteracy	*Sun. Times*	10.4.94
The 3Rs scandal	*Daily Mail*	24.1.95
Study shows half of adults illiterate	*Guardian*	21.1.97

We were interested in what we could deduce from newspaper photos about literacy practices in contemporary societies and in how these images compared with the photos we collected in the course of our ethnographic research. In Barton *et al.* (1993) we listed the features about literacy practices that we had noticed from our own photographs. These were mostly descriptive statements that had emerged from discussions, such as *showing that you are literate can be a statement of your social identity and status* and *lots of writing is not done on paper.* They were intended to be thought provoking but were not analysed any further.

At first we collected and examined the media images in the same intuitive way that we had looked at our own photographs: we clipped out 'interesting' images and put them side by side, grouping and labelling them in ways that seemed to make sense. From this process came an additional set of themes. We noticed *Literacy as Threat* in images which depict the 'paperwork stress' associated with money, exam results or legal proceedings. *Literacy as Defiance* was shown in images of oppositional literacy practices, such as graffiti, demonstrations and political protests.

In other images literacy objects such as cheques, letters, identity papers, lottery tickets, ballot papers, and medical paperwork are given, received and shown. These emphasised the role of *Literacy as Evidence* in legal and bureaucratic power structures.

We noticed the frequent images in which literacy signifies that a person has a particular status. These are often of politicians, stockbrokers, businessmen, judges, barristers, doctors, academics, committee members, clerics or media people. Typical pictures show the person carrying papers/newspapers/folders under their arm or posing with papers or books around them. We called this *Literacy as Accessory.*

Related themes were *Literacy as Display* in images where the literacy signifies individual or group identity, whether on banners, slogans on clothes (T-shirts and hats mainly, but also face paint, and badges) and *Literacy as Ritual Public Gesture*: images of the symbolic role of the signature (its legal power within political and business deals, its social status in autographs) and the 'commemorative' role of literacy within public celebrations and ceremonies (wreaths, plaques, graves, rolls of honour, trophies and certificates).

We were struck by the emotional force of many of the media images, and by the public nature of the practices represented, in contrast to the more personal literacies emphasised within education. In this respect these media images had more in common with our ethnographic literacy photographs than with the images to be found in promotional literature about literacy. However, our early intuitive surveys of different newspapers suggested that there are consistent differences between them in the kind of practices depicted that are connected to patterns of news coverage. At this stage we felt the need for better definition of the images we were collecting and a better understanding of what kind of sample we were looking at. How frequently do images of literacy practices appear as a percentage of all images in the papers? And how are they patterned in different kinds of newspapers? These questions led us to attempt a more systematic analysis of newspaper images of literacy.

We decided to concentrate on four newspapers for the systematic pilot study. Our aim was to select 100 images depicting aspects of literacy practices from each of these papers as our experience suggested that this would be a big enough sample to begin to see recurrent patterns and themes in a given paper. From our earlier experience we expected to have to search through 20 or more issues of each paper to reach this target number. In fact, one of our first discoveries was that when we applied systematic and inclusive criteria to selecting images, there were many more in each issue of the papers than we had noticed before. The maximum number of issues we needed for any of the papers was five. This meant that we got to know individual issues of the papers very well indeed.

Comparing ethnographic photographs and media photographs

As sources of data about literacy practices, ethnographic photographs and media photographs are clearly different in status. Several points seem important to mention here before I go on to discuss the content of the images we collected:

(a) Our move from ethnography to media analysis has been a move from *creating* pictures for research purposes to systematically *classifying existing* ones. As I will discuss later, the process of creating a corpus of photographs is selective in ways that we may not be aware of and which tends to reinforce our guiding theory. Systematically analysing an existing corpus of photographs, however, makes us confront that theory and challenges the boundaries we have been working within.

(b) There is a difference in who is documenting the literacy practices and why – researcher/informant or photojournalist and editors? The ethnographic researcher is interested in *direct documentation* of literacy practices, capturing the 'visual traces' of such practices. Media photographs are *socially salient, public representations* of literacy practices created by photojournalists and editors as part of creating newsworthy messages and meanings. The literacy practices represented in the images are therefore recontextualised within a discourse of news.

Actually, in both cases, literacy practices are being mediated, both by the producer of the image and by the technological form of the image itself: we are always looking at representations. Nevertheless, it is possible to make inferences from these representations about the literacy practices that exist in contemporary societies, since both types of photograph are created with a documentary intent, to offer information and comment on some aspects of reality. They are not offered as fictional images.

(c) *Ethnographic and media photographs are selected according to different criteria.* The ethnographer looks for 'typical' or 'critical' literacy moments, in order to document the everyday rather than the extraordinary. Newspaper photographs are selected according to news values, the ideology and readership of the paper. Highly valued photographs are those that depict novel, extreme, shocking, elite persons or negative events (Bell 1991). However, as Stuart Hall reminds us – what is 'newsworthy' would not be understandable without a background of shared assumptions of what is normal or typical practice. 'News stories often pivot around the unexpected, the problematic, but an event is only unexpected because it breaches our normal expectations of the world' (Hall 1981, p. 235). Therefore news also tells us about common culture and stereotypes. For this reason, news stories, even though they focus on atypical events can still provide information about common literacy practices. For example although the photograph from the Russian election was part of a story about the novelty of the practice of casting a ballot for the women depicted in it, it is assumed that this practice is a familiar part of the everyday world of the *Guardian* newspaper reader.

(d) *The ethnographer and the photojournalist exert different degrees of control over the images they produce.* The photojournalist typically has more awareness of the visual language of professional photography, and media images are typically more deliberately and skilfully constructed than ethnographic ones. Posed pictures, re-enactments and montages are more acceptable within newspapers (within the limits of certain conventions) than within ethnographic research – although some artifice is still involved in visual ethnography. Compared with the ethnographer, the photojournalist has little control over how their pictures will be used: sub-editors decide captions and headlines and integrate the pictures with a story that the photographer may have little or no knowledge of and even re-use the same photograph matched with different stories at different times.

(e) *There is an integral relationship between the pictures and the text in a news item:* media photographs are designed to be 'read' as part of a carefully constructed narrative that almost always includes extended written text and often juxtaposes several pictures. Ethnographic photographs, in contrast, are assumed to be meaning-bearing in themselves and are often accompanied by only very brief written captions or explanations (Edwards 1992). In practice, however, ethnographic photographs (as Barton *et al.* (1993) have noted) seem to invite questions, explanation and discussion, which may be either oral or written.

(f) *A variety of relationships are possible between the photographer and the photographed,* both within journalism and ethnography. These can range from the unknowing and potentially exploitative relationship of the candid shot, to the knowing collaboration where participants are involved in both the construction and interpretation of the image.

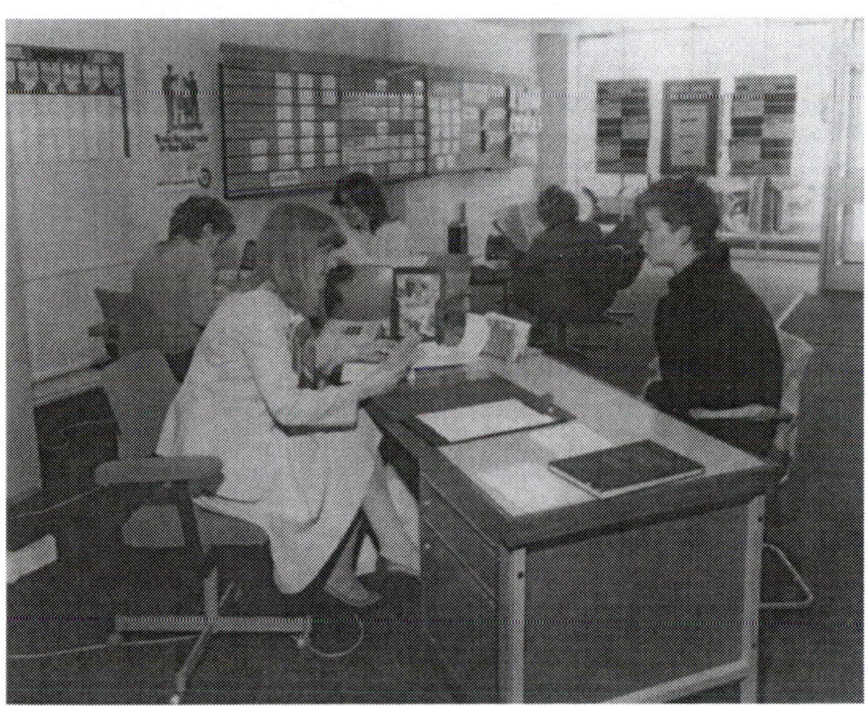

Figure 2.1 Activities in the job centre

Figure 2.2 Footing the bills

Figure 2.3 Giant cheque

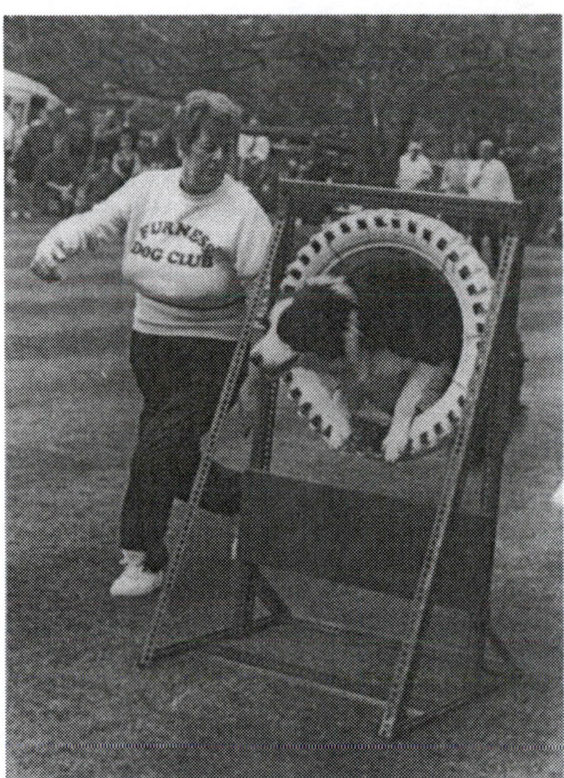

Figure 2.4 Furness dog club

Extending definitions of the elements and boundaries of a literacy event

The process of systematically searching and sorting newspaper images of literacy, (rather than picking out images we liked or which looked interesting) has lead to a number of useful difficulties in applying the framework of literacy as social practice. Our initial assumptions have proved to be too vague and simplistic and we have been forced to elaborate them and take account of all kinds of images that initially seemed like marginal cases. In fact, such cases can reveal a great deal and making sense of them is a powerful way of pushing at theory, developing a more flexible framework for analysis that includes features we might have previously overlooked.

In this section I demonstrate how the working concepts of literacy events and practices have been challenged and extended by systematic analysis of existing photographs. I will use a few, key photographs to illustrate the points I want to make.

The analysis started from a theory of literacy as social practice and has made some use of the concepts introduced by Gunther Kress and Theo van Leeuwen in their book *Reading Images: The Grammar of Visual Design* (1996). I have some hesitations about the very structured approach offered by a theory of visual design, in that it can lead to convoluted distinctions and arguments which may serve the analyst's purposes while having little apparent relationship to the strategies of users and producers of the images. Overall, however, I agree with Carey Jewitt (1997) who argues that the advantage of using a systematic approach to analysing images such as that offered by Kress and van Leeuwen is that it enables the researcher to offer a clear account of the process by which readings of an image can be justified and challenged. It offers a procedure for analysis and for presenting data derived from images.

The perspective of social semiotics is attractive in that it recognises the existence of regularities in the meanings signified by particular features of images, whilst understanding these as cultural resources that are drawn on and created by producers and viewers of the images in particular contexts and social relationships. It therefore avoids, to some extent, the structuralist limitations of more traditional semiotic approaches.

Selecting images from the newspapers was a far more complex process than we had imagined. The original idea was to only include examples of actual 'literacy events' as defined by Shirley Heath (occasions in which a piece of writing is integral to the nature of participants' interactions and their interpretative processes). However, what counts as an 'interaction' between people and texts turns out to be problematic. There are many images where some written text is present and significant in identifying settings and/or participants in the image although no active literacy event is taking place (e.g. business signs in the background, wearing an identification badge). Even more marginal, are the images in which the literacy element seems entirely incidental to the main focus of the narrative but still represents a trace of a literacy practice that *could* be drawn on as the focus of a different story (e.g. a car registration plate, or a logo on a T-shirt).

We ended up classifying the sample of media photographs into four main types in terms of their literacy content: (1) interactions between people and texts; (2) literacy in the environment; (3) writing on the body; and (4) reproductions of documents. The frequency with which these categories occurred in our data is shown in Table 2.3. Some of the photographs contained several of the categories. In this case we prioritised them so that if there was a literacy event present, the photo was classified under this heading. This means that the figures in categories 2, 3 and 4 underrepresent the actual occurrence of these depictions of literacy in our corpus.

I will discuss each of the four categories in turn and show what happens to our notions of participants, settings, artefacts, activities, events and

Table 2.3 Frequency of occurrence of different kinds of literacy practices represented in a corpus of 400 images, drawn from a sample of 4 different newspapers

Name of newspaper	*Total images in sample of papers examined – around 5 or 6 issues of each paper*	*Total literacy images found in sample (as % of all images in paper)*	*Interactions between people and written texts*	*Literacy in the environment*	*Writing on the body*	*Reproduction of document*
Daily Telegraph	441	100 (23%)	42	33	21	4
Daily Mail	632	100 (16%)	23	31	36	10
Lancaster Guardian	283	100 (35%)	45	23	30	2
Westmoreland Gazette	434	100 (23%)	41	31	26	2
TOTAL	1790	400	151 (38%)	118 (30%)	113 (28%)	18 (5%)

practices. In each case I will argue that these notions change and the changes tell us something more about literacy practices: who can participate and how, how literacy-related artefacts and resources are used, the relationship between specific settings and the broader domains of which they are a part.

Interactions between people and written texts

These were the images closest to our original prototypical literacy events They include images where a time-bounded interaction between people and texts or other literacy-related artefacts is taking place. As Table 2.3 shows, they are the biggest single category of images (38%) but they are not the majority of the images we collected. Examples of images classified under this heading are to be found in Figures 2.2 and 2.3.

- *Participants* The participants in these images are always animate and mainly human. It can be problematic to decide exactly who is involved in the literacy event where there are queues or crowds of people depicted. Animals can be incorporated into literacy events (as in a race horse with writing on the saddle-cloth).
- *Settings* The physical setting is not always clear enough to give a full description of where the event is taking place. In some cases the immediate setting may not be clear although the domain of activity is very obvious (in sports pictures for example). Sometimes the physical setting may be domestic, while the domain of the literacy practice is not (e.g. reading a legal document, disputing bills). This shows the permeability of domains of practice and their unstable relationship with the immediate physical location.
- *Artefacts* A wide variety of material resources is involved in these literacy events. These include papers and other writing surfaces such as gravestones, banners and trophies; writing tools, including computers and spray cans, but also accessories such as desks, shelves of books and office paraphernalia in general. It is difficult to know where to draw the boundaries of such accessories. For example, shelves can be storage or display spaces for books but also for many other non-literacy-related artefacts.
- *Activities* We began by thinking in terms of activities as simply reading and writing, but a very large number of newspaper images involve people displaying, holding, inspecting, possessing or giving, discussing and disputing written texts of various sorts. The media make special use of the function of *Literacy as Evidence* and have appropriated this for their own ends. It is the basis for many specially composed images as I will go on to discuss later.

Literacy in the environment

There was a great deal of literacy in the background environment of the images which was not directly referred to in the narrative of the news item. In some cases it is obvious that the literacy elements had been intentionally included in the image, to identify people, locations and affiliations. In other cases they appear to be entirely incidental.

Three in ten of the literacy images we collected were of this type. Many are commercial and regulatory signs (traffic signs and other 'DO NOT' notices), symbols of ownership and identity such as name plates or car registration plates. These are typically on buildings, and also appear on vehicles and animals. People are surrounded by these signs and labels, but at the moment that is captured in the photograph they are ignoring, or not interacting with them.

However, these signs and labels still signify the existence of the practices and purposes that have generated them – practices which are taken for granted but are extremely important and pervasive in social life. People are in some way *incorporated* into these practices without having to engage actively in reading or writing as such. Sometimes they are merely surrounded by them. This seems to provide a way of connecting the notion of 'events' with the idea of the 'visual environment' which otherwise might be quite separate.

- *Participants* No *animate* participants need be in these images, so if we wish to say that there are participants in these images, we may have to extend the notion to inanimate objects as Kress and van Leeuwen do (e.g. planes, hotels, bottles). Where people and animals are included, it is not apparent that they are participating in the literacy practice. There is no visible evidence of active participation. Incorporation may be a better term to describe their relationship with the literacy practice.
- *Settings* A variety of immediate locations are apparent. The setting is an essential part of the image or is the entire image.
- *Artefacts* The artefacts present in the images are identifying signs and labels on buildings, vehicles and consumer products (especially food and cosmetics); office accessories; shelves of books; public notices and posters designed to inform and/or regulate behaviour.
- *Activities* No literacy activities are apparent in these images. Where animate subjects are included they are passively juxtaposed with the written texts, sometimes sitting in/on a labelled object or climbing on it. Where the body of a person or animal is in physical contact with the literacy artefact (touching or leaning on it) we have included this as a literacy event, though the distinction is obviously shaky. Borderline cases we have struggled with include all kinds of labelled vehicles (such as wheelchairs, canoes and horses). It was the flimsiness of this

distinction between being in physical contact with and being in the vicinity of literacy artefacts that made us feel we needed to include background signs and labels as part of literacy practices. In these cases it is the literacy activities themselves that have to be inferred – those involved in composing and producing the signs (in a spatially and chronologically removed setting/domain) and the (incidental) reading of them, possibly in the photographed setting.

Literacy on the body

These images include the large amount of writing which can be seen on people's clothing; for example sponsors' names, brandnames, writing as patterns on clothing, tattoos and body painting. It also includes badges which identify people, such as those worn by people at conferences or as part of a work-related uniform. Twenty-eight per cent of the literacy images we collected depicted writing on the body.

This writing is an extension of the extremely widespread practices of decorating the human body with a variety of visual semiotics long studied by anthropologists (see Blanchard 1994). Wearing text is not a one-off event but may extend over a long period of time. The nature of the statement being made varies. Sometimes it is a voluntary and personal statement of social identity (as for example in Figure 2.4, *I am a member of the Furness Dog Club*) or ideological/sociopolitical affiliation (for example *Save the Whales*). In many cases however, it is a required statement of institutional affiliation connected with an official identity (tax adviser, policeman, member of the Manchester United football team). Many occupations require the wearing of specially marked uniforms; sponsorship deals often require the wearing of brand logos and this imposed marking is akin to the branding of property (including animals and slaves) and to the public branding used to shame those defined as deviant – as in a recent report of prostitutes in the US having to wear special sweatshirts with slogans identifying them, dunce's caps, etc. An interesting further complication to the meanings of writing on the body is when football strips, including the sponsor's brand name, become appropriated by fans and used as voluntary statements of solidarity with their team.

- *Participants* Participants in these images are mainly human, but may also be other animals. Where inanimate objects are marked with text these have been included under *literacy in the environment.*
- *Settings* The predominant domain is sport, with some business and leisure settings. *Public* inscription is an essential element: this writing exists to be seen by others. (There are of course many other markings on body and clothes which are specifically designed *not* to be seen in public and so are unlikely to appear in newspaper photographs.)

- *Artefacts* The body is used as a writing surface. This may be the *skin* itself, from branding, tattooing, painting, and all the subtle variations such as marks in body sweat; *clothing* of all sorts – writing is printed on clothing and sewn into it; things are pinned to or draped over clothing, including special artefacts like sandwich boards and identification tags that have been made specifically for the display of written text on the body. The degree of permanency of the marking varies.
- *Activities* If there is any literacy activity depicted in these photographs, it is the act of wearing/displaying the message. Different meanings arise from this, dependent on how far this is a *voluntary* display of personal identity, solidarity or affiliation or an imposed identity or role.

Reproductions of documents

The use of written documents as images in their own right underlines the function of literacy as evidence and its usefulness in the context of news. This was a minor category in our corpus (only 5% of the images) but these representations have occurred in other newspapers we have examined and were part of other images in our collection that also contain prototypical literacy events. Examples are front pages of newspapers or popular magazines used to cross reference the story to a previous publication, a frequent strategy used in the tabloid press. In other items the image is of a document (a letter, medical form or legal document) without people or a surrounding visual context. In these cases the function of the document coincides with the function of the photographic image as a *witness* to the actuality it represents: 'this really happened, see for yourself'.

- *Participants* There are no animate participants in these images. The reproduced texts themselves are the only participants in the image.
- *Settings* Often no physical surroundings are apparent in the image, but the domain of practice is clear from the content/type of document and is clearly identified in the accompanying text.
- *Artefacts* The documents themselves.
- *Activities* No activities are depicted in these images. The documents are displayed as evidence and the only interaction is between the reader and the journalist. This interaction between reader and journalist is part of all media images. In this group of images it is the only interaction and is used to represent a common literacy event from the everyday world, namely the written document as witness. This is where the function of *literacy* as evidence and *photographs* as evidence coincide and the media make use of their documentary role.

Conclusions

Looking for visual traces of literacy practices in newspaper photographs demonstrates without a doubt that literacy is part of social practice. The photographs provide a wide variety of examples from the public arena of what this might mean. Analysing such pictures systematically demands that we operationalise the underlying concepts and pin them down to specific instances. This causes some difficulties especially with the idea of literacy events which implies active participation and interaction between people.

We have found images that we wish to classify as representing traces of literacy practices but which have no visible animate participants; settings which show a disjuncture between the immediate physical circumstances and the relevant domain. A variety of resources are shown as 'accessories' to literacy events and it is not always clear whether to include them within the boundaries of the literacy event (for example, a shelf on which books and other objects are stored); in some images the only literacy-related 'activities' are that human beings are in the vicinity of a written text or wearing one and in these cases the notions of 'event' and 'activity' become uncomfortably stretched.

Many of the photos we have collected suggest, therefore, that we need to reconsider ideas of what *interaction* may consist of in a literacy event and perhaps the adequacy of the notion of *event* itself. We need a form of description that acknowledges that people can participate in literacy practices in a range of ways, some of which involve a very passive role. By the same token, what seem to be inert texts in the background of an image, can be active in a variety of ways in shaping and signifying the meanings of social practices. We also need ways of specifying the relationship between domains of practice and the physical settings in which people move and act and some way of incorporating the time dimension of peoples' encounters with texts – in short, to allow for displacements of space and time (see Chapter 3 in this volume).

It is also clear from the variety of posed and artificially constructed images in our collection, that the media appropriate literacy practices for their own ends. They make use of the functions of literacy as *display* and *evidence* to create specially fabricated literacy events for the newspaper reader in order to represent real-life happenings in a convincing and entertaining way, as in the giant cheque displayed in Figure 2.3. In turn, people who wish to advertise their cause or product through the media respond by wearing appropriate T-shirts and logos, displaying banners and creating photo-opportunities that will get noticed by the press.

In summary, this study of newspaper photographs has provided visual evidence of a wide range of everyday, public literacy practices, and confronted us with the need to refine the terms we use to describe and account for these. In addition, it shows how the process of public photography both creates and interacts with everyday literacy practices, thereby revealing a great deal about the underlying significance (meanings and values) of literacy, especially as it relates to themes of public ritual, display and evidence.

Note

1 The research on which this paper is based has involved several members of the Literacy Research Group over the last year or so. In particular, Rachel Rimmershaw and I obtained funding from the Nuffield Foundation to carry out pilot work on newspaper photographs during the summer and autumn of 1996. We were assisted in this project by Stella Proctor, Janet Elleray, David Barton and Kathy Pitt. Where I use 'we' in this paper I am acknowledging the ideas developed by this group.

References

Barton, D., Hamilton, M., Ivanič, R., Ormerod, F., Padmore, S., Pardoe, S. and Rimmershaw, R. (1993) 'Photographing Literacy Practices', *Changing English,* Vol. 1 No. 1.

Barton, D. and Hamilton, M. (1998) *Local Literacies: Reading and Writing in One Community,* Routledge pp. 127–40.

Bell, A. (1991) *The Language of News Media,* Oxford: Blackwell.

Blanchard, M. (1994) 'Post-Bourgeois Tattoo: Reflections of Skin Writing in Later Capitalist Societies', in L. Taylor (ed.) *Visualising Theory: Selected Essays from V.A.R. 1990–1994,* London: Routledge, pp. 287–300.

Duranti, A. (1988) 'The Ethnography of Speaking: Toward a Linguistics of the Praxis', in T. Newmeyer (ed.) *Linguistics: The Cambridge Survey. Vol. IV; Language: The Socio-Cultural Context,* Cambridge: Cambridge University Press, pp. 210–28.

Edwards, E. (1992) *Anthropology and Photography 1860–1920,* London: Yale University Press and Royal Anthropological Institute.

Gee, J. (1992) *The Social Mind: Language, Ideology and Social Practice,* New York: Bergin and Garvey.

Giddens, A. (1984) *The Constitution of Society,* Cambridge: Polity Press.

Hall, S. (1981) 'The Determination of News Photographs', in S. Cohen and J. Young (eds) *The Manufacture of News: Social Problems, Deviance and the Mass Media,* London: Constable.

Hamilton, M. and Davies, P. (1993) 'Literacy and Long-term Unemployment: Options for Adult Guidance, Support and Training', *British Journal of Education and Work* 6(2): 5–19.

Hamilton, M. and Rimmershaw, R. (1996) 'Exploring Public Images of Literacy', Final Report to the Nuffield Foundation.

Heath, S. (1982) 'Protean Shapes in Literacy Events', in D. Tannen (ed.) *Spoken and Written Language: Exploring Orality and Literacy,* Norwood, NJ: Ablex.

Hodge, R. and Jones, K. (1996) 'Photography in Collaborative Research: "Insider" "Outsider" Images and Understandings of Multilingual Literacy Practices', Centre for the Study of Language in Social Life Working Paper 83, Lancaster University.

Jewitt, C. (1997) 'Images of Men: Male Sexuality in Sexual Health Leaflets and Posters for Young People', *Sociological Research Online* 2(2), http://www.socresonline.org.uk/socresonline/2/2/6.html.

Kress,G. and van Leeuwen, T. (1996) *Reading Images: The Grammar of Visual Design*, London: Routledge.

LaTour, B. (1993) *We Have Never Been Modern*, Hemel Hempstead: Harvester Wheatsheaf.

Myers, G. (1996) 'Out of the Laboratory and Down to the Bay: Writing in Science and Technology Studies', *Written Communication* 13: 5–43.

Prosser, J. (1995) 'Photography in Educational Research: Constructing a Methodology', paper presented at the Annual Conference of the British Educational Research Association, Lancaster University.

Prosser, J. (ed.) (1997) *Image Based Research* London: UCL Press Ltd/Taylor & Francis.

Silverstone, R and Hirsch, E. (eds) (1994) *Consuming Technologies*, London: Routledge.

Smith, D. (1993) *Texts, Facts and Femininity: Exploring the Relations of Ruling*, London: Routledge.

Street, B. (1984) *Literacy in Theory and Practice*, Cambridge: Cambridge University Press.

Street, B. (ed.) (1993) *Literacy in Cross-Cultural Perspective*, Cambridge: Cambridge University Press.

van Leeuwen, T. (1993) 'Genre and Field in Critical Discourse Analysis: A Synopsis', *Discourse and Society* 4(2): 193–223.

3

THE NEW LITERACY STUDIES AND TIME

An exploration

Karin Tusting

This chapter, inspired by the title of the Lancaster Literacy Research Group's theme year 'Expanding the New Literacy Studies', explores one direction in which the theory of New Literacy Studies might fruitfully be expanded. The word 'exploration' underlines the fact that I am in no way attempting to develop a coherent theory of 'literacy and time'. Rather, in this chapter I work through some of the implications of considering time as an important element of literacy practices, exploring some of the ways in which this focus could develop the theory of literacy practices further.

A focus on time as a significant element in all social practices can contribute to a more insightful understanding of aspects of socially situated literacy practices. Adam (1990) in her book *Time and Social Theory* argues for the need for an active and complex focus on time in all social research. I will briefly present her arguments, which form the theoretical background for this exploration, before moving on to consider literacy studies in particular with respect to these ideas, drawing on the 'six facets' of literacy studies outlined by Barton and Hamilton in Chapter 1. Finally I will demonstrate in practical terms the insights that can be gained from a focus on time, drawing on my own current research about the literacy practices of a Catholic community to illustrate the theoretical points made.

Time and social theory

Adam's argument begins with the claim that social scientists have traditionally had a narrow conception of time. Those working with positivist approaches in particular have largely limited the idea of 'time' to its being merely an abstract measure, a quantitative, linear, invariable measuring stick against which 'lived experience' can be set and quantified; a concept which takes little or no account of people's experiences of the variable and subjective nature of time as they live it.

Social theorists working within more interpretivist traditions have nuanced this concept somewhat, often attempting to account for or describe some of the ways in which time is experienced as lived reality rather than as abstract measure. This is often expressed in terms of dualisms or dualities, loosely along the lines of comparing 'natural' (for which read linear, invariable, quantifiable) time with 'human' time as it is experienced in social life: Adam cites Young's (1988) distinction between linear and cyclical time, Jaques' (1982) distinction between intent and succession, Elias' (1984) distinction between experiential and structural time and Bergson's (1910) distinction between *durée* and *temps*.

However, even these approaches have their shortcomings as Adam points out. First, time is too complex a concept to be dealt with in terms of simple dualities, a point that will be further developed below. And second, despite the focus on the different types of time that are experienced, these dualities still distinguish between 'social' time – the subjective, complex, shifting time of human experience – and 'natural' time, which somehow still exists 'out there' as an absolute linear measure. This positivist conception of time is therefore seen as being 'real' time, with humans' subjective experience being simply a construction of the human mind. Adam claims that the reverse is true; that the concept of a time line divided into equal intervals within which events occur only exists itself as a human construct, and that in the natural sciences the concepts of relativity, the central importance of the observer's position and the qualitative experience of time have replaced the positivist image of an objective time line.

She begins by demonstrating that while this concept of linear 'clock' time is often seen by social scientists as being the basic 'scientific' conception of time, in the natural sciences this idea has been superseded. In the nineteenth century scientists, particularly experimental scientists, were indeed working within this paradigm; but in the twentieth century it has been challenged by developments in the physical sciences in particular. Einsteinian theories of relativity have destroyed the idea that such a thing as an 'absolute' time may exist, showing instead how any measurement or experience of time is always relative to the position of the observer. The 'linear measuring rod' concept of clock time is a time that is, in theory at least, reversible. However, thermodynamic theories and theories of dissipative systems show that time can never in reality be reversible; the arrow of time moves inexorably in only one direction. Quantum physics has shown that any experience of time is fundamentally affected by the framework of the observer. Modern physics, the 'hardest' of the natural sciences, has posed fundamental challenges to the idea of 'natural' time as being an absolute, linear, reversible measuring rod, and instead shows how the 'natural' time of the physicists has more in common with the 'social' time of the social scientists; in both worlds, all experience of time relates to the relativity and subjectivity of the observer, and there is no absolute measure of time in nature that can be separated from this experience.

After examining conceptions of time from the physical sciences Adam moves closer to human experience in examining biological time. She stresses the fact that although similar things occur over and over again in the biological world – cells reproduce in the same way, processes of growth and decay follow a continual cycle – this does not imply that 'biological time' itself is cyclical. Rather she stresses the fact that biological time is characterised by 'rhythmic repetition', that is to say that similar events continually recur but 'the same' event can never happen more than once. This enables change – for example evolutionary change – to happen within the framework of continually repeated similar events, as small changes in one cycle can develop into vast differences many cycles later.

Another weakness Adam identifies in social scientific thought is the division into 'past', 'present' and 'future'. Tracing the history of this division back to St Augustine, she demonstrates how Western philosophy has often seen this temporal division as a distinction between the real and the ideal, where only the present is 'real', and the past and the future, not currently being experienced, only exist as ideas in people's minds. This concept is rejected. Instead, through her analysis of biological time she demonstrates how both 'past' and 'future' are constructed in the flow of present experience.

It is not only humans who construct the past and the future in the present through social practices involving memory, foresight and anticipation. Many animals learn over time: dogs remember that getting into a car leads to an unpleasant experience after one trip to the vet's and refuse to enter the car again; birds construct nests for chicks as yet unborn; salmon return to the spawning grounds of their youth to breed, drawing on their past to construct the future. The effects of these actions construct the past and the future as part of the flow of present experience, whether or not the animals themselves are aware of the abstract concepts of 'past' and 'future' positioned as 'unreal' in the Western tradition. A more useful conceptualisation of time that does not reify the distinction between past, present and future is to acknowledge the way in which 'past' and 'future' are emergent in 'present'; a continually revocable past is constructed in an emergent present, which is at the same time constructing and extending into the future. History is constructed and reconstructed in a constantly emergent present, while the contingent nature of the future is transcended by such activities as planning.

The other main weakness of social scientific conceptions of time has been their analytical dualistic approach. To split human experience of time into two or three categories – the distinction between past, present and future for instance, or the distinction between linear and cyclical time – is to miss out on the complexity of the different types of time within which we exist at every moment. Imagine for example someone waiting for a bus, already a few minutes late for work, engaged while waiting in the literacy practices of reading a newspaper and checking the bus timetable. The experience of 'being late' could affect their experience of the passage of time in at least two ways: the wait for the bus might seem agonisingly long, while the watch on their wrist might seem to be registering the minutes flying by to make them later and later, giving a simultaneous experience of time passing very quickly and very slowly; a paradox that, when lived, does not seem to hold any internal contradictions. In reading the newspaper they are constructing the past in the present, experiencing the accounts of events of the previous day or week. In thinking about the day ahead of them they are constructing the future in the present. Random events such as noticing a familiar perfume on a passer-by might reawaken memories from their own life-history, whether in their recent past or in their early childhood, with events in the present reconstructing the distant past unexpectedly. In the simple act of waiting for a bus to go to work they are participating in rhythmic repetition of cyclically-patterned events with the same thing happening at the same time every day – 'routine' time. And over the course of their life they will have picked up implicit cultural knowledge about what to do in the particular circumstance of waiting for a bus; their present demeanour is being constructed on the basis of memory of all the previous instances of rhythmic repetition of this event that have gone into constructing this person's way of waiting for a bus – an emergence of the past in the present very different from the active reconstruction of past events implied in the reading of a newspaper. In checking the bus timetable to see when the next bus is due they are using a literacy practice to gain knowledge about institutional time, the routines of the bus company. And this is only the beginning of an analysis of the times at play in this moment; any event in human existence can be spoken of in terms of innumerable different aspects of time, many of which are intimately interrelated in sometimes paradoxical ways.

According to Adam, theories of time which try to take account of this multiplicity of aspects have been few. Adam's analysis, like the example above, demonstrates that time can be seen as having a very large number of aspects, which interrelate in complex ways; any attempt to impose a universal duality or typology will inevitably miss important aspects of time, and cannot address the interrelatedness of these aspects. Dualities and typologies have a tendency to hierarchise, reify differences and suggest clear-cut separations between different 'times' which are at best unhelpful, at worst misleading. Instead, Adam argues for a conceptualisation of time in social theory in forms of interdependent 'levels', giving access to the multiplicity of aspects of time that may be relevant.

She also claims that most social theorists should widen the time frames with which they are working. We are not merely affected by or living with 'human' time, that is to say the sociotemporal order (Zerubavel 1981). We are living examples of biological and physical times; our reliance on technology means the hugely fast speeds of sub-atomic time and communications at the speed of light are an everyday part of our existence; the existence of nuclear weaponry means that all our futures could be shadowed by an end to our time as a species. We need to expand our time frames to encompass all of these aspects if we are to have a theory of time which can deal with the multiple aspects of time lived in social life.

Time and the New Literacy Studies

The key points of Adam's argument which I want to develop with respect to the theory of literacy practices are the following: the conceptualisation of time as having multiple interrelating levels; the idea of the past and the future being constructed and controlled in an emergent present; and the fact that experiences of time are always relative to the place and framework of the observer. These points will inform the following discussion, which draws on the six facets of the New Literacy Studies outlined by Barton and Hamilton in Chapter 1 of this volume. Each facet will now be examined in turn with respect to the implications of a complex social theory of time for the theory of literacy practices.

Literacy is best understood as a set of social practices; these can be inferred from events which are mediated by written texts. These social practices cannot be directly observed; they are a theoretical construct, a pattern which theorists impose on recurrent or regular literacy events. There is therefore a danger that practices can come to be seen in a rigid, structural way, when the events they pattern are dynamic and changing. An understanding of the way in which the past and future are emergent in and constructed in the present enables us to move beyond this static idea and see the way in which patterns may be both regular and dynamic.

The past and future are emergent in the present; and in the same way, literacy practices are emergent in and constructed in present events. Constructions of how literacy practices have been in the past, and how they will be in the future, will change as the present emerges, and are themselves relative to the point of view of the observer. So, while regularity can be observed in the repetition of literacy events, it is possible that both the events and people's experiences and expectations of these literacy practices change over time. This change does not imply a weakness in the theory of literacy practices; rather the essentially situated nature of the practices drawn on requires them to change as the situation changes. This conceptualisation enables us to keep the idea of structured or patterned literacy events while freeing us from the tyranny of imposing a static structure on dynamic events.

There are different literacies associated with different domains of life. Barton and Hamilton define these domains in terms of place, giving examples of home, school and workplace as being particular domains with particular literacy practices. Domains can also be identified in terms of time. Zerubavel

(1981) demonstrates that time is an important boundary marker, particularly when synchronising the different roles that people play in our complex, multifaceted modern lives. He claims that time is now such a clear marker of different domains that we can usually tell the time without a clock, simply by observing the practices going on around us. He examines practices in hospitals, where nurses define their roles depending on whether they are in 'their' time or working their shift; despite the fact that they may be in the same place with the same people, their practices and roles change in time. In fact, a literacy event – the writing of the day's report – is the boundary marker between these two domains; once the report has been written the nurse is 'on her own time'. Similarly, Kapitske (1995) demonstrates how the literacy practices of Seventh Day Adventists change radically on the Sabbath; time is used as a marker between sacred and profane domains and between sacred and profane literacy practices.

Literacy practices are patterned by social institutions and power relationships, and some literacies are more dominant, visible and influential than others. This 'patterning' of practices by institutions and power relationships is not a powerful, static grid imposed on dynamic events, but is again emergent in the present, constructed through a constructed past and constructing the future. This means that these patterns do not exist beyond the recurrent present events that constitute them. Instead, they emerge through these present events 'in' time, rather than being imposed from 'outside' time. Memories of these recurrent events make up a constructed past, which is reconstructed every time it is recalled or drawn upon as a resource; it is through drawing on the resource of this constructed past, drawing on memories of recurrent events, that it becomes possible to construct these patterns. And the constructed patterns are themselves drawn on in the constitution of future events.

In terms of power relations, this is a very significant realisation since it enables us to conceptualise change while retaining the fact that the power relations influencing these patterns are very real. 'Some literacies *have become* more dominant, visible and influential than others' might be a more helpful representation, since focus on how this has taken place over time can lead to a richer understanding of the power relations and dynamics involved. Given that one of the key concerns of the New Literacy Studies has been to challenge the dominant 'ideological' or 'autonomous' models of literacy (Street 1984), an understanding of how these autonomous models have become powerful over time is a key weapon in the critical armoury, enabling us to develop ideas about how these power relationships can themselves be challenged and changed in time.

Literacy practices are purposeful, embedded in social goals and cultural practices. In order that the full implications of this statement be realised it is necessary to situate 'social goals' in the constructed future and 'cultural practices' as having been constructed through recurrent events in the past and emergent in the present. This will be seen later in the analysis of the literacy practices associated with a parish newsletter, where literacy plays a key part in the synchronisation of community activities to achieve shared social goals.

One of the key 'social goals' which necessitates the instantiation of literacy practices in literacy events is the transcendence of the transience of time; the use of literacy practices to create history. This leads us into the next precept, which is that *literacy is historically situated.* This means that literacy practices have to be seen as being embedded in the particular history of the society in which they are instantiated. But for something to be seen as historically situated it is necessary that some construction of the past be drawn on, in order to conceptualise what is meant by the society's 'history' in the first place. This itself happens in literate societies through literacy. The essentially temporary nature of lived reality can be made permanent through literacy. It is largely through literacy that we construct records, communicate with people in the future, and leave traces of our presence. Our conceptualisation of history relies to a great extent on literacy artefacts created in literacy events in the past, with our participation in literacy events in the present allowing us to reconstruct that past. The past is continually reconstructed in the present, partly through the repetition and mediation of literacy practices.

Indeed it could be argued that the whole 'point' of literacy, the need to create writing in the first place, springs from the need to construct written historical records of temporary social existence. Spoken language is ephemeral, while written language is more permanent, and is therefore portable through time. Even something as informal and on the face of it non-historical as 'writing a shopping list' is a means of recording transitory thought processes, reconstructing the present in the future or the past in the present: the 'past' transitory thought processes involved in checking the amount and type of food in the kitchen and deciding what more is needed for the coming week are made permanent and portable through writing the result down on the list, so that instead of needing to go through these complex thought processes again at the 'present' time of 'being in the supermarket' it is possible to simply refer to the historical record of the results of the thought processes in the past and reconstruct the results in the present. Literacy is historically situated; and in literate societies, history is to a great extent situated in literacy.

Literacy practices change and new ones are frequently acquired through processes of informal learning and sense making as well as formal education and training. This 'change' involves many different aspects of time, and Adam's call for attention to the multiplicity of times is important here. First, there is the time frame of an individual's life history. Over the course of a lifetime the literacy practices of an individual will inevitably change as they engage in different social practices and education. But this precept also applies to the wider time frames within which literacy practices develop. Historically, literacy practices change; as has already been pointed out, literacies become dominant over time, and these developments relate to wider processes of social change. Since, as I have already pointed out, literacy practices do not 'exist' but are instead continually emergent in events, this leads to the possibility of gradual change, as events are never repeated exactly; this focus again allows the concept of practice more flexibility as opposed to 'practice' being a rigid theoretical structure imposed on events.

At this point it is useful to illustrate these ideas by drawing on empirical research, in order to demonstrate how a focus on time and literacy can give insight into literacy practices. This illustration will draw on my current research, an ethnographic study of the role of text in the construction and maintenance of Catholic identity within one particular Catholic community. I will focus on one aspect of the construction of Catholic identity – preparation of children for First Holy Communion – and one aspect of the maintenance of community identity over time – the use of the parish newsletter to synchronise community activities – in order to demonstrate how a focus on literacy and time can give insight into the meanings and functions of literacy practices within this community.

I should point out that while I accept Adam's arguments that attention to the multiple and interrelating aspects of time is necessary in social scientific research, I take the position that it is neither possible nor desirable to attempt to analyse *all* the temporal aspects of a particular phenomenon. Instead, based on the premise underlying this book as a whole – that the situated nature of practices is key to understanding them – I would argue that those aspects of time which it is significant to address with respect to any particular event or practice are those which appear to be most relevant to the people involved in the practice, and that the aspects of time the social scientist should address should be influenced by the context of the event as a whole. With respect to the two sets of practices I am dealing with here, I am focusing on the aspects of time which I see as being meaningful for the people involved in the practices. With this in mind, the two aspects of time addressed with respect to preparation for First Holy Communion are first, the investment of time in literacy practices as a measure of commitment and second, the use of literacy practices as markers in an individual's life history; to take one's First Communion is to pass an important boundary stage, and literacy is used as a means of keeping a permanent record of this boundary crossing. The analysis of the newsletter shows one way in which community identity is maintained over time, a process of 'rhythmic repetition' which contrasts with the linear progressive nature of the First Holy Communion preparation.

Literacy, time and preparation for First Holy Communion

Entry into the Catholic Church is marked by three important sacramental occasions: Baptism, First Holy Communion and Confirmation. Each of these 'sacraments of initiation' is taking the person one stage further into membership of the Church. A child is baptised as soon as possible after birth, First Holy Communion takes place at around the age of seven or eight, and Confirmation takes place at the age of twelve or thirteen. Although Baptism is the formal means by which someone 'becomes' a Catholic, First Holy Communion is the point at which children, having reached the age of individual responsibility (seven years old), can participate in the Eucharistic sacrament, thus entering full communion with the community. These sacraments are seen as gifts from God; preparation for the sacraments is very important so that the child fully understands the nature of the gift they are receiving, and makes a conscious choice to receive the sacraments and progress further to becoming a full member of the Catholic Church. (Of course there are also many informal means by which a child takes on a Catholic identity, which I will not focus on here. I will also not address the different means by which adult converts are included in the community in detail; adults pass through the same boundary changes but clearly in a different way.)

A lot of time is spent by children and parents engaged in literacy events in preparation for the sacraments. For First Holy Communion, children spend nine months attending regular preparatory sessions; a commitment that is both stressed by the priest during the ceremony and mentioned in that week's newsletter announcing the ceremony: 'Over the past year they, together with their parents have been preparing for this great event in their lives' (see the newsletters in Appendix 3.1; Figure 3.1 and Figure 3.2). This investment of time is not only a measure of the education that is needed to understand the meaning of the ceremony, but also an indication of the commitment expected of the children (and their parents) to the gift of the sacrament and the process of being included in the Church community.

During these sessions children listen to and speak with catechists who prepare them for their First Communion, working through chapters in a textbook designed for this purpose. A significant amount of time in these classes is also spent in literacy events which produce literacy artefacts to be used for public display. These artefacts are different in every session, but can include for example paper 'hands of friendship' on which individual children write their names and those of their friends, or short prayers collaboratively written in small groups. These literacy artefacts are displayed on a large board placed at the back of the cathedral, which is added to after every session in the months leading up to the ceremony. They can be seen as being permanent and material evidence of the temporal investment that has been required from candidates and their parents. Literacy has been used to turn a transient and private event – the First Communion preparation session – into an enduring and public 'proof' of this temporal commitment.

The display board is designed to keep the wider parish community aware of the children's progress through the First Communion programme. It also includes photographs and names of individual children, so that parishioners can see which children make up this year's cohort. This display is a feature of the cathedral for at least six months of every year, and is thus a literacy artefact that achieves its goals through endurance in time. In the development of Catholic identity, which is a community identity, it is important not only that the individual concerned becomes a member of the community, but also that the community as a whole is aware of and welcomes these new members. The inclusion of the display board in the literacy environment of the cathedral is one way in which this social goal is met.

In addition to this permanent display the parish also organises recurrent events involving the children's literacy artefacts aimed at fulfilling the same social goal. At regular intervals throughout the year Sunday Masses are designated 'Celebration Masses', during which priests ask for the parish community's prayers for the candidates, so that the community as a whole is invited to participate in their progress. During these Masses some of the literacy artefacts that have been produced in the children's preparation sessions are included in the church service. For example, posters of trees with the words 'sorry', 'forgiveness' and 'love' decorating their 'leaves' were carried up to the altar by children during one Celebration Mass. On other occasions children read out prayers they have written themselves.

After the preparation comes the ceremony itself, during which literacy is used to transcend time by keeping a permanent record of the occasion. This ceremony is such a significant milestone in the child's process of becoming part of the Catholic community that it is very important that this be recorded, making a transient present event permanent in the future. Communion candidates are each given a certificate recording the date and place of the ceremony. Relatives and friends give cards of congratulations, as they would on a birthday or other special occasion. All those attending the Communion Mass are given a special hymn sheet with the names of the candidates on the front; again this enables a permanent record to be kept and also marks the service as special. At regular weekly services no hymn sheets are distributed, hymn books are used instead; whenever a separate sheet is distributed the Mass is marked from the beginning as being special in some way.

So, this demonstrates how literacy practices are a significant aspect of preparation for First Communion, an important boundary in an individual's life history, in the journey towards becoming a full and active member of the Catholic community. The investment of time in literacy practices is a measure of the individual's and family's commitment to the significance of this boundary crossing, and is demonstrated through the public display of the literacy artefacts produced by the candidates during this investment of time. The display also signals their progress to existing community members, as an enduring feature of the literacy in the environment of the cathedral, and the recurrent literacy events of Celebration Masses fulfil the same function. Literacy practices and artefacts are used to keep a record of the ceremony of First Holy Communion itself, extending the present into the individual's future and thus creating a record of their past. This demonstrates the importance of literacy in achieving the social goals associated with this process of preparation, the specific nature of the literacies associated with the particular domain of preparation for First Communion, the patterning of these literacy practices by the wider social relationships of family and parish, and the key importance of time in all these areas.

Literacy, time and the parish newsletter

The above analysis has examined the roles of literacy and time in one of the key 'boundary stages' associated with taking on Catholic identity. But identity is not something that is merely bestowed on an individual passing a particular stage. Community identity is maintained over time through continual renewal of the links that bind communities together. I will examine here one of the ways in which literacy is used to maintain community identity over time – the way the weekly parish newsletter is used to synchronise community activities at various levels. This weekly newsletter, a piece of A4 paper, printed on both sides and folded into a booklet, is distributed to everyone coming into Mass on a Saturday or Sunday, and copies are left at the back of the church for visitors who come to the Cathedral at times outside the regular Masses. These newsletters can be seen to play an important role in the maintaining of community identity. Here, I will analyse two newsletters (reproduced as Figure 3.1 and Figure 3.2 in Appendix 3.1) to demonstrate how this literacy artefact seems in part to be produced with the goal of synchronising peoples' activities in time.

One of the important aspects of community identity is the knowledge that many people are doing the same thing at the same time. Anderson (1983) writes about the importance of the emergence of print in the development of 'national identity'; knowing that many people, who you will never meet, are reading the same piece of paper as you in the same national language, and obtaining knowledge about these people through the medium of print, allows a link to be made between large numbers of people that could not have been made in the days before widespread print literacy. In the same way, the distribution of this newsletter to all those coming to

Mass in any one parish is a marker of identity, with everyone going to Mass at the same weekend reading the same newsletter. The Mass is one of the focal points of community identity for a Catholic community. Through the newsletter, each person can take away a physical record of their participation in this focal moment, which will remain in their homes through the week, tucked into the kitchen noticeboard or in a pile of papers on a desk; this presence of particular texts in the home is itself a marker of identity.

So it can be seen, merely from examining the practices of distribution of this newsletter, that it can play a part in the maintenance of a community identity by being something that everyone has an identical copy of. Examining the text of the newsletter more closely can tell us more about the literacy practices involved with it, the community's orientation to time, and the interaction between the two. I shall here focus on the use of the newsletter to synchronise the activities of the community in time at various levels.

Synchronisation in time is an important part of community identity, constructed in part by groups of individuals being involved in the same activities at the same time. In this community various events go on throughout the week involving various different groups of people, most of whom would usually also go to Mass at the weekend. The Sunday newsletter therefore plays an important role in disseminating synchronising information to all those involved in community activities.

This synchronisation happens on many different levels. On an individual level, on the back of every newsletter is a section entitled 'Ministries for the coming week'. This is a reminder to those parishioners who take on particular responsibilities – reading at Mass, cleaning the cathedral, preparing coffee after the Sunday Mass, organising the Children's Liturgy, and distributing Communion – that their turn is coming up in the following week.

The times of various regular group meetings in the parish are also printed on the back of the newsletter. These serve both an informative function, reminding those involved in regular activities of activities which they would expect to happen, and a 'display' function; by including these activities in the newsletter, and therefore displaying them even to those who are not involved, they are validated as being part of the wider flow of parish life, and acknowledged as being part of the life of the wider community.

Group meetings which are not regular are published inside the newsletter, the inside pages being the main body of the paper. Special events such as a 'Music Day' for those involved with the musical part of the Mass, an 'Education Mass' for those involved with teaching, and a reunion of those who have been involved with the Enquirers' Group are advertised here, with dates and times. This is unlikely to be the only place in which this information is disseminated – for example the Music Day would be publicised at choir practices and other musical meetings; but again the newsletter serves as a central node in which all the community's activities can be synchronised.

Events involving the parish as a whole are also advertised within this newsletter; important events like a Spring Fayre, the parish's most important fund-raising event, are advertised repeatedly, with temporal references like 'Only two weeks to go to the Spring Fayre' ensuring that everyone is aware when the event will take place. So the newsletter is used not only to synchronise activities of groups within the parish community but also to synchronise the activities of the parish as a whole.

Mass times throughout the parish are published on the front of the newsletter. As with the regular group meetings, most if not all of those attending these services will not need reminders of their timing, since going to Mass is a regular repeated activity usually occurring at the same time every week. However the times are published on the front of the newsletter, taking up about half of the surface area of the front page. It is possible that this is because of the central importance of the religious service as being that which unites the community as a whole, with the announcement of times being not so much a matter of synchronisation as a marker of significance.

Particular actions within the Mass are also synchronised by means of the newsletter. The section 'Mass responses', which includes responses to particular parts of the Mass which vary each week, and the section 'Today's Readings' are both used to signal what is to be done during those parts of the service which vary week by week. It is implicitly expected that people will know when is the appropriate time to say these responses or to look up these readings since this is not indicated in the newsletter. This has a particular implication in terms of literacy practices involving the newsletter, in that there are 'right' and 'wrong' times through the service to be seen reading it, despite the fact that it is given to you as you enter the church at the beginning of Mass. For example, you will rarely see people looking at the newsletter during the time when the priest consecrates the Communion bread and wine, this being one of the most sacred parts of the ceremony, while before the Mass officially begins it is quite common to see people reading their newsletters – an instance of literacy practices as a marker of the difference between sacred and profane time.

So far I have concentrated largely on synchronisation of what could be seen as 'public' activities. There is also evidence in the text of the newsletter of attempts to synchronise people's private activities. In particular, the newsletter appears to play an important part in trying to synchronise the prayer life of large numbers of people, running from the local level of the parish community to the global level of the Catholic Church as a whole.

On the parish level, most newsletters include a 'Thought for the Day', such as the following:

> We are constantly being tempted to put people and things before God. Our Lady is given to us as a model, she hears the will of God and keeps it. There must be no weakening on our part as we remember that we live in spiritual tents. 'Here are my mother and my brothers. Anyone who does the will of God, that person is my brother and sister and mother.'

This 'thought' usually draws on one or some aspects of the Mass readings of the day. Here, the reference to 'spiritual tents' might seem bizarre unless put into the context of one of the readings which uses this expression metaphorically; this is a synchronisation which only works when people attend Mass as well as reading the newsletter. In a small way, this is an attempt through literacy to give the parish a common spiritual focus at one particular point in time.

The private prayer activities of the entire world-wide community of Catholics are synchronised in a similar way. There are two striking examples of this in the newsletters I am examining here. The Fourth Sunday in Easter, 20 April 1997, was designated as 'World Day of Prayer for Vocations', meaning that on this day the entire Catholic community throughout the world was intended to be praying for vocations to the priesthood. A prayer for vocations is printed on the front of this newsletter (Figure 3.1), with advice on how to decide if one has a vocation. This is a vast example of synchronisation of private activities through literacy practices.

A similar example is demonstrated in the 27 April newsletter (Figure 3.2), in which is printed the Pope's Intention for May. These intentions are part of the 'cycle of prayer' of the Catholic Church. Coming from the Vatican and being disseminated through the national centres of every country in the Catholic world, this cycle of prayer has a different focus and theme for each month of the year; an attempt to synchronise the prayer of the global Catholic community both in church and in their daily lives. The month of May has traditionally been dedicated to the Virgin Mary; hence the reference to Our Lady in the quote above, and the intention:

> That Mary's faith be an encouragement for all those who seek to know and accomplish God's will and for the promotion of woman in accordance with the model of Mary, Mother of Jesus and Mother of the Church.

Versions of this intention will have been disseminated in various ways throughout the Catholic community world-wide on this day. This is an attempt through literacy to synchronise private prayer throughout the world for the entire month of May.

The printing of this intention is accompanied with advice on how to accomplish this devotion to the Virgin Mary during this month. This is encouraged to be through two special forms of prayer devoted to Mary, the Angelus and the Rosary. The most interesting part of this injunction is the way in which the recommendation to pray the Rosary regularly is phrased (the 'decades' referred to in the quote are the blocks of ten 'Hail Marys' that make up the Rosary):

> Saying the Rosary, this can be fitted in for example, a decade in the morning as you get up and prepare the breakfast, a decade on the way to work or school or cleaning up, a decade at lunch time, a decade before or during tea or as you wash up and a decade in the evening.

This is an attempt through literacy to synchronise people's private activities of prayer with their more public activities of going to work, eating dinner together, etc. It assumes that everyone reading it will follow a common schedule, which assumption already creates a commonality between people in the community. It acknowledges that people may find it difficult to fit in a special time for prayer, and attempts to show how prayer can be fitted in to this schedule. This is a particularly powerful representation of how literacy is used to synchronise both public and private community activities, and how the institutional voice of the Catholic Church is mediated through literacy at a local level.

I would not like to claim that these attempts to synchronise private prayer activities actually result in every Catholic who reads the newsletter incorporating these intentions into their prayer practices. Rather, the fact that the institution of the Church makes these requests of the Catholic population through the medium of the newsletter gives an interesting indication of the relations of power which are presupposed to exist between the institution and the individual, which extend to the institution having the right to attempt this synchronisation; whether or not it actually has effects in individuals' lives is another question.

The distribution and reading of the parish newsletter is only one of the many literacy practices which contribute to the construction of community identity, and the synchronisation of community activities in time is only one way in which this is achieved. Therefore the analysis above can offer only a very limited insight into a series of very complex processes. However despite these limits, it has been demonstrated that a focus on only one aspect of time – synchronisation – and on only one type of text – the parish newsletter – can still show that time can be a significant aspect to address, in an analysis of literacy practices; in particular that an examination of time and literacy practices can demonstrate the patterning of these literacy practices by the social institutions and power relations associated with the domain in which this text is situated and the social goals which different groups and institutions within this domain are trying to achieve.

Conclusions

I have demonstrated here how 'time' is an important if implicit aspect of the new literacy studies, and that focusing on time and literacy can give useful insights into literacy practices. In a brief analysis of a few aspects of literacy, identity and time in the Catholic community, I have attempted to demonstrate some of the ways in which this focus can be helpful, looking in particular at the literacies used in two domains of life within this community.

Through an analysis of the literacy practices involved in preparation for First Holy Communion, I have demonstrated how an investment in time is used as a measure of commitment and how literacy artefacts are produced as a material 'proof' of this commitment; how these literacy artefacts are used both permanently and in recurrent literacy events to achieve the social goal of community awareness of candidates' progress; and how literacy is used to transcend the temporary nature of the ceremony itself and create a permanent historical record of a once-only event.

An analysis of the practices around the parish newsletter has demonstrated the use of literacy to synchronise events in time, in order to achieve the social goal of maintenance of community identity both at a local level, synchronising the activities of the parish community, and at a global level, through the dissemination through literacy of the institutional voice of the Catholic Church.

This analysis has demonstrated the necessity of a notion of time that allows for its complex nature; the word 'time' is used to describe many different phenomena, as was demonstrated both in the theoretical discussion which opens this chapter and in the illustrative analyses. The particular aspect of time that I would like to stress in terms of developing theory in the area of literacy studies is the way in which a consciousness of change over time can free us from a common underlying dichotomy, in which 'practices' are seen as being 'static structures outside time' and 'events' as 'dynamic actions in time'. While the concepts of 'events' and 'practices' are key to our work, it is necessary to be continually aware that literacy practices emerge through the rhythmic repetition of similar literacy events. Constantly bearing in mind the temporal nature of literacy practices can give us a more flexible conceptualisation of what a practice 'is'.

Acknowledgements

I would like to thank members of the Lancaster Literacy Research Group for their comments on earlier drafts of this paper, particularly David Barton, Mary Hamilton and Roz Ivanič for their detailed comments. I would also like to thank the members of the church community for their ongoing help and cooperation with this research, in particular those who read and commented on the final draft of the chapter, and who gave permission to reproduce copies of the newsletters.

References

Adam, B. (1990) *Time and Social Theory*, Cambridge: Polity Press.

Anderson, B. (1983) *Imagined Communities: Reflections on the Origin and Spread of Nationalism*, London: Verso.

Bergson, H. (1910) *Time and Free Will*, London: Swan Sonnenschein (cited in Adam (1990)).

Elias, N. (1984) *Uber die Zeit*, trans. H. Fliessback and M. Shroter, Frankfurt: Suhrkamp (cited in Adam (1990)).

Jaques, E. (1982) *The Form of Time*, London: Heinemann (cited in Adam (1990)).

Kapitske, C. (1995) *Literacy and Religion: the Textual Politics and Practice of Seventh Day Adventism*, Amsterdam: John Benjamins.

Street, B. (1984) *Literacy in Theory and Practice*, Cambridge: Cambridge University Press.

Young, M. (1988) *The Metronomic Society*, London: Thames and Hudson (cited in Adam (1990)).

Zerubavel, E. (1981) *Hidden Rhythms: Schedules and Calendars in Social Life*, Berkeley: University of California Press.

Appendix 3.1

TODAY'S READINGS

Acts 4:8-12; Psalm 117; 1 John 3:1-2; John 10:11-18.

THOUGHT FOR THE DAY

In an age when sheep can now be cloned into identical copies. Jesus stands out as that shepherd who knows our uniqueness, our individual likes and habits. The closeness he has with the Father mirrors his nearness to us. If we listen for his voice, then he promises us a better pasture.

TODAY IS WORLD DAY OF PRAYER FOR VOCATIONS

Much of our year is spent in encouraging and fostering leadership within our parishes, by inviting people to respond to active involvement in the life and mission of the Church. Today, we are asked to concentrate on one aspect of vocation - priesthood and religious life. We pray that many people will respond to God's call to commit their lives to service as priests, sisters and brothers.

THE VOICE

How does one decide the happy but scary question: Is God calling me?

There are five principles:

1. Stay where you are! Pray and think, allow the idea to come ad go a bit. If it's authentic, it will grow.
2. Be ready for doubt - this will help to strengthen and confirm a call.
3. Continue to pray. read the Gospels and walk with Jesus as a disciple. Get acquainted with him.
4. Listen to the Lord with another trusted person.
5. Lean forward gently. The call of God attracts and draws, by following in little choices we are prepared for a move in our life.

MASS RESPONSES

PSALM:

The stone which the builders rejected has become the corner stone.

GOSPEL ACCLAMATION:

Alleluia, alleluia! I am the good shepherd, says the Lord; I know my own sheep and my own know me. Alleluia.

PLEASE PRAY FOR

THE SICK

Bishop B. F[redacted], B[redacted] D[redacted], M[redacted] J[redacted], H[redacted] F[redacted]

LATELY DEAD

M[redacted] V[redacted], C[redacted] K[redacted], C[redacted] B[redacted], W[redacted] W[redacted]

ANNIVERSARIES

H[redacted] G[redacted] McB[redacted], D[redacted] D[redacted], T[redacted] P[redacted] M[redacted], J[redacted] D[redacted], Mgr B. L[redacted], Canon H. M[redacted], Fr F. M[redacted].

MINISTRIES FOR THE COMING WEEK

CATHEDRAL

READERS

Sat E. M[redacted]
P. F[redacted];
Sun: S.R[redacted],
M.R[redacted];
6.30pm:E.G[redacted],
C. M[redacted].

COFFEE

McG[redacted] Family

CLEANERS

T. C[redacted],
F.M[redacted] Sr C[redacted],
C.B[redacted].

CHILDREN'S LITURGY

?

EUCHARISTIC MINISTERS

P.B[redacted],T.H[redacted],K.B[redacted], D.S[redacted].
Sr C[redacted],G.S[redacted], M.M[redacted],S.V[redacted].
J.B[redacted],T.G[redacted], J.J[redacted],C.G[redacted]

ST. THOMAS MORE

Readers

Sat. J.D[redacted]
OSU
Sun.L.W[redacted]
K.W[redacted]

Offertory

Sat. P&T McL[redacted];
Sun. E[redacted] family

CHILDREN'S LITURGY R. W[redacted]

ST. PETER'S CATHEDRAL & ST. THOMAS MORE

FOURTH SUNDAY OF EASTER (YEAR B)
WORLD DAY OF PRAYER FOR VOCATIONS

THE CATHEDRAL

Sunday Masses
Vigil: Sat 6.30pm
Sunday: 10.30am & 6.30pm
Children's Liturgy: 10.30am
Weekday Mass : 12.05pm
Monday - Saturday in the Cathedral
Confessions
Saturdays: 11am - 12noon,
4pm - 5pm.
Exposition of the Blessed Sacrament
Saturday, 9.30am - 12noon

ST. THOMAS MORE

Sunday Masses
Vigil: Sat. 6.30pm
Sunday: 9.15am
Weekday Mass
Monday - Friday 9am.
Confessions
Saturday: 6.00 - 6.20pm

NAZARETH HOUSE

Sunday Evening Prayer and Benediction at 4.30pm.

PRAYER FOR VOCATIONS TO THE PRIESTHOOD

"The harvest indeed is great, but the labourers are few. Pray ye therefore the Lord of the harvest that He send labourers into His harvest." (Luke 10:2)
O God, Who didst from eternity appoint Thine only begotten Son to be the High Priest of the human race, pour forth we beseech Thee Thy Holy Spirit upon Catholic families in every land, that vocations to the priesthood may be multiplied.
Give unto us priests, O Lord. Give us priests after Thy own Heart:-
To offer up the unceasing sacrifice of the Mass;
To lead the little ones to Thee;
To strengthen the faith of believers;
To preach the gospel to the ignorant;
To bring forgiveness to repentant sinners;
To give the bread of life to starving souls;
To comfort the suffering, to help the dying;
To spread the Kingdom of Heaven in our midst.
O Mary, Queen of the clergy, pray for us;
obtain for us an increase of holy priests.

GO OUT TO THE WHOLE WORLD, PROCLAIM THE GOOD NEWS TO ALL CREATION

20th April, 1997 Tel: 61860

ST BARNABAS SOCIETY APPEAL

At All Masses in the Cathedral and St Thomas More this weekend. We hope that you will contribute generously towards this worthwhile cause.

THE MAYOR'S SERVICE OF THANKSGIVING

We welcome to the Cathedral this afternoon, Sunday 20th April at 2.30pm, the Mayor and members of the City Council for this Service of Thanksgiving at the end of her Mayoral year. We hope that many parishioners will make a special effort to attend.

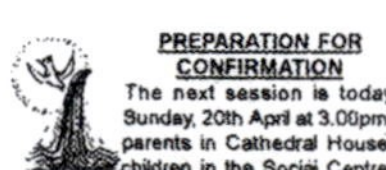

PREPARATION FOR CONFIRMATION

The next session is today Sunday, 20th April at 3.00pm: parents in Cathedral House, children in the Social Centre.

CATHEDRAL LINK

Please leave any items for the next edition at Cathedral House before Sunday 27th April.

SCOUTS' SERVICE

Friday 25th April at 7.30pm in the Cathedral. We extend a warm welcome to all Scouts in the area to this Service.

CARDS AND GIFTS FOR FIRST COMMUNION AND CONFIRMATION

After all Masses next Sunday (27th April) at the Cathedral and the following Sunday at St Thomas More (4th May) we will have for sale a number of cards and gifts suitable for first Holy Communion and Confirmation; orders can also be taken.

PLEASE TAKE A POSTER FROM THE BACK OF CHURCH TO DISPLAY IN YOUR HOME WINDOW AND ONE FOR YOUR LOCAL SHOP TO ADVERTISE THE SPRING FAYRE

SOCIAL GROUP

Will meet on **Tuesday 22nd April at 7.00pm** in Cathedral House. An open meeting to which all parishioners are welcome to plan the Spring Fayre.

THE R.I.B.A.AWARD

Alison Grant, the North Regional Director of the Royal Institute of British Architects presented Bishop B[redacted] in the Cathedral last Saturday with a bronze plaque which is their award for excellence in architecture. This was in recognition of the restoration and re-ordering work carried out in the Cathedral. The bronze plaque will be installed in the porch of the Cathedral soon. This is a very much coveted award which we feel was well deserved for the work carried out in the Cathedral.

CATHEDRAL SPRING FAYRE

Saturday 10th May
1.00pm
Cathedral Social Centre

Please can you help by donating goods to sell on the stalls, raffle prizes, time on the day to set up or run a stall? We need you!
contact M[redacted] W[redacted] ([redacted]) if you can help in any way. Goods for stalls can be left at Cathedral House or the Convent.

"COME AND SEE"

Women of the L[redacted] diocese are invited to a weekend of prayerful reflection at Castlerigg Manor, Keswick on May 16th - 18th. Cost £54. For more details contact P[redacted] W[redacted], Tel: [redacted].

THE FAITH & JUSTICE COMMISSION

Have organised a study day to be held at L[redacted] University Chaplaincy Centre on Saturday May 17th, 10am-4pm entitled: 'RECONCILATION WITH THE EARTH - FROM PRINCIPLES TO PRACTICE'. See poster at the back of church for details or contact S[redacted] S[redacted] (tel: [redacted]).

BRAHMS
A GERMAN REQUIEM

Presented by the University College of St M[redacted] to mark the hundredth anniversary of Brahms' death on Sunday 27th April at 8.00pm in the Cathedral.
Tickets £6.50 and £2.50 on the door.

CATHEDRAL PRIMARY SCHOOL

Mrs B[redacted] H[redacted] our Deputy Head, has been appointed Headteacher at St J[redacted]'s primary school W[redacted]. We wish first of all to congratulate Mrs H[redacted] on her appointment as Headteacher and also to thank her for the excellent contribution she has made to the Cathedral School. It is worth noting that not only has the Cathedral School provided excellent teachers for our children but has also prepared its teachers for posts of greater responsibilities in other Catholic Schools.

NEW TEACHER FOR THE CATHEDRAL SCHOOL

Miss M[redacted] R[redacted], well known to St Thomas More community has been appointed to the Cathedral School. She will take up her new appointment in September.

What's On at the Cathedral & St Thomas More

UCM MEETING

Monday 21st April, 2pm in the Convent.
UCM Mass on Friday April 25th at 12.05pm in the Cathedral.

S.V.P. MEETING

Wednesday 23rd April at 7.00pm in Cathedral House.

CHOIR

every Friday, 7.30 - 8.30pm Conference Room

JUNIOR YOUTH GROUP

Friday, 6-7.30pm, Social Centre.

SENIOR YOUTH GROUP

8.00 - 9.30pm in the Cathedral Social Centre

400 CLUB WINNER

£100:
Mr C[redacted]

100 CLUB WINNER

Mr J. A[redacted]
Half year and full year subscriptions now due.

COFFEE

After 10.30am, Mass. All Welcome

TABLE TOP

Every Sunday in the Social Centre 11am - 2pm.

POPMOBILITY

Monday 7.00pm in the School Hall.

SENIOR CITIZENS

Tuesday, 2-4pm Social Centre

BINGO

Wednesday 7.15pm Social Centre

ENQUIRERS COURSES

CATHEDRAL: Thursday at 7.30pm in Cathedral House.

MEDITATION GROUP

Each Thursday, 3.00-4.00pm, Ursuline Convent.

BELLRINGERS

Practice night 7.30-9pm every Thursday

PARISH COUNCIL

The next meeting will take place on Thursday 24th April at 7.30pm in Cathedral House.

Figure 3.1 Newsletter 20 April 1997

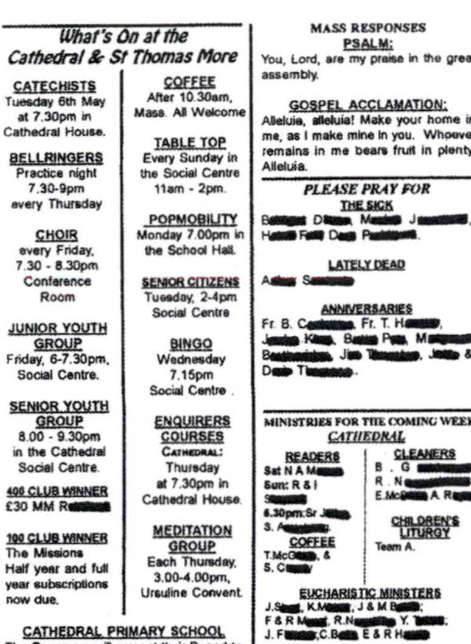

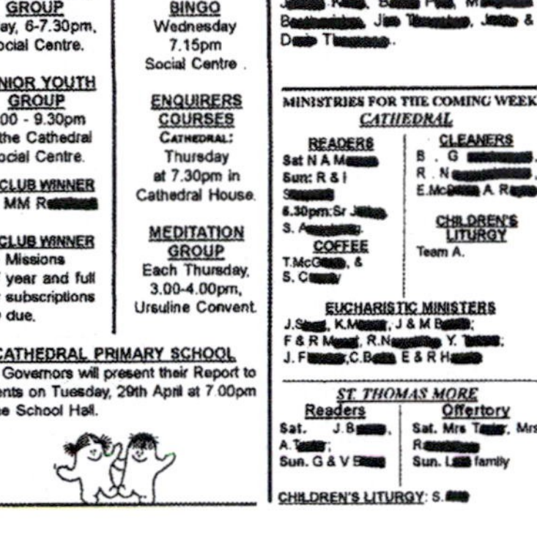

What's On at the Cathedral & St Thomas More

CATECHISTS
Tuesday 6th May at 7.30pm in Cathedral House.

BELLRINGERS
Practice night 7.30-9pm every Thursday

CHOIR
every Friday, 7.30 - 8.30pm Conference Room

JUNIOR YOUTH GROUP
Friday, 6-7.30pm, Social Centre.

SENIOR YOUTH GROUP
8.00 - 9.30pm in the Cathedral Social Centre.

400 CLUB WINNER
£30 MM R■■

100 CLUB WINNER
The Missions
Half year and full year subscriptions now due.

COFFEE
After 10.30am, Mass. All Welcome

TABLE TOP
Every Sunday in the Social Centre 11am - 2pm.

POPMOBILITY
Monday 7.00pm in the School Hall.

SENIOR CITIZENS
Tuesday, 2-4pm Social Centre

BINGO
Wednesday 7.15pm Social Centre .

ENQUIRERS COURSES
CATHEDRAL: Thursday at 7.30pm in Cathedral House.

MEDITATION GROUP
Each Thursday, 3.00-4.00pm, Ursuline Convent.

CATHEDRAL PRIMARY SCHOOL
The Governors will present their Report to Parents on Tuesday, 29th April at 7.00pm in the School Hall.

MASS RESPONSES

PSALM:
You, Lord, are my praise in the great assembly.

GOSPEL ACCLAMATION:
Alleluia, alleluia! Make your home in me, as I make mine in you. Whoever remains in me bears fruit in plenty. Alleluia.

PLEASE PRAY FOR

THE SICK
B■■ D■■, M■■ J■■, H■■ F■■ D■■ P■■.

LATELY DEAD
A■■ S■■

ANNIVERSARIES
Fr. B. C■■, Fr. T. H■■, J■■ K■■, B■■ P■■, M■■ B■■, J■■ T■■, J■■ & D■■ T■■.

MINISTRIES FOR THE COMING WEEK

CATHEDRAL

READERS
Sat N A M■■
Sun: R & I S■■
6.30pm:Sr J■■ S. A■■.

COFFEE
T.McG■■, & S. C■■

CLEANERS
B . G■■.
R . N■■.
E.McG■■ A. R■■

CHILDREN'S LITURGY
Team A.

EUCHARISTIC MINISTERS
J.S■■, K.M■■, J & M B■■;
F & R M■■, R.N■■ Y. T■■;
J. F■■,C.B■■ E & R H■■

ST. THOMAS MORE

Readers
Sat. J.B■■. A.T■■;
Sun. G & V B■■

Offertory
Sat. Mrs T■■, Mrs R■■
Sun. L■■ family

CHILDREN'S LITURGY: S.■■

ST. PETER'S CATHEDRAL & ST. THOMAS MORE

FIFTH SUNDAY OF EASTER (YEAR B)

THE CATHEDRAL
Sunday Masses
Vigil: Sat 6.30pm
Sunday: 10.30am & 6.30pm
Children's Liturgy: 10.30am
Weekday Mass : 12.05pm
Monday - Saturday in the Cathedral
Confessions
Saturdays: 11am - 12noon; 4pm - 5pm.
Exposition of the Blessed Sacrament
Saturday, 9.30am - 12noon

ST. THOMAS MORE
Sunday Masses
Vigil: Sat. 6.30pm
Sunday: 9.15am
Weekday Mass
Monday - Friday 9am.
Confessions
Saturday: 6.00 - 6.20pm

NAZARETH HOUSE
Sunday Evening Prayer and Benediction at 4.30pm

PRAYER FOR VOCATIONS TO THE PRIESTHOOD

"The harvest indeed is great, but the labourers are few. Pray ye therefore the Lord of the harvest that He send labourers into His harvest." (Luke 10:2)
O God, Who didst from eternity appoint Thine only begotten Son to be the High Priest of the human race, pour forth we beseech Thee Thy Holy Spirit upon Catholic families in every land, that vocations to the priesthood may be multiplied.
Give unto us priests, O Lord. Give us priests after Thy own Heart:-
To offer up the unceasing sacrifice of the Mass;
To lead the little ones to Thee;
To strengthen the faith of believers;
To preach the gospel to the ignorant;
To bring forgiveness to repentant sinners;
To give the bread of life to starving souls;
To comfort the suffering, to help the dying;
To spread the Kingdom of Heaven in our midst.
O Mary, Queen of the clergy, pray for us,
obtain for us an increase of holy priests.

27th April, 1997 **Tel: 61860**

L■■ Roman Catholic Diocesan Trustees Registered - Registered Charity No: ■■

FEASTS THIS WEEK
Thursday 1st May is the feast of St Joseph the Worker.
Friday is the first Friday of the month there will be EUCHARISTIC DEVOTIONS for all Special Eucharistic Ministers and Readers on **Friday in the Cathedral at 7.00pm.**

POPE'S INTENTIONS FOR MAY
That Mary's faith be an encouragement for all those who seek to know and accomplish God's will and for the promotion of woman in accordance with the model of Mary, Mother of Jesus and Mother of the Church.

MARY MODEL AND MOTHER
Elizabeth recognised Mary's threefold blessedness:
- Blessed in God's choice;
- Blessed in her fruitfulness;
- Blessed in her full acceptance of God's word.

She received God's revelation, co-operated totally, gave flesh to God's word, proclaimed his praise, observed the love of the Lord, diligently sought the Lord and stored up every detail to be pondered in mind and heart.

THE GROUND RULES FOR DEVOTION TO MARY ARE THREE:
1. The recognition of what God did in her as an individual and as a model of the Church.
2. Imitation of her co-operation with grace in faith and obedience.
3. Trust in her as our mother.

We recommend and encourage you to have some form of devotion to Mary during May.

For example, reciting the Angelus each day at 12 0'clock and 6pm. Saying the Rosary, this can be fitted in for example, a decade in the morning as you get up and prepare the breakfast, a decade on the way to work or school or cleaning up, a decade at lunchtime, a decade before or during tea or as you wash up and a decade in the evening. Below are printed the mysteries on which we are encouraged to meditate and the days on which they are said.

(Each decade consists of 1 Our Father, 10 Hail Mary's and 1 Glory Be to the Father.)

THE FIVE JOYFUL MYSTERIES
(Monday & Thursday)
1. The Annunciation
2. The Visitation
3. The Nativity
4. The Presentation in the Temple
5. The Finding of the Child Jesus in the Temple.

THE FIVE SORROWFUL MYSTERIES
(Tuesday & Friday)
1. The Prayer and Agony in the Garden
2. The Scourging at the Pillar
3. The Crowning wiht Thorns
4. The Carrying of he Cross
5. The Crucifixion and Death of Our Lord.

THE FIVE GLORIOUS MYSTERIES
(Wed., Sat., Sun.)
1. The Resurrection
2. The Ascension of Christ into Heaven
3. The Descent of the Holy Spirit on the Apostles
4. The Assumption
5. The Coronation of the Blessed Virgin Mary in Heaven and the Glory of all the Saints.

BEREAVEMENT GROUP
Meeting on Tuesday 19th, at 7.30pm in Cathedral House. We encourage all bereaved to come to these very helpful sessions. The question we would like to ask for Tuesday night is, 'When you were grieving what did someone do that you really appreciated and what do you wish had been done but wasn't?'

CARDS AND GIFTS FOR FIRST COMMUNION AND CONFIRMATION
On sale today after all Masses at the Cathedral and the following Sunday at St Thomas More (4th May) a number of cards and gifts suitable for first Holy Communion and Confirmation; orders can also be taken.

"THE PRESENT"
The DiocesanYouth Service Newsletter is available at the back of church for all young people and those working with youth or interested in youth issues.

CATHEDRAL SPRING FAYRE
Saturday 10th May
1.30pm
Cathedral Social Centre

Only 2 weeks to go to our second most important fund-raising event in the year. Please can you help by donating goods to sell on the stalls, raffle prizes, time on the day to set up or run a stall?

WE NEED YOU!

contact M■■/■■ (■■)if you can help in any way. Goods for stalls can be left at Cathedral House or the Convent. *Please take a poster to display today!*

DIOCESAN PILGRIMAGE TO LOURDES JULY 17TH-24TH
There are still a few places available on the coach from L■■. Details on the church noticeboard, or Phone Fredom Travel: ■■ ■■, or G■■ T■■ ■■ for booking forms.

MUSIC GROUP
Will meet next Thursday at 7.00pm in the Conference Room.

PREPARATION FOR MARRIAGE
All those intending to get married within the next 6 months are invited to attend the preparation course which starts today, Sunday, at 3.00pm in Cathedral House.

THANKS
"E■■, M■■ and A■■ M■■ send their warmest thanks to all those who so kindly came to E■■'s funeral. Their presence added something very special to the Service."

ST BARNABAS SOCIETY APPEAL
Many thanks to all who gave so generously last Sunday to this appeal.

'RECONCILATION WITH THE EARTH - FROM PRINCIPLES TO PRACTICE'.
If you are concerned about 'global warming' or pollution of our atmosphere and waters or even about recent food scares, and you want to know what you can do, why not attend the conference at L■■ University on May 17th. The two keynote speakers will be Fr Sean McDonagh and Dr Ed Echlin. The day will cost just £5 for those who are waged, £1 for the unwaged.
See poster at the back of church for details or contact S■■ S■■ (tel: ■■).

Figure 3.2 Newsletter 27 April 1997

4

THERE IS NO ESCAPE FROM THIRD-SPACE THEORY

Borderland Discourse and the in-between literacies of prisons

Anita Wilson

In this chapter I shape the discussion around my belief that within incarcerative environments, theoretical aspects of literacy and prison need to be seen beyond the binary contexts of autonomous singularity or social multiplicities. I propose that acknowledgement of a 'third space' allows fresh and original perspectives to be recognised regarding such an environment, its Discourse and the influences of its literacy-oriented activities, practices and materials.

To effect this acknowledgement requires me to advance three topics for discussion:

- First, to propose that the two notions of *Prison as autonomous entity* and *prisons as social environments* are bound up in the realities of closed institutions and that theoretical issues around both need to be recognised, addressed and included in any discussion on the place of communicative practices within penal establishments.
- Second, to propose that the two notions of *Literacy as autonomous* and *literacies as sociocultural constructs* are similarly bound up in the realities of closed institutions and that both contribute to the generation of communicative practices within penal establishments.
- Third, to draw a theoretical framework around salient aspects of autonomy and social multiplicities within which to make visible a *third space* – a space which supports its own culturally-specific discourse, generated, influenced and sustained by the interrelation of these notions of prison and literacy.

During my discussion, I prioritise prison before literacy. This is a deliberate decision on my part as I feel that the reader's existing knowledge of the former will be significantly outweighed by knowledge of the latter and my intention is to inform and explore rather than to reiterate existing theory. All illustrations, however, remain literacy-oriented. I intend my understanding of various terms such as 'Prison', 'prisons', 'Literacy', 'literacies', 'autonomous' and 'third space' to unfold during the development of my discussion although the reader could refer now to my final section 'Third-space theory' to pre-empt such clarification.

Before moving to the first topic I provide a short resumé of my research sites and methodologies in order to acquaint the reader with my position and how I see the position of others in my work.

Who we are and the spaces we inhabit – a brief summary of my research environments and those who know more about it than I do!

Researching at the conjunction of two institutions – Lancaster University's Linguistics Department and a number of prisons in England and Scotland – has provided me with a unique opportunity to engage with literacy-related issues surrounding means of communication which exist within and between the jails of both England and Scotland. I focus only on male prisoners, adult and young offenders.

My work has developed over a number of years, emerging as an ethnographic study of the various literacies which are contained within the setting of prisons and has been conducted at a pace dictated more frequently by the impositions of incarcerative rather than academic time.

While the site to which I have gained most access is a Young Offenders Institution in the North of England housing young men between the ages of 15 and 21, my collection of data has been gathered by way of general observations, personal interaction and sustained written communication with young and adult prisoners in a number of establishments. During this time I have formed and re-formed my own opinions and these have been engaged with, supplemented, validated, overruled and contested by the contributions of a considerable number of male prisoners nationwide. It is also fair to say that I have had invaluable cooperation from many members of prison staff at all grades whose contributions have been substantial. And while this chapter is primarily concerned with prisoners I include references to non-prisoners where considered relevant. Any quotations I use during the course of these discussions are included with the knowledge and permission of the authors.

I want to begin by proposing that it is of primary importance to accept that both Prison as autonomous entity and prisons as social environments are bound up in the realities of closed institutions.

Prison — * — prisons

There is no question as to the existence of a perception of Prison – with a capital P – as an autonomous institutional construct. It is manifested judicially by sending people 'to Prison' and in mainstream society people often refer to others as being 'in Prison' or having a 'Prison record'.

Prison is organised around an overarching set of Official Rules and has a number of Statutory Instruments in the shape of Command Papers and Standing Orders which are applied universally to all those in 'Prison'. Such regulation carries an implicit assumption that all establishments and those within them can be incorporated within an abstract and encompassing administration without any regard for difference or differentiation, and used by the Prison system to reduce its population to a dehumanised, discrete and passive unit as a means by which to effect management and control.

Government statistics support this traditional view within publications such as the *Report on the Work of the Prison Service* (Home Office 1991) or surveys such as *The Second Prison Survey* (Scottish Prison Occasional Papers Report No. 10/1994, Wosnick, Gemmell and Machin 1994) and *Literacy Behind Prison Walls* (National Center for Education Statistics USA, Haigler *et al.* 1994). Individuals are subsumed within these publications, emerging only as numbers or comparative charts. Throughout this discussion then, I use the term 'Prison' with a capital P in an overarching collective sense in order to distinguish it from any reference I make to individual prison establishments.

Many Prison literacy-related activities and practices consolidate the autonomous view. The system imposes numerous forms of dehumanising controls over all who live and work within it. It imposes uniform labelling by age such as 'Juvenile' or 'Young Offender', it reduces status to 'remanded', 'sentenced' or 'convicted' and prisoners are categorised by security levels A, B, C or D using abstract codes and numbers. Those who exercise control are equally depersonalised, reduced to titles such as 'Governor 1' or 'Principal Officer' while staff are reduced by replaceability or substitution in their day to day work to an arbitrary manifestation of what Bourdieu (1991) refers to as 'rites of institution' and 'symbolic ritual'.

For example, in the standard reception procedure imposed for receiving prisoners into the jail, each prisoner is required to sign away his personal belongings, his own clothes, and any sense of social identity, exchanging his name for an impersonal number and living space. Staff are similarly reduced to the repetitive completion of standardised forms and identified only by role in an operation where they may be impersonally interchanged or replaced without any threat to the power of the process. Such procedures are deeply embedded within a model of Prison as autonomous and resonate with Goffman's (1961) and Wallace's (1971) criteria for totality and institutionalism.

However, it is my experience and the views of many prisoners that while those of us with knowledge of 'inside' have an awareness of the existence of

Prison, the environment in which prisoners and staff find themselves is not only one of symbolism and asocial autonomy. We are all only too aware of the existence of the relevant structures of imposition and power, but also note the heterogeneousness of the prison estate and the multiplicity of social (and anti-social!) interactions both within and between the plurality of establishments.

I am supported in my view that prisons – in the plural – need to be viewed through a lens of social diversities as well as that of institutional determinism as illustrated by the written correspondence between myself and two prisoners – one from Scotland and one from the South of England, quoted below;

> *'All prisons ARE different, very much so. Even though a jail may be the same category as another, none are alike. Contemporary theory seems to lump us all together within the institution of "prison," – whose contemporary theory ?!?!?! . . .'*
>
> (personal correspondence Keith. 24/1/97)

> *'Close study would indicate that inmates at Perth prison would reflect local attitudes and values different in distinct ways from inmates in an Edinburgh or a Glasgow prison just as citizens of those cities have their differences.'*
>
> (personal correspondence A.T. November 1996)

These opinions support my proposal that prisons are organic and social environments.

Prison itself challenges the notion of perceived stasis and occasionally imposes its own statutory changes. During my study, for example, modifications to official rules have been imposed in English jails regarding the volumetric control of prisoners' property. This ruling has influenced – among other things – the number of books a prisoner may hold in possession. Increased governmental emphasis on drug awareness and matters of security has also generated revised staff practices regarding incoming mail, and the detection of 'acid tabs' on stamps or on envelope glue is now curtailing the availability of stamps and stationery. But such changes still remain within the traditional construction of Prison as they are universally imposed and implemented regardless of any disparity between establishments.

It would be misrepresentational however, to suggest that any prison is an environment which is only either institutionally or socially constructed. Those operating within the prisons are aware of both the outside worlds they have left behind and the perceived threat of Prisonisation which the system tries to impose.

Rather than forget the former or be drawn into the latter, acquired knowledge of both allows prisoners the opportunity to create a 'third space' in which to live their everyday lives in the prisons. This notion of a 'third space' I have expanded from Bhaba's work (1994), the nature of which will become apparent as my discussion progresses and which I introduce by a literacy-focused example observed at one Young Offender establishment:

> During one of my visits a prisoner was returning to the jail having been to court. He is an experienced car thief, had been remanded for further reports and on leaving the court en route for the prison had been told by the police that his trainers were to be 'held for forensic investigation'. This meant that on his return to the jail he would be required to wear prison issue shoes until such time as his trainers were returned to him. Prison shoes are notoriously 'uncool', no-one wants to wear them and as this young man has an image to retain, he stated that as an act of rebellion, he would rather wear nothing on his feet rather than be seen in them. Not to wear shoes however, he knew would place him in contravention of Prison Rules. Officers on duty insisted that he take a pair, allowed him to choose whether he would prefer brown or grey and proceeded informally to customise them for him with a felt-tip pen in order to transform them into 'Adidas prison trainers' by drawing 3 stripes down the outside edge. The defacement of prison property however, as they knew, is also in contravention of the Prison Rules. The young man still protested. He was not going to wear them – especially if they were Adidas – if he had to wear them at all he wanted them changing to 'Nikes'!

Such an event cannot be read either from a purely inside-institutional nor outside-social perspective. Institutionally, the symbolic actors all display knowledge of Prison Rules – such as the regulations governing footwear and the defacement or destruction of prison property – but the 'rule-keepers' knowingly take on the role of 'rule-breakers', changing themselves and the rules to the social practices associated with trainers. Socially, the cultural rules of 'training shoe literacy' and 'getting a new pair of shoes' are also known to all parties but the events, in being reappropriated, are drawn into an alien environment where they should not apply.

I want to propose that all those involved are engaged in a literacy-related activity, with a culturally-appropriate Discourse, situated in a culturally-approved space, which embodies but transcends the practices and ideologies from which it is formed. I feel that it is within such a third space that the majority of those within the prisons live out their day to day realities.

I develop these notions throughout the discussion and intend the diagram below to visually clarify the issue to date.

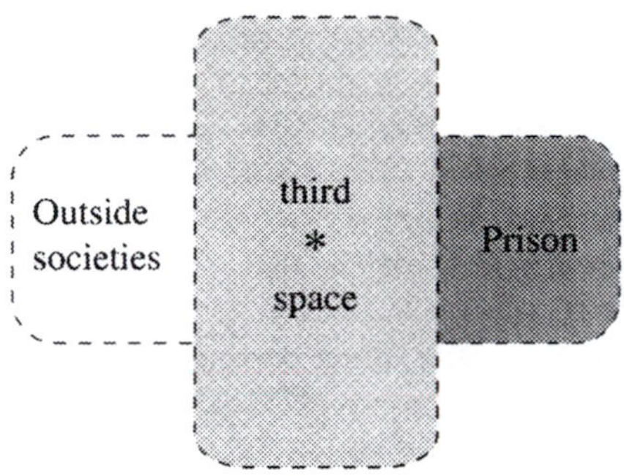

My second proposal is that the constructions of Literacy as autonomous and literacies as sociocultural constructs are both of relevance and that each contributes to the generation of communicative practices within penal establishments.

Literacy — * — literacies

Street (1984, 1993), describing an autonomous model of literacy, suggests that proponents of such a view see Literacy as 'a single thing with a big L and a single Y' (1993, p. 81) seeking to make written language superior to spoken and linking Literacy to cognitive development and social change. In line with the theme of this volume, I want to expand the model of 'autonomous Literacy' to include its distantiation from the social, its perception of itself as a discrete unit and – with specific reference to prisons – its subsequent use as a means of impositional control.

This model of 'autonomous Literacy' has much in common with the model of 'autonomous Prison' which I created above. Like Prison, the autonomous view of Literacy is situated in institutional ideology and in its traditionally educational manifestation has statutory rules regarding standards, assessment and evaluative criteria. It assumes, like Prison, that it can be imposed and that it exists in a vacuum detached from social interaction, removed from social or cultural difference.

Street observes that 'the ways in which literacy skills are assessed have been largely in line with this (autonomous) model' and the assessment of Prison Literacy often makes links between perceived lack of educational achievement, truancy and exclusion, retaining the notion that low levels of education, low levels of Literacy and low levels of morality are intrinsically interconnected. This is reflected in studies such as that undertaken by Hagell and Newburn (1994) which attempted to link negative educational careers to persistent young offenders. Studies such the UNESCO Institute for Education Report of 1992 or the American survey of 1994 by Haigler *et al.* reduce prisoners to statistics and use autonomous Literacy to sustain the belief that prisoners' abilities are significantly below those of the 'free' community – a belief I have already argued against in other work (Wilson 1996).

Singular Literacy is manifested at individual establishments in the wording of officially administered documentation, the standardised testing of all incoming prisoners and the statistical recording of prisoners' abilities, suggesting that autonomous Literacy is linked to and given significant credence by the institution of Prison.

To present the counter-claim that there are many literacies would be to state the obvious in a chapter relating to the theme of 'Expanding the New Literacy Studies' and Street's counter-proposal of an 'ideological' model has led the way not only to acknowledge the diversity of literacies in their social settings but to draw attention to the significance of attendant issues of power, authority and social differentiation. Progressive empirical work undertaken by Heath (1983) and continued in contemporary studies cited by Barton and Ivanič (1991) and Street (1993) has forced a recognition of the multiplicity of literacies which both constitute and are constituted by the social settings in which they exist. Such projects and the events and practices embedded within them have drawn attention to ideologically-oriented environments and sociocultural implications and I continue to draw on the social relevances of the New Literacy Studies at many levels of my work.

I have noted elsewhere the multiplicity of writing which is undertaken by prisoners (RaPAL Bulletin, Wilson 1993) and my ongoing research shows the considerable variety and patterns of literacies which exist in the prison environment – literacies which include the textual and the visual and which I head up under interrelated titles such as 'emotional literacies', 'symbolic literacies' and 'subversive literacies'. These are intentionally abstract as more concrete terms carry with them conventional meanings and interpretations which within the environment I am trying to describe – where young men are allowed to wear Nike prison shoes – are being constantly redefined.

Official Prison Literacy for example – by which I mean the vast quantity of standardised and universally administered documentation – remains within Street's (1993) notion of 'dominant' autonomy only while it remains within its approved parameters. An official standardised canteen form given out to every prisoner at a set time on a given day, supplied for ordering items from the Prison shop, escapes from its concept as an 'imposed' or 'constrained' activity (Barton and Ivanič 1991) when it becomes transformed into a shopping list embedded within the social practices of its recipients. This is particularly apparent when it is humorously reappropriated (as I have seen) to include a request for machine guns, grappling hooks, large-breasted women or substantial quantities of illicit substances! Once acted upon or interacted with, such forms become reappropriated into the realms of subversive, vernacular, symbolic or other patterns of literacies.

In addition to being reappropriated, I have also noted that literacies themselves influence the cultural mores of the environment in which they are embedded. The extract below is an example of the cultural hybridity of outside and inside activities and practices which are involved when writing a letter in prison:

> *'last week I wrote a letter for an illiterate guy to his Mum and I said 'say this and that' but he knew what he wanted to say and would not let me rephrase anything, so I wrote it as he spoke it . . . he wanted to pay me some roll-up tobacco or Rizla or chocolate but I told him to get me an envelope and a carrier bag (as both would not cost him anything – the envelope being prison issue and the bag to put my sewing in)'.*
>
> (personal correspondence with Ronnie)

The space in which this interaction takes place allows for the outside practices of letter-writing and sewing to be combined with the inside realities of institutional currency and cultural identity in a specific way. The activity of '*sewing*' for example, along with other conventionally female-gendered outside activities such as writing poetry, listening to 'sentimental' music and the buying and sending of 'emotional' greeting cards and letters are accorded cultural credibility within this predominantly male-orientated third-space environment to the extent that not to engage in them might be seen as a marginal position.

While I agree with Street's defence that the 'ideological model subsumes rather than excludes the work undertaken within the autonomous model' (1993, p. 9) I feel that not only has the model and existence of a Discourse of autonomous Literacy often been overlooked in studies which have been concerned with the social nature of vernacular literacies but that to reduce the discussion of communicative practice to an either/or detracts from the very real possibility – at least within the prison environment – that people not only have an awareness of Prison and prisons but, as the examples above have shown, choose to reappropriate both Prison Literacy and outside literacies as a means by which to determine the culturally-specific space and features of their everyday lives.

I would like to offer a further instance of a specific event in order to illustrate the interplay between the two models, reproducing both the scenario and the letter in which it was embedded. I quote from my ongoing journal.

> '8th August 1995 – *down* [the punishment block] *after adjudications* [disciplinary proceedings] *as the Governor is doing his rounds a piece of paper is squeezed through the gap in the door of one cell (Mr B******'s).*

*It is intended for the Governor (Dear Sir) but it is intercepted by an officer who reads it, shakes his head and is about to screw it up and put it in the waste bin. I ask him if it is alright to look at it . . . It is a letter to the Governor and one of the saddest things I have read. This is a boy with a lot on his mind – he spends large amounts of his time copying the words of songs from his Walkman onto pieces of paper – he addresses his letters to his father as Sir X **** . . . on a housing estate in X******** – the psychiatrist says that he is perfectly healthy mentally – I don't think so'.*

The letter is as follows:

Dear Sir

I am a Transvestite like Dressing up in Women clothes See you Soon you big Sexy ger

So much Love

to All the World

Im a TranSvestite

Queen v Lee Show the world

Show the Judge this boy is

A Transit Van

Just as to merely acknowledge and separate out Prison from prisons is an inconclusive endeavour, so the division into Literacy and literacies would fail to recognise the culturally legitimate 'space' which allows this interaction to take place.

There is no question that the writer of this letter draws on his knowledge of both the Discourse of Prison and the Discourse of outside societies or that he has an understanding of the place of both Literacy and literacies to inform the Discoursal environment he is positioned within. His is a 'third-space' world where the outside social event of posting a letter is combined with the inside institutional restrictions of communication; where he knows he must address the 'symbolic other' in the conventionally accepted letter-writing manner of 'Dear Sir' but may challenge symbolic authority by the informal and unconventional content of his correspondence; where the austerity of solitary confinement in Prison can still support a literate and creative form of social communication.

In my work then, I feel that it is the use of various literacies within this world which are as important as any division over the meaning or the dichotomy of terms. I have found that by looking at such use or uses raises an awareness of the crucial part that literacies play in the creation of a culturally-validated third space and the generation of the Discourse it requires.

The visual representation below illustrates my suggestion:

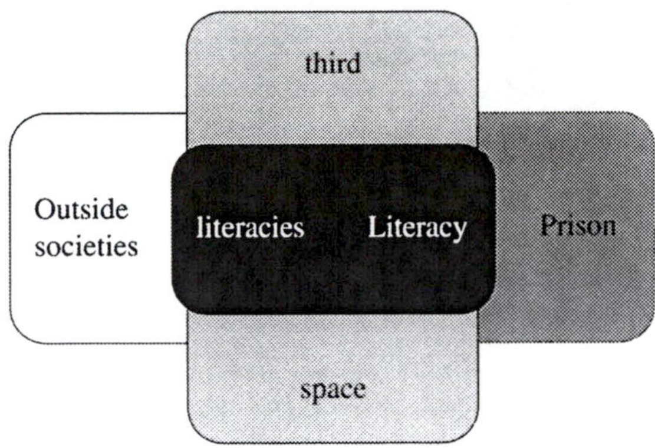

Thus far, I have discussed and ultimately linked Prison/s and Literacy/ies in order to acknowledge a third space – a space where representatives of the Prison system vandalise government property for the benefit of prisoners over whom they are instructed to retain institutional control; where seemingly autonomous Literacy and social literacies can be successfully reappropriated by a psychiatrically disturbed youth in solitary confinement; and within which an adult male can credibly exchange his educational expertise for an envelope and a bag for his embroidery!

However, such events and practices are not pre-existent, but are continuously created, learned and validated only within the third space of the prison environment. Neither do they exist in a vacuum and there are implicit codes of behaviour and rules of engagement which go to make up what I propose as the Discourse of this specific environment in which they exist. Just as I have proposed that the acknowledgement of a third space bridges the gap between Outside and Prison and that the Literacy and literacies within it exist between social and institutional worlds so I suggest that its culturally-specific Discourse bridges both outside and inside worlds.

The addition of this Discoursal element completes my model – as illustrated on p. 64.

However, while it has been thoroughly introduced by real world events and original data, it requires theoretical underpinning and a refinement of the terms in order to both confirm its validity and to facilitate its future

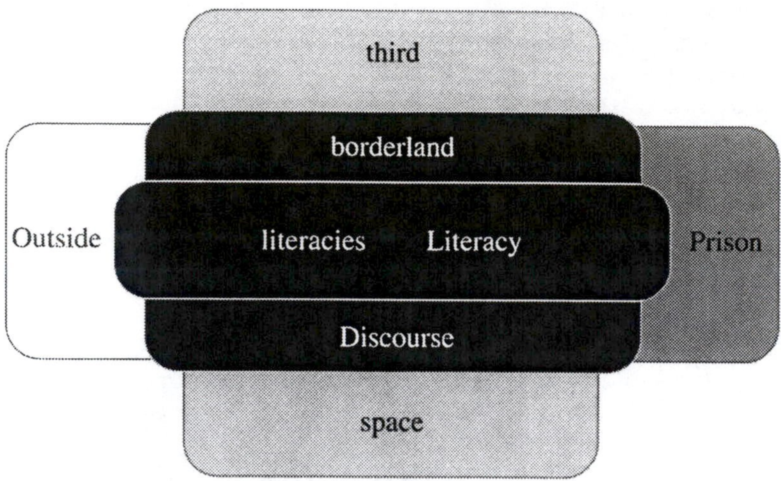

expansion into other domains of literacy studies. The final section seeks to address specific issues of theoretical definition and as my title suggests 'there is no escape from third-space theory'!

Third-space Theory — * — Theoretical Issues

My model has progressively built upon issues of environment, literacies and the Discourse of prisons and its generation has required me to draw on theories from a number of sources. The concluding illustration below shows my refined terms and I use this final section to explain how these terms came about.

The 'third-space' Prison Community

The notion of the third space as a site in which to locate prison literacies, I have appropriated from work by Bhaba (1994) wherein he draws attention to the need to reconsider the perceived homogeneous nature of cultural identity, proposing that the recognition of a third space provides 'the precondition for the articulation of cultural difference' (p. 38). Although grounded in broader issues around migration, national identity and disenfranchisement I have found Bhaba's work to have considerable resonance with my perception of prisoners who I see often as being divested of their preferred identities, finding themselves in a cultural vacuum and yet seeking to retain a sense of personhood. I take his notion forward by acknowledging it and placing it within the specific domain of prison life.

I see my third space as a place which supports a variety of social networks because I have come to understand that such is the perception retained by those who live in it and because I have observed that the majority of its practices – particularly those relating to literacies – are of an interactive nature. I also see it as a place which provides an opportunity for those who operate within it to form groups distinctive and culturally-specific enough for them to be identified as communities. Discussion between prisoners and myself requires me to make plain however that my perception of community has little in common with any traditional sociological reading of homogeneity or egalitarianism (challenged successfully by Cohen 1985 and discussed in depth in Wilson 1999) but one that allows prison community membership to be retained on a stronger or weaker basis. This broad framework thus dispenses with traditional divisions between remanded and sentenced prisoners and allows for the inclusion of both prisoners and non-prisoners.

This 'mish-mash' community I have named as 'mushfake' – a term described by Mack (1989) as used by American prisoners to describe items they have fashioned from whatever is available to them such as hats made out of underwear or artefacts made from spent matchsticks. I abstract this singularly appropriate term to describe the 'mushfake' prison community which I see as constructed from whatever particular outside and inside practices are available.

This 'mushfake prison community' can operate on two levels – the local and the global. My informants have suggested that all prisons are different and the mushfake community of any one prison is manifested according to the specific ethos of that particular establishment. As one of my illustrations showed, the currency for writing a letter was an envelope and a carrier bag to put sewing in, although it might have been roll-up tobacco, Rizlas and some chocolate. Likewise, from my observations, the storage of personal letters can vary between a cardboard box, a filing system, a drawer or a plastic bag. However, I would contend that some exchange rate for letter-writing or the storage of personal letters is present in all jails and that there is sufficient cultural assonance between establishments to apply the concept of 'Prison Community' as an encompassing term.

To acknowledge its presence at both levels allows each prison community's 'real-time' manifestation but also acknowledges what Cohen (1985) refers to as its universal 'symbolic' qualities.

Literacies and the degree to which they are embedded in shared practices further convince me of the validity of an overarching term. In the personalisation of 'private' space, for example, I have found that while the choice of books and posters may vary between staff observation posts and prisoners' cells, the use of literacy-orientated material artefacts to turn an impersonal environment into one which has salience for the occupants is common to all members of the Prison Community.

Taking a broad reading, this Prison Community and its patterns can be seen to extend beyond the confines of any establishment, hence my intentional visual 'overlaps' on the visual representation.

To clarify, I therefore use the term 'prison community' in lower case when referring to a particular establishment and Prison Community using capitalisation when referring to the general concept. I am, therefore, taking the term beyond Clemmer's seminal work *The Prison Community* (1940) which, although an ethnographic study of impressive quality, was confined to the observations of a single establishment.

Borderland Discourse, meta-knowledge and the identity kit

I reappropriate Gee's theory of 'borderland Discourse' (1990) for the 'third-space' Prison Community because I feel it to have particular relevance to the environment of my study. His description of 'borderland' as a place between home and school used by children marginalised by mainstream ideologies is akin to the liminal space described by Bhaba and the third space which I have identified as relevant to prisons.

His term 'Discourse' – not 'discourse' with a small 'd' as a general term describing some form of interaction – he describes as:

> a sort of 'identity kit' which comes with the appropriate costume and instructions on how to act, talk, and often write so as to take on a particular social role that others will recognise.
>
> (Gee 1990, p. 142)

I apply this term to the communicative force which drives the Prison Community and informs the literacies of prisons within it.

Gee also suggests that the ability to acquire knowledge of any new Discourse is assisted by having a 'meta-knowledge' of existing Discourses which can

> lead to the ability to manipulate, to analyse, to resist while advancing.
>
> (Gee 1992, p. 117)

This is particularly salient to the way in which prisoners read the Prison Discourse they are being forced to address in the light of the Discourses of the outside societies they have left. Choosing to remain 'maladapted' to Prison Discourse allows prisoners to create an 'identity kit' by which to negotiate their entry into the borderland Discourse of the Prison Community.

Drawing on aspects of contemporary outside worlds provides the means by which to sustain the 'mush-fake' nature of the Prison Community and its Discourse, illustrated by my example of the scenario with the customising of trainers. At the time of the incident, credibility in the outside world was no longer to be achieved wearing Adidas trainers. This change of cultural marker explained why my informant was so adamant that his Prison shoes be customised to Nikes in order to bring him into the borderland Discourse of his prison community as a street-wise non-Prisonised individual.

In-between literacies

The final issue, one which I have intentionally placed at the centre of this model, concerns the various literacies which both influence and are influenced by borderland Discourse and the Prison Community. Just as Bhaba recognises elements of an in-between cultural space and Gee identifies events in the in-between of Discoursal space, I place literacies as central to the maintenance of a space which exists between outside and inside worlds.

However, just as borderland Discourse involves culturally-specific thoughts, acts, opinions, events and practices, so in-between literacies embedded within it retain a culturally-specific understanding that expands beyond the mere acts of reading and writing. Taking the illustration of the hand-written letter on p. 62 as an example, elements of visuality become relevant wherein the physical appearance and visibility of the literacy artefact play a significant part in the credence of the activity. The form, content and production of the artefact itself play a significant role in its interpretation by its various audiences.

As further proof, newspapers are 'swung' between cell windows by means of unravelled blankets, not only to share the activity of newspaper reading but to use the artefact as a means of ballast in order to effect a line of communication between prisoners' cells. Letters and cards used to personalise Prison cells are promoted almost to the level of visual icon. Books become a vehicle not only for reading in order to pass the time but as a means of passing information to other prisoners by writing messages and graffiti poems on the inside covers and blank pages.

It is significant to note however, that Prison Rules forbid articles to be 'swung' from cell to cell, but this does not deter prisoners from breaking the Rules in order to read the newspapers or to retain lines of communication. Prison wages are such that a prisoner makes a conscious financial sacrifice if he wishes to buy stamps and writing paper in order to ensure he has a collection of letters and cards with which to personalise his space. Prison punishments are such that time can be added on to a custodial sentence if a prisoner is found guilty of defacing Prison property and yet prisoners continue to make marks of personal social identity through graffiti statements and poems written on Prison books. Such practices are so commonplace that it would seem that considerable assessment is made by those entering the jails when choosing between joining the 'borderland' Discourse of Prison as Community or the 'dominant' Discourse of the Prison as Institution.

These literacy-related activities and practices become a central part of the 'identity kit' which prisoners choose to adopt in order to retain aspects of their outside lives rather than become absorbed into the institutional ideology of Prison.

Conclusions and thoughts for expansion

I have noted – and feel strongly – that my observations may provide valuable insight into the reassessment of time spent in jail and it is because of my protracted involvement with some prisons and many prisoners that I have become aware of one of the most salient findings of my work to date. I have found that the longer a man remains in Prison the stronger he seeks to retain his ties with his outside worlds. The more competent he becomes at engaging with rules of borderland Discourse the more he draws on his distant knowledge of outside societies. A man serving a long sentence keeps pets, he cooks, he grows plants, he writes longer letters, he reads more books, he enrols at University or college, he takes up painting, calligraphy, writing books or poetry.

He writes and tells me that the fight against Prisonisation is subtle and complex:

> *'it is a silent battle, not with a recognisable enemy, but with our minds. To win we have to pamper our minds, cater for them, bribe them, keep them occupied or lose them. If we lose our minds, we lose ourselves and the battle. It is a battle I will not lose'.*
>
> (personal correspondence 29/4/94)

My work acknowledges that the literacies of the Prison Community are not merely linguistic constructions embedded within theoretical frameworks, they are fundamental to the maintenance of an environmental and Discoursal space which might be the difference between keeping or losing your mind.

References

Barton, D. and Ivanič, R. (1991) *Writing in the Community*, London: Sage.

Bhaba, H.K. (1994) *The Location of Culture*, London: Routledge.

Bourdieu, P. (1991) *Language and Symbolic Power*, Cambridge: Polity Press.

Clemmer, D. (1940) *The Prison Community*, London: Holt, Rinehart & Winston.

Cohen, A.P. (1985) *The Symbolic Construction of Community*, London: Tavistock Publications.

Gee, J.P. (1990) *Social Linguistics and Literacies – Ideology in Discourse*, London: Falmer Press.

Gee, J.P. (1992) *The Social Mind – Language, Ideology and Social Practice*, London: Bergin & Garvey.

Goffman, E. (1961) *On the Characteristics of Total Institutions: The Inmate World in the Prison – Studies in Institutional Organisation and Change*, ed. D. Cressey, New York: Holt, Rinehart & Winston.

Hagell, A. and Newburn, T. (1994) *Persistent Young Offenders*, London: Policy Studies Institute.

Haigler, K.O., Harlow, C., O'Connor, P. and Campbell, A. (1994) *Literacy Behind Prison Walls*, Washington: US Department of Education.

Heath, S. (1983) *Ways with Words: Language, Life and Work in Communities and Classrooms*, Cambridge: Cambridge University Press.

Home Office (1991) *Report on the Work of the Prison Service*, London: HMSO.

Mack, N. (1989) 'The Social Nature of Words: Voices, Dialogues, Quarrels', *The Writing Instructor* 8, Summer.

Street, B.V. (1984) *Literacy in Theory and Practice*, Cambridge: Cambridge University Press.

Street, B.V. (ed.) (1993) *Cross-Cultural Approaches to Literacy*, Cambridge: Cambridge University Press.

Unesco Institute for Education Report (1992) *Basic Education in Prisons*, Feldbrunnedstrasse 58, Hamburg.

Wallace, S.E. (1971) *Total Institutions*, Transactions Inc., USA.

Wilson, A. (1993) 'A Creative Story about Prison Writing', *Research and Practice in Adult Literacy* 21, Summer.

Wilson, A. (1996) 'Speak Up, I Can't Write What You're Reading', *Journal of Correctional Education* 47(2), June.

Wilson, A. (1999) 'Reading a Library – Writing a Book: The Significance of Literacies for the Prison Community', Unpublished PhD dissertation, Lancaster University.

Wosniak, E., Gemmell, M. and Machin, D. (1994) *The Second Prison Survey*, Edinburgh: Scottish Prison Service.

5

BECOMING JUST ANOTHER ALPHANUMERIC CODE

Farmers' encounters with the literacy and discourse practices of agricultural bureaucracy at the livestock auction

Kathryn Jones[1]

Transcribed excerpt of a conversation between two livestock auction staff (30/3/95)	English version of a conversation between two livestock auction staff
Stan: **mae nw'n deud fedri di gael dy stopio ar y ffordd wsti**	Stan: they say you can get stopped on the road you know
John: **'dyw!**	John: no!
Stan: **os wyt ti heb .**	Stan: if you haven't got .
John: **heb un o'r rhain?**	John: haven't got one of these?
Stan: **. heb y fform wedi llenwi ynde**	Stan: . haven't got the form filled in
John: **mae 'di mynd yn rhyfedd ..**	John: it's got awful ..
Stan: **o mae 'di mynd yn ofnadwy hefo fforms wan**	Stan: oh it's got dreadful with forms now

In this chapter, my purpose is to show how the processes of 'globalisation' and 'disembedding' that are characteristic of contemporary society are realised in part through discursive practices and, specifically, bureaucratic literacy practices. I draw on my own empirical research with Welsh farming people in north-east Wales to make connections between the local historic literacy practices of their day-to-day farming activities and larger national and international social processes. I also show how written texts and literacy practices are constitutive of the social practices of organisation and control as they are realised by transnational bureaucratic systems. The data that I am using in this chapter come from a cattle sale at the Ruthin Farmers' Auction where Stan and John, quoted above, were working. I look closely at how the organisational procedures of the livestock auction are carried out linguistically through people's use of talk and texts. The notion of 'talk around texts' is used within New Literacy Studies to emphasise how reading and writing are often inseparable from talk. I think it is important to be more precise about what 'talk around text' involves and from my data, I have identified text *articulation, negotiation* and *inscription* as being strategies people accomplish through talk to mediate textual bureaucracy.

This chapter is divided into four sections. The first section called 'Gwaith papur ("paper work") and bureaucracy' looks at how the increasing amount of paper work involved in farming is part of the ongoing bureaucratisation of the agricultural industry and how written texts are crucial to the functioning of large-scale bureaucracies. The next section takes 'Agricultural bureaucracy' as an example of a large scale bureaucratic system which operates transnationally through the practices of a number of interconnected organisations and shows how this bureaucratic system has become disembedded from the locally situated context of the Welsh farmers in this study. The third section, 'Becoming incorporated into MAFF bureaucracy', focuses on how individual farmers become incorporated into the agricultural bureaucratic system when they take their cattle to be sold at their local livestock auction. In the fourth section, 'Accessing agricultural bureaucracy's discursive order', I show how this process of accessing a bureaucratic system is accomplished discoursally through texts and talk. Finally, I summarise how the concerns of this chapter can extend our understanding of literacy as a social practice.

Gwaith papur and bureaucracy

During the fieldwork for my research on the literacy practices of Welsh users, I have worked with, and talked to, many farmers and other people involved with the agricultural industry in north-east Wales[2]. 'Mae wedi mynd yn ofnadwy hefo fforms wan' or, literally, 'its got dreadful with forms now' sums up many people's response to the increasing amount of form-filling and other paper work that is now involved in routine farming practices. In the data extract at the beginning of this chapter, the forms Stan and John were talking about were the (then new) *animal movement forms* (animal movement form was the auctioneers' name for this form) which farmers had to fill in every time they took their cattle to be sold at auction. For most farmers, this form was just one more form in an increasing amount of Ministry of Agriculture Fisheries and Food (MAFF) bureaucracy they had to deal with. From MAFF's perspective on the other hand, the ongoing bureaucratisation of the agricultural industry was a necessary development as part of the process of centralising and controlling agricultural production and food markets within the European Union (EU). Although many farmers agreed with the need for agricultural reform, the increased amount of gwaith papur this involved for them personally was generally seen as a burden.

Theories of bureaucracy

The process of the bureaucratisation of contemporary society is well documented. Theories of bureaucracy stem from the work of Max Weber, the German sociologist who first defined bureaucracy as 'a hierarchical organization designed rationally to co-ordinate the work of many individuals in the pursuit of large-scale administrative tasks and organizational goals' (Weber 1978, quoted in Fairclough 1989, p. 212). The 'ideal type' of bureaucracy which Weber understood to be rational and, by implication, objective and neutral has subsequently come to be seen as ideological and serving the purposes of particular groups (Sarangi and Slembrouck 1996). The 'rationality' which shapes the practices of a bureaucracy is, therefore, an ideological rationality. In the bilingual context of Wales, one dimension of the ideological rationality of bureaucratic institutions has, until recently, been that English was the only accepted language for official texts and proceedings. The *1967 Welsh Language Act* was a significant challenge to the hegemony of English in this domain because it legislated that written texts produced in Welsh had 'equal validity' in law with texts produced in English. The most recent *1993 Welsh Language Act* now requires that all public sector institutions treat the Welsh and English languages on 'a basis of equality' in the service they provide to the public (HMSO 1993). As a result of this legislation, an increasing number of the written texts produced by public sector institutions are being produced in Welsh as well as English.

Bureaucracy has always been understood as a mechanism for exerting power and control over a population. Control has been characterised as the 'supervision of the activities of the subject population' (Giddens 1990, p. 58). Some forms of supervision or surveillance are direct, as in the practices of prisons, schools or some kinds of workplace, as described by Michel Foucault in the *Archaeology of Knowledge* (1972). At other times, control or supervision operates indirectly through the accumulation and control of knowledge (Giddens 1990, p. 58). Amassing information about individuals and keeping records of this information is one dimension of surveillance and control. Historically, the practices of collecting, recording and storing data about individuals have been almost exclusively mediated by written texts. Writing and literacy practices have been central to achieving administrative and managerial purposes since the earliest historical times (Goody 1977; McArthur 1986). The contemporary use of more and more powerful computer technology in many bureaucratic contexts makes the textual manipulation of information about individuals increasingly comprehensive.

The sociologist Dorothy Smith has commented how bureaucracy 'is *par excellence* that mode of governing which separates the performance of ruling from particular individuals, and makes organization independent of particular persons and local settings' (1993, p. 213). In the experience of most people, bureaucracies are large, faceless organisations that operate elsewhere from their local context. At a local level, employees of a bureaucratic institution take on the position of what Anthony Giddens (1990) calls the 'facework commitment' on behalf of the faceless institution they represent in their meetings or 'encounters' with individual customers, clients and members of the public. This distance between local reality, or the 'local historic order' as Garfinkel, Lynch and Livingston (1981) call it, and the abstract bureaucratic system which is used to document, evaluate and control that reality constitutes the 'disembedding' of institutions. By 'disembedding' Giddens means the 'the "lifting out" of social relations from local contexts of interaction and their restructuring across indefinite spans of time and space' (Giddens 1990, p. 21). This condition of disembeddedness partly constitutes the tensions between local and the more global social practices that are said to characterise much of contemporary social life. One of the ways in which this disembeddedness is realised is through the inscription of locally historic action and circumstances into a disembedded text time (Smith 1993).

The second and third sections of this chapter look in some detail at the discursive accomplishment of bureaucratic disembedding as it occurs at the livestock auction. Before then, the following section outlines how the contemporary agricultural bureaucracy, which the farmers and auction workers involved in my research deal with in their day-to-day working lives, operates at different institutional levels.

Agricultural bureaucracy

EU legislation and MAFF

The Ministry of Agriculture Fisheries and Food (MAFF), the government ministry with responsibility for agricultural issues within the UK, is a large-scale bureaucratic institution whose bureaucratic practices are largely concerned with administering and controlling agricultural aid schemes. Following the UK's membership of the European Economic Community (EEC) in 1973, these agricultural aid schemes have been managed in line with the EEC's (now the EU's) Common Agricultural Policy. In 1992, as part of the reform of the Common Agricultural Policy, the EEC legislated that, rather than aid schemes being administered separately by each Member State, some schemes should be integrated and managed directly from Brussels:

> in realigning the existing market measures a[s] part of the reform of the common agricultural policy, the Community is opting, to a

> large extent, in both the crop and livestock sectors, for direct aid to producers . . . in order to adapt to the new situation and improve their effectiveness and usefulness, it is necessary to set up a new integrated administration and control system covering the aid schemes for arable crops, beef and veal, sheepmeat and goatmeat, as well as specific measures for farming in mountain, hill and certain less-favoured areas.
>
> (Council Regulation (EEC) No. 3508/92, The Council of the European Communities 1992)

Integrating the bureaucracy involved in managing agricultural aid on a EU-wide basis has been another step in the globalisation of farming practices with the mechanism for administering aid schemes becoming disembedded further from the local context in which individual farmers are going about their daily job of farming. The consequence of these bureaucratic reforms is further 'rationalisation' of operational and classificational procedures as these are set out in the EEC legislation:

> given the complexity of such a system and the large number of aid applications to be processed, it is essential to use the appropriate technical resources and administration and control methods . . . as a result, the integrated system should comprise, in each Member State, a computerized data base, an alphanumeric identification system for agricultural parcels, aid applications from farmers, a harmonized control system and, in the livestock sector, a system for the identification and recording of animals.
>
> (ibid.)

Putting such a complex and detailed system for collecting and manipulating data into action has only been achievable using, what the EEC legislation refers to as, 'high-performance' computerised data bases (ibid.). Developments in computer and satellite technology have also been incorporated within this bureaucratic system to achieve the EU's purpose in instigating redefined bureaucratic goals and procedures. This purpose was 'to combat fraud in the CAP arable and livestock schemes and to ensure that there is fair competition in Europe' (MAFF-produced explanatory booklet on *The Integrated Administration and Control System 1995*, MAFF 1995, p. 3). EEC legislation specifies that the high-performance computerised databases should allow cross-checks to be made as part of the surveillance and control of aid applications. Surveillance satellites are also employed to check that farmers are using their land for the purposes they claim financial aid for. A recent article in the *Guardian* newspaper quotes, for example, the case of Italian farmers whose claims for subsidy for growing durum wheat exceeded the amount they were actually growing:

> Only 1.9 million acres of durum wheat – used in spaghetti-making – were being grown when claims were being made for 4.2 million acres. The European Commission's spy in the sky, intended to combat such fraud, also revealed that Italy and Greece were claiming subsidies for non-existent olive trees.
>
> (Bannister 1997, p. 26)

MAFF is the centralised institution that oversees the implementation of these bureaucratic reforms in the UK. It operates in Wales through the Agricultural Division of the Welsh Office (WOAD). There are also regional and local MAFF offices in various parts of Wales, as there are in England and Scotland. Within the structure of this disembedded system, the MAFF employees take on the position of institution 'delegates' (Giddens 1990). As delegates, they take part in administering a bureaucratic system which, ultimately, they have no responsibility for and no control over. There is some direct contact between MAFF's regional employees and the farmers who are administered and controlled by their policies. At other times, MAFF bureaucracy is mediated by other institutions, principally the two agricultural unions in Wales: The National Farmers' Union (NFU) and Farmers' Union of Wales (FUW). Both unions advise farmers on the implications of EU and MAFF bureaucratic reforms and give support and help with filling in aid application forms. Other organisations placed in an intermediary position are livestock auctions like the Ruthin Farmers' Auction.

Organisation in the middle: the livestock auction

One of the consequences of establishing the Integrated Administration and Control System was the need to have a subsidiary system for identifying all cattle with a unique alphanumeric code and keeping records of the movement of each head of cattle. The legislation that enforced this amendment to EU policy was *The Bovine Animals (Records, Identification and Movement) Order 1995*. Before this legislation, farmers were already keeping a record of the birth, death, acquisition and sale of all their cattle. This legislation extended the period of time these on-farm records had to be kept from three to ten years. The *1995 Order* also amended previous legislation by insisting that farmers now 'informed' auctioneers 'in writing' of the details of the cattle they brought to the market for sale:

> (4) It shall be the duty of the owner or person in charge of any bovine animals to inform in writing –
>
> (a) the person who, in relation to a market to which they are moved, is the market operator,

. . .
of the following particulars-

(i) the ear tag number of each animal;
(ii) the date of the movement;
(iii) the place from which the movement was made
(iv) the place to which the movement was made.

(*The Bovine Animals (Records, Identification and Movement) Order 1995*, Article 5, paragraph 4, HMSO 1995)

This legislation also introduced the auction's legal obligation to collect and keep the farmers' written declarations about the identification and movement of their cattle for a period of 6 months. Farmers were not informed directly about this new legislation by MAFF. Instead, farmers were told by the auction staff whose job it became to collect written declarations at the auction. To facilitate this procedure, the auction, on the advice of the Livestock Auctioneers' Association, produced a form of their own to serve as the farmers' written declaration about the animals that they brought to market. Figure 5.1 is a reproduction of the form produced by the Ruthin Auction. This form is in English. If this had been a MAFF/WOAD text it would have been produced as a bilingual form or a form with separate Welsh and English versions. Being a private sector organisation, the livestock auction was not required to produce texts such as this in Welsh as well as English. When I spoke to one of the auctioneers about this, he explained that they were just beginning to change their practice of producing all their written texts in English – a practice that dated back to the founding of the company at the end of the previous century. He explained that in response to their shareholders' requests, they had, for example, just produced their annual report in Welsh as well as English. As yet, however, they had no plans to produce Welsh or bilingual versions of the *animal movement form.*

Auction staff: Stan as bureaucracy delegate and mediator

Implementing the 1995 Order at the auction brought about changes in the work responsibilities of some of the auction staff who had to collect, check and (initially) fill in the animal movement forms for farmers. Stan was specifically employed by the auction to do this work. Stan was retired and, at the time of the fieldwork for this research, in his early seventies. He had grown up and lived locally in the rural district outside Ruthin on a smallholding where, until the late 1970s, he and his wife had kept some milking cows. Stan had spent most of his working life employed by a local agricultural retail company, the Vale of Clwyd Farmers. It was because of his long experience of dealing with farmers, his 'meticulousness' with paper work, and the fact that he was a Welsh-user that, the auctioneers said, he

THE BOVINE ANIMALS (RECORDS, IDENTIFICATION & MOVEMENT) ORDER 1995

ADDRESS FROM WHICH CATTLE MOVED & HOLDING NUMBER

Name : ....

Address : ....

....

Holding N°. : ....

ADDRESS OF PREMISES TO WHICH MOVED : *FARMERS AUCTION CO.,* *, CLWYD*

DATE OF MOVEMENT / SALE :

This form must accompany all cattle to market. It must apply to all cattle, including calves.

Auction Lot N°.	Official Ear Tag	Freeze Brand	Breed	Sex M /F	Age (Cattle) Date of Birth (Calves)	CID/CCD Status
	/					
	/					
	/					
	/					
	/					
	/					
	/					
	/					

DECLARATIONS

1. I hereby declare that I am the owner/owner's agent of the animal(s) described above and that to the best of my knowledge the particulars shown on this form are true and complete.
2. I further declare that the Auction Lot Numbers are currently marked with the Official Ear Tag Numbers and that any CID/CCD's relating to these lot numbers are correctly matched.

or

3. I authorise the auctioneers to act on my behalf without any responsibility attached to this action in respect of ear numbers or CID/CCD's.

CALVES

4. Calves : None of the calves are the progeny of a dam in which BSE is suspected or has been officially confirmed.
5. Calves : None of the calves are from a herd in which there is / has been present a case of EBL, notified and confirmed within the last 3 years.
6. Calves : None have been brought to a market before this day. Calf N°............... was presented

at .... Market on ..../........../........ (being a date within 28 days of today).

Signature of Owner / Agent :

BSE FREE CATTLE DECLARATION

7. Cattle : I hereby declare that the animals described above are from holdings in which BSE has not been diagnosed in the last 6 years.

or

8. Cattle : (Purchased animal) During it's lifetime this animal has only lived on the holdings listed:

Holding of Birth Holding N°. :..Herd N°. :...

Address :..

....

Intermediate Holdings :..

Signature of Owner / Agent :

Figure 5.1 The Animal Movement Form

was taken on for this part-time work at the auction. In his work, Stan was positioned as a MAFF delegate who undertakes the face-work commitment of MAFF's bureaucratic system, mediating the literacy practices that incorporated farmers within its abstract bureaucratic order.

To show how farmers become incorporated into MAFF's abstract bureaucratic system through the animal movement form, the following section provides a brief account of the way cattle sales are organised at the auction.

Becoming incorporated into MAFF bureaucracy

Selling cattle at market[3]

Local farmers like Dewi Wilkinson in Figure 5.2, sold their heifers and old dairy cattle (barrens) at the livestock auction in Ruthin. Dewi's oldest son worked at the auction on Thursdays and Fridays and so it was usually he who drove the cattle by truck the four miles from their farm to the auction. On arrival at the auction, farmers bringing cattle for sale took their trailers round to the unloading and loading bays (unloading *and* loading bays and cattle section are the auction staff's names for these parts of the auction) at the side of the auction's cattle section. The cattle were unloaded from their trailers and herded by their owners and some of the auction staff into pennie (pens) or corlannau (sheep folds) in the cattle section where they were kept until they were taken to the sale ring to be sold. This process of unloading and penning the cattle was referred to by the auction staff as 'bwcio mewn' ('booking in'). Bwcio mewn was when the cattle were identified with 'lot number stickers' (see Figure 5.2). These lot numbers, together with the names and addresses of the farmers, were then recorded on what was called the auction's 'sale sheet' (see Figure 5.2).

According to the auctioneers, bwcio mewn, and the written texts and practices it involved, had been a part of the auction's sale routine for many years. In October 1995, farmers bringing their cattle to the auction encountered an additional dimension of MAFF bureaucracy – the animal movement form incorporated into the bwcio mewn process. For the farmers selling their barren cows[4], Stan was the 'face' of this new bureaucracy. He told them about their new form-filling obligation. Stan questioned farmers to fill in the animal movement form, and he also gave them extra copies of the form to take home so that, in future, they could fill them in themselves before coming to the auction.

On the day that I observed him at his work, Stan had been doing this job for several months. By then, many of the farmers brought the animal movement forms with them to market. Stan collected forms from those farmers and checked that they had completed them properly. Stan filled out the form with the farmers who hadn't brought their own (see Figure 5.2) and gave them extra copies to take home.

The livestock auction showing the open air 'cattle section' on the left

Dewi Wilkinson with his cows on the farm

A cow's back with lot number sticker and sprayed with a strip to indicate that it is being sold as 'BSE free'.

Stan (right) filling in the animal movement form and Herbie (left) with the sale sheets asking a farmer about the ear tag number of his cattle.

Pen	Desc.	Res.	Seller	Buyer	Price	£	p.

The auction sale sheet

Figure 5.2 Selling cattle at the livestock auction

Mid morning on Thursday 30 March 1995 in the cattle section of the auction. Sound of chains clinking and cows lowing as they were unloaded off the trailer. Stan (S) approached a young farmer (F3) in his early 20's as he was opening up his trailer to get the cattle out.

Transcript of original encounter	English version of original encounter
1. **S: su'dach chi . tywydd garw**	1. **S: how are you . dreadful weather**
2. **F: (xxx)**	2. **F: (xxx)**
3. **S: 'dach chi 'di dod â** form **do?**	3. **S: you've brought a** form **have you?**
4. **F3: na s'gyn ' ai 'run**	4. **F3: no I haven't got one**
5. **S:** [os] **s'gyn chi 'run . .na'i roi rei i chi at (xx) sydd yn hollol (xx)**	5. **S:** [if] **you haven't got one . I'll give you some for (xx) which is completely (xx)**
6. **F3:.s'im isio roi lawr ffor' 'cw ?**[a]	6. **F3: don't want to put** [the cows] **down that way?**[a]
7. **S: lawr ffor hyn . . be 'di'r enw ?**	7. **S: down this way . . what's the name?**
8. **F3:** I. G. Roberts	8. **F3:** I. G. Roberts
9. **S:** [*wrth ysgrifennu*] I.G. ?	9. **S:** [*writing*] I.G. ?
10. **F3: ia . wel** [*buwch yn brefu*] I.G , B **a** S **'dwch ?**	10. **F3: yes . well** [*cow lowing*] I.G, B **and** S ?
11. **S:** [*ysgrifennu enwau yn y rhan o'r fform ar gyfer enwau gwerthwyr*]	11. **S:** [*writing names in section of form which requires the sellers' names*]
12. **K** [*i F3*]: **su' mae**[b]	12. **K** [*to F3*]: **hello**[b]
13. **F3** [*i K*]: **o su' mae . ti'n iawn ?**	13. **F3** [*to K*]: **oh hello . y'alright?**
14. **K: o'n ni'n meddwl dyle bo' fi'n dy 'nabod di .. Cae Afon**[c]	14. **K: I was thinking I should know who you are .. Cae Afon**[c]
15. **S** [*i F3*]: **Cae Afon?**	15. **S** [*to F3*]: **Cae Afon?**
16. **F3: Cae Afon**	16. **F3: Cae Afon**
17. **S:** number (xx). .holding number three six	17. **S:** number (xx). . holding number three six
18. **F3:** oh double nine . triple nine	18. **F3:** oh double nine . triple nine
19. **S:** triple nine . oh double nine **?** .	19. **S:** triple nine . oh double nine ? .
20. **F3: ia .** nine **wedyn**	20. **F3: yes . then** nine
21. **S: y .** number **'i chlust 'i ?**	21. **S: er . her ear** number **?**
22. **F3: 'dach chisio'r** herd **neu'r llall ? .** herd number **dach chi isio ia ?**	22. **F3: d'you want the** herd [*number*] **or the other ? .the** herd number **you want is it?**

THE BOVINE ANIMALS
(RECORDS, IDENTIFICATION & MOVEMENT) ORDER 1995

ADDRESS FROM WHICH CATTLE MOVED & HOLDING NUMBER

Name : ....

Address : ....

....

Holding N°. : ....

ADDRESS OF PREMISES TO WHICH MOVED : *FARMERS AUCTION CO., . CLWYD*

DATE OF MOVEMENT / SALE :

This form must accompany all cattle to market. It must apply to all cattle, including calves.

Auction Lot N°.	Official Ear Tag	Freeze Brand	Breed	Sex M /F	Age (Cattle) Date of Birth (Calves)	CID/CCD Status
	/					
	/					
	/					
	/					
	/					
	/					
	/					
	/					

DECLARATIONS

1. I hereby declare that I am the owner/owner's agent of the animal(s) described above and that to the best of my knowledge the particulars shown on this form are true and complete.
2. I further declare that the Auction Lot Numbers are currently marked with the Official Ear Tag Numbers and that any CID/CCD's relating to these lot numbers are correctly matched.

or

3. I authorise the auctioneers to act on my behalf without any responsibility attached to this action in respect of ear numbers or CID/CCD's.

CALVES

4. Calves : None of the calves are the progeny of a dam in which BSE is suspected or has been officially confirmed.
5. Calves : None of the calves are from a herd in which there is / has been present a case of EBL, notified and confirmed within the last 3 years.
6. Calves : None have been brought to a market before this day. Calf N° .... was presented at ....Market on ..../........./........ (being a date within 28 days of today).

Signature of Owner / Agent :

BSE FREE CATTLE DECLARATION

7. Cattle : I hereby declare that the animals described above are from holdings in which BSE has not been diagnosed in the last 6 years.

or

8. Cattle : (Purchased animal) During it's lifetime this animal has only lived on the holdings listed:

Holding of Birth Holding N°. : ....Herd N°. : ....

Address : ....

....

Intermediate Holdings : ....

Signature of Owner / Agent :

The animal movement form before it was filled in by Stan

Transcription conventions: **Text in this font = originally spoken in Welsh**; text in this font = originally spoken in English; [*italics in square brackets*] = my commentary; (xxx) = unintelligible speech; . = a pause; . . = a longer pause

Welsh	English
23. **S: y . ia**	23. **S: er . yes**
24. **F3:** 'A' seven one five seven	24. **F3:** 'A' seven one five seven
25. **S:** 'A' seven one five seven **ia (xxx)** number seven one five seven	25. **S:** 'A' seven one five seven **yes (xxx)** number seven one five seven
26. **F3: y . saith tri pump 'dio**	26. **F3: er . it's seven three five**
27. **S: saith tri pump**	27. **S: seven three five**
28. **F3: tri pump . saith dau un dau**	28. **F3: three five . seven two one two**
29. **S: saith dau un dau . iawn .** [*darllen y golofn nesa ar y fform*] breed . fresian	29. **S: seven two one two . right** [*reading the next column on form*] breed . fresian
30. **S: be 'di hoed nw ?**	30. **S: how old are they ?**
31. **F3:** no idea	31. **F3:** no idea
32. **S: saith saith . wyth . 'beth felly ?**	32. **S: seven seven . eight .something like that?**
33. **F3: (xx) ia**	33. **F3: (xx) yes**
34. **S:** BSE free?	34. **S:** BSE free?
35. **F3: na 'dyn**	35. **F3: no they're not**
36. **S: nagoedd .** [*swn troi tudalenau*] **. yr ola' 'ma gynta 'dach chi'n roi ia ?**	36. **S: no they weren't .** [*sound of pages turning*] **you're putting this last one first are you?**
37. **F3: ia . a wedyn**	37. **F3: yes . and then**
38. **S:** [*wrth ysgrifennu*] **yr ola gynta' . . iawn**	38. **S:** [*while writing*] **the last one first . . right**
39. **F3: ia** [*swn giatiau metel yn agor i ollwng y gwartheg drwyddynt*]	39. **F3: yes** [*sound of metal gates opening to let the cows through*]

THE BOVINE ANIMALS
(RECORDS, IDENTIFICATION & MOVEMENT) ORDER 1995

ADDRESS FROM WHICH CATTLE MOVED & HOLDING NUMBER

Name : ....

Address : ....

....

Holding N°. : ....

ADDRESS OF PREMISES TO WHICH MOVED : *FARMERS AUCTION CO.,* *. CLWYD*

DATE OF MOVEMENT / SALE :

This form must accompany all cattle to market. It must apply to all cattle, including calves.

Auction Lot N°.	Official Ear Tag	Freeze Brand	Breed	Sex M /F	Age (Cattle) Date of Birth (Calves)	CID/CCD Status
	/					
	/					
	/					
	/					
	/					
	/					
	/					
	/					

DECLARATIONS

1. I hereby declare that I am the owner/owner's agent of the animal(s) described above and that to the best of my knowledge the particulars shown on this form are true and complete.
2. I further declare that the Auction Lot Numbers are currently marked with the Official Ear Tag Numbers and that any CID/CCD's relating to these lot numbers are correctly matched.

or

3. I authorise the auctioneers to act on my behalf without any responsibility attached to this action in respect of ear numbers or CID/CCD's.

CALVES

4. Calves : None of the calves are the progeny of a dam in which BSE is suspected or has been officially confirmed.
5. Calves : None of the calves are from a herd in which there is / has been present a case of EBL, notified and confirmed within the last 3 years.
6. Calves : None have been brought to a market before this day. Calf N° .... was presented

at .... Market on ..../........../....... (being a date within 28 days of today)

Signature of Owner / Agent :

BSE FREE CATTLE DECLARATION

7. Cattle : I hereby declare that the animals described above are from holdings in which BSE has not been diagnosed in the last 6 years.

or

8. Cattle : (Purchased animal) During it's lifetime this animal has only lived on the holdings listed:

Holding of Birth Holding N°. :...Herd N° ....

Address :..

....

Intermediate Holdings :..

Signature of Owner / Agent :

A representation of the animal movement form as it was completed by Stan

Figure 5.3 Stan completing the *animal movement form* with a farmer

Notes

a The farmer was checking with Stan which direction he should herd his cattle as he unloaded them from his trailer.

b su'mae / hello – I recognised that this farmer was the younger brother of an old school friend of mine and since I was watching him being questioned by S. made our previous acquaintance known.

c Cae Afon is a (fictitious) farm name. The name of Farmer 3 is also fictitious.

d This is not a scanned copy of the original animal movement form as it was filled in by Stan for Farmer 3. It is a representation of that form that I have produced myself by copying the text Stan produced from the transcript and the photographs I took of forms filled in by him.

Transcription conventions: **Text in this font = originally spoken in Welsh**; text in this font = originally spoken in English; [*italics in square brackets*] = my commentary; (xxx) = unintelligible speech; . = a pause; . . = a longer pause

The preceding extract from the audio recordings[5] I made at the auction is an example of Stan completing the animal movement form with a young farmer. I shall go on to focus on the insights this recording provides into the discoursal process of becoming incorporated into MAFF's bureaucratic discourse order in the next section of this chapter.

Accessing agricultural bureaucracy's discursive order

Bwcio mewn: an access point to agricultural bureaucracy

Bwcio mewn at the auction can be seen as one of what I shall call the 'access points' (a term taken from Giddens 1990, p. 83) to agricultural bureaucracy, where a farmer becomes part of the abstract bureaucratic discourse order[6] of MAFF. In this event, the animal movement form is the text that mediates MAFF bureaucracy. The form was devised for collecting and recording factual information about the farmer and his livestock. The production of a factual record of the identification and movement of farm animals is an important part of the process of transforming the physical and locally situated activities of a farmer's work into the abstract conceptual and classificational order of MAFF's bureaucratic and discursive courses of action.[7] In the process of filling out the form, the physical actions of taking livestock to market and so on involved in the movement and sale of animals, are factualised as nominalisations of material processes (Halliday 1985): *ADDRESS FROM WHICH CATTLE MOVED; ADDRESS OF PREMISES TO WHICH MOVED, DECLARATIONS* and *BSE FREE CATTLE DECLARATION* (see Figure 5.1 on p. 77). These real-time, local historic processes become nominalised as atemporal classificationary facts within the 'text time' of this form. Factualising information is a discursive means of standardising and homogenising the identities of all the farmers who are incorporated within MAFF and EU agricultural bureaucracy. Factualising locally situated material processes is also, I suggest, partly how the disembedding of globalisation is accomplished discursively.

For the farmer, the process of 'accessing' or becoming a part of MAFF's bureaucratic system at the auction is a discoursal process mediated by Stan. This process can be seen as a set of bilingual literacy and discourse practices involving three interconnected and overlapping dimensions:

- Stan's *articulation* of the identificational categories of the animal movement text;
- Stan and Farmer 3's *negotiation* of the facts for the text;
- Stan's *inscription* of the negotiated facts on to the form.

These three interconnected dimensions are represented in Figure 5.4.

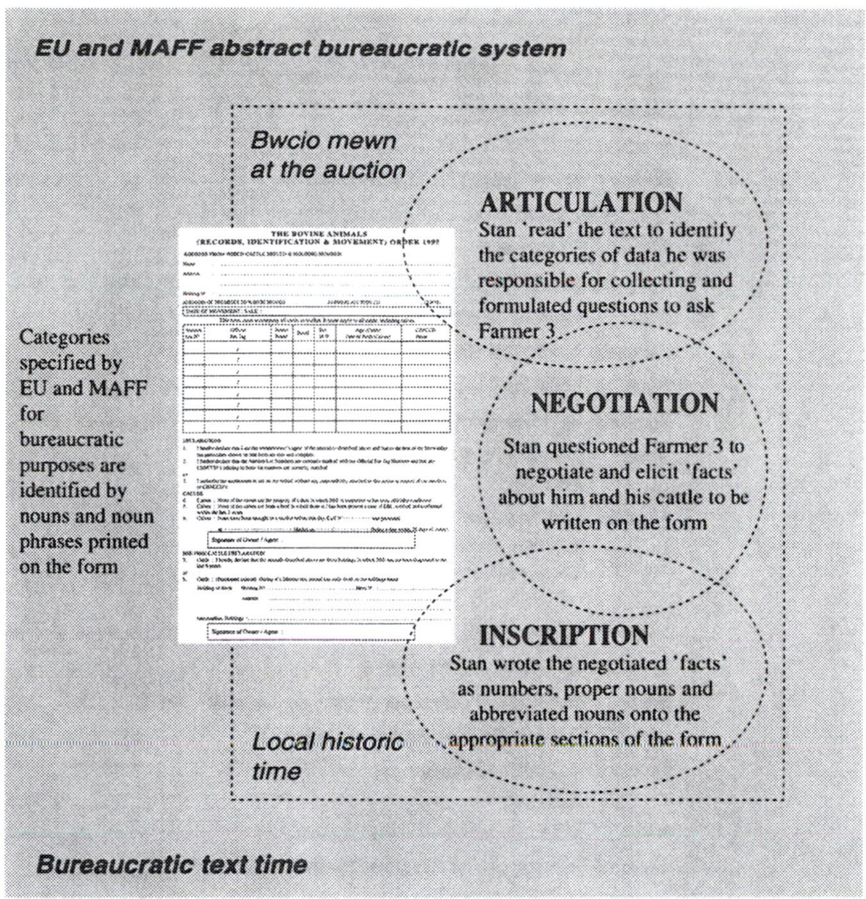

Figure 5.4 A representation of the discursive process of 'accessing' MAFF's agricultural bureaucratic system

Figure 5.5 is a visual representation of the way the processes of *articulating, negotiating* and *inscribing* are accomplished discoursally in the encounter between Stan and Farmer 3. On the left of Figure 5.5 are the identificational categories used in MAFF's bureaucratic order, as they appear in the animal movement form. In the central column is the excerpt from the locally situated encounter at the auction where Stan and Farmer 3 negotiate facts about the farmer. On the right are the identificational and categorical facts as Stan inscribed them on to the form.

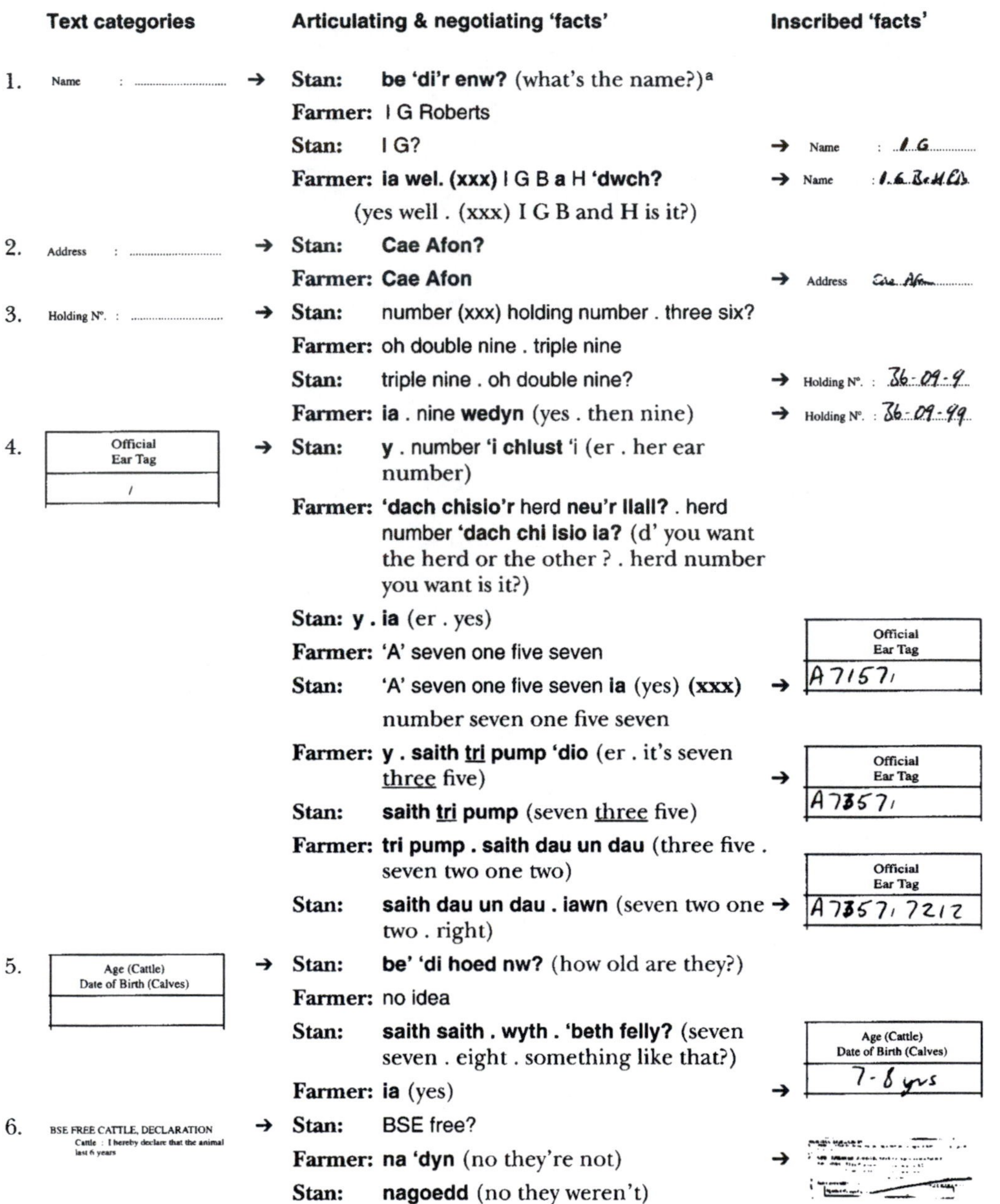

	Text categories		Articulating & negotiating 'facts'	Inscribed 'facts'
1.	Name :	→	Stan: **be 'di'r enw?** (what's the name?)[a]	
			Farmer: I G Roberts	
			Stan: I G?	→ Name : I G
			Farmer: **ia wel. (xxx)** I G B **a** H **'dwch?** (yes well . (xxx) I G B and H is it?)	→ Name : I.G. B.H.
2.	Address :	→	Stan: **Cae Afon?**	
			Farmer: **Cae Afon**	→ Address Cae Afon
3.	Holding N°. :	→	Stan: number (xxx) holding number . three six?	
			Farmer: oh double nine . triple nine	
			Stan: triple nine . oh double nine?	→ Holding N°. : 36-09-9
			Farmer: **ia** . nine **wedyn** (yes . then nine)	→ Holding N°. : 36-09-99
4.	Official Ear Tag /	→	Stan: **y** . number **'i chlust** 'i (er . her ear number)	
			Farmer: **'dach chisio'r** herd **neu'r llall?** . herd number **'dach chi isio ia?** (d' you want the herd or the other ? . herd number you want is it?)	
			Stan: **y . ia** (er . yes)	
			Farmer: 'A' seven one five seven	
			Stan: 'A' seven one five seven **ia** (yes) **(xxx)** number seven one five seven	→ Official Ear Tag A7157/
			Farmer: **y . saith tri pump 'dio** (er . it's seven three five)	→ Official Ear Tag A7357/
			Stan: **saith tri pump** (seven three five)	
			Farmer: **tri pump . saith dau un dau** (three five . seven two one two)	
			Stan: **saith dau un dau . iawn** (seven two one two . right)	→ Official Ear Tag A7357/ 7212
5.	Age (Cattle) Date of Birth (Calves)	→	Stan: **be' 'di hoed nw?** (how old are they?)	
			Farmer: no idea	
			Stan: **saith saith . wyth . 'beth felly?** (seven seven . eight . something like that?)	
			Farmer: **ia** (yes)	→ Age (Cattle) Date of Birth (Calves) 7-8 yrs
6.	BSE FREE CATTLE, DECLARATION Cattle : I hereby declare that the animal last 6 years	→	Stan: BSE free?	
			Farmer: **na 'dyn** (no they're not)	→
			Stan: **nagoedd** (no they weren't)	

Figure 5.5 Articulating, negotiating and inscribing MAFF's bureaucratic facts

Note

[a] Transcription conventions: **Text in this font** = originally spoken in Welsh; text in this font = originally spoken in English; (text in brackets) = English version of original Welsh; (xxx) = unintelligible speech; . = a pause

Talking textual bureaucracy into being: text interpretation and articulation

Articulating textual categories into talk involved two strategies. First, reformulating nouns and noun phrases printed in English on the form into oral questions of relational processes of identification in Welsh. And second, reading out noun phrases directly from the text as elliptical questions or prompts in English. The bilingual character of this discourse is not unexpected in an event where Welsh is the code preferred by the participants for their oral interaction and English is the code of the bureaucratic text they are interpreting and inscribing. This pattern of code mixing appears throughout my data (collected from a wide range of other work, and non-work contexts) when Welsh-users were dealing with texts written in English. This kind of code-mixing did not occur, however, when the written texts and the spoken interaction were in Welsh.

Reformulating parts of a text into talk and 'reading out' other bits would also be expected in a monolingual event. In this bilingual context, code mixing highlights how the discursive formations of the written text are mixed up with those of the oral interaction between Stan and this farmer. I think the bwcio mewn event is constituted by a particular configuration of the complex discourse formations that make up what I am calling the 'farm world discourse' through which farmers live their lives. For the Welsh farmers in my study, their farm world discourse is bilingual. During bwcio mewn, as I shall go on to show, elements of bureaucratic discourse in English from the text are mixed up with elements of an '*agos ati*' (literally, 'close to you') discourse in Welsh with which Stan and the farmer negotiate bureaucratic facts and some of the controlling purpose of this bureaucratic encounter. Different and conflicting subject positions and interpersonal relations operate within each discourse. We can also locate agos ati discourse elements in this encounter as being a feature of the local historic discourse order which are conspicuously absent in the disembedded bureaucratic discourse of the animal movement form.

Stan managed complex 'personal/professional' interpersonal relationships with the farmers he dealt with. He told me that he knew most of the farmers who came to the auction. Some he knew very well as friends, neighbours, members of the same chapel. Others he knew from his years working for the Vale of Clwyd Farmers. In this event, Stan was also positioned as a delegate of the agricultural bureaucratic system and had some institutional power. The farmers were positioned as the legal owners of cattle whose farming practices were being monitored and controlled by the system Stan represented. Each farmer also had particular personal relationships with the auction staff.

As a bureaucracy mediator in this encounter, Stan engaged with the animal movement form in a professional capacity. To mediate the fact gathering purpose of the text, Stan reformulated the identificational noun and noun phrase, categories of 'Name', 'Official Ear Tag' and 'Age (Cattle)' as be 'di'r enw? (what's the *name*?), [be 'di] number 'i chlust 'i? ([what's] her *ear* number?), and be 'di hoed nw? (literally – what's their age?). When asking the farmer for a name, Stan formulated an impersonal question rather than, for example, be 'di'ch enw chi? (what's your name?). Stan's question was appropriate in this context since the name that had to be recorded on the form needed to match the name of the owner of the cattle and was not necessarily the name of the person bringing the cattle to market. With the other two questions, Stan seems to be reappropriating the factual bureaucratic discourse of the text into what I am calling the agos ati element of this farm world discourse where the question forms are highly elliptical as is typical of 'less formal' spoken Welsh and the cattle are referred to as 'she' and 'they'. This agos ati discourse seems to be mediating and mitigating some of the controlling dimension of the bureaucratic text.

At other times, during his mediatory dialogue with the MAFF discourses of the text, Stan also took on the text's bureaucratic voice by articulating MAFF terminology as it appeared in the text. One example is the noun phrase Stan articulated unchanged from the form to formulate the elliptical question '[Are they] BSE free?'. 'BSE free' were the first two words of the nominalised heading of *BSE FREE CATTLE DECLARATION* which, together with the additional contextualisation cues of rising intonation and looking up at the farmer, signalled Stan's request for confirmation or denial of this statement. On other occasions that morning I recorded Stan requesting the same information asking a farmer: ''dyn nw'n BSE free?' (are they BSE free?) [1/2 B235]; or checking ''di ddim yn BSE?' (she's not BSE?) [auction extract 3 l.141 1/2 A093] and reformulating in Welsh: 'yn lân 'di?' (she's clean is she?) [1/2 B346] to a fellow auction worker. Another classificational noun he voiced directly from the text is 'Holding No.' which he articulated as 'holding number . three six?' (see Figure 5.5).

Being inscribed into the bureaucratic system: writing orally negotiated facts into text

Figure 5.5 demonstrates how the text inscribed by Stan on to the form was (almost exclusively) the words and numbers Farmer 3 gave Stan in response to his questions. The farmer had some expertise of the agricultural bureaucracy that he was dealing with at the auction.[8] He had some prior knowledge of the identificational categories used for agricultural bureaucracy forms. We can see this, for example, in the way he answered Stan's first question in the 'appropriate' way for this record of animal movement. This was typical, I noticed, of all the farmers Stan questioned. When asked, 'be 'di'r enw?' (what's the name?), Farmer 3 gave the initials and surname of the household members in whose name these barren cows were kept. He did not give their first names or just his own name which he could have done but which would not have been appropriate here since MAFF records and data bases are kept with individuals identified by their initials and surname only. Also for these records, the name of the owner of the cattle was required and not the name of the person bringing them to market. This selection of appropriate name for the bureaucratic discourse of the written text contrasts with the names used between Stan and the farmers who referred to each other more familiarly through their agos ati discourse by their first names or first name and farm name when they were not form filling. The farmer knew what Stan meant by 'holding number', knowing this number by memory. He was also familiar with the alphanumeric cattle identification code used on the new official ear tags. These ear tags had two sets of numbers: on the front the 'herd number' (the term used in MAFF literature) and on the back another number identifying the animal itself. Farmer 3 initiated the use of MAFF terminology (in English) to clarify with Stan which ear number he wanted for the form: 'herd number 'dach chi isio ia?' ([it's the] herd number you want is it?).

In this encounter, Farmer 3 took on the position of a farmer with some expertise in agricultural bureaucratic discourse. Not only did he answer Stan's questions but also oriented his answers to the categorical order and discourse formation of the agricultural bureaucratic system. Part of this orientation included providing facts about himself and his livestock in English rather than in Welsh. He voiced the initials of the names using English rather than Welsh phonetic values. He also gave the holding number and ear tag numbers in English. This pattern of using English for initials and figures is common throughout my data – particularly for bureaucratic and commercial encounters where, for most people, English was the predominant language of commercial and bureaucratic discourse. The only use of Welsh for numbers in this encounter was when Farmer 3 switched to Welsh, using this code contrast and stress on the word tri (three) to signal the place where he had made a mistake with the ear tag number (see Figure 5.5). This is also the only example in my bwcio mewn recordings of Welsh being used for these numbers.

For the most part, this farmer was compliant with the way he was positioned by this encounter with MAFF discourse. This may be because he was already familiar with this bureaucratic positioning. The farmer also had to comply because, unless he completed this form, he could not sell his cattle at the auction. Paul Davies (1994) reports on the resistance and compliance of unemployed people with the bureaucratic literacy practices of the Employment Service. In contrast with this farmer, most of the unemployed people in Davies' study had little or no expertise of the Employment Service's bureaucratic discourse and consequently felt threatened by it. I think Farmer 3 shows some resistance to the process of being bureaucratised in his (as I interpret it) non-co-operational answer 'no idea' to Stan's question 'be 'di hoed nw?' (how old are they?). Answering Stan's question in English also seems to me to be the farmer's way of managing some resistance to the way he was being positioned with a code-switch to English which distanced him from the otherwise agos ati-ness of Stan's question in Welsh.

Some concluding thoughts about literacy as a social practice

Making connections between empirical data and social theory provides insights into literacy practices as being constitutive of larger social processes. In my research, the literacy practices of bwcio mewn at the auction are partly constitutive of social organisation and control as it is realised in the specific context of agricultural bureaucracy. Literacy practices, specifically the process of negotiating and inscribing factual information, are also constitutive of the disembedding of local historic material processes and interpersonal relations which are part of the globalisation of the contemporary social order.

Focusing on the discourse of bwcio mewn gives some additional insights into the interrelationship between talk and texts in literacy events and can help refine the notion of 'talk around text'. In this bwcio mewn context I have characterised this relationship as involving *articulation, negotiation* and *inscription.* I have shown how talk articulates discursive elements of texts. Sometimes these elements of a text's discourse are incorporated unchanged into local historic talk and would be called 'manifest intertextuality' in Norman Fairclough's (1989, 1992) framework for discourse analysis. At other times, a text's discourse can be reappropriated into a different discourse element, as Stan reappropriated bureaucratic discourse elements in English into elements of a Welsh agos ati discourse. Talk can also mediate and mitigate the controlling dimension of a text, as again with an agos ati discourse. Texts embody and mediate the conceptual and categorical order of a bureaucratic system. Inscribing talk into text incorporates local historic processes and circumstances within the discursive order of an abstract and disembedded bureaucratic system.

Finally, this chapter shows how a literacy mediator mediates more than the immediate processes of articulating and inscribing the discursive order of a text. Literacy mediators are also positioned within the larger social structures of which their mediatory literacy practices are a part. In this context, Stan as a mediator of bwcio mewn literacy practices was positioned as a 'delegate' of the agricultural bureaucratic order. He also provided the 'facework commitment' of an otherwise faceless bureaucratic system. Thinking of literacy mediators in this way extends our understanding of the way people's individual literacy practices constitute larger social structures and social processes.

Notes

1 I would like to thank all the auctioneers, staff and farmers at the Ruthin Farmers Auction for their support in carrying out this research. On this occasion, my special thanks go to Mr Stanley Jones (Stan), Mr Paul Roberts, Mr Dewi Wilkinson and Mr Herbert Watson (Herbie) who have helped me make sense of agricultural bureaucracy and livestock auction practices. In accordance with their wishes and approval real names are used in this chapter.

2 The fieldwork for this research was conducted with people living and working in Ruthin (a small market town), Bontuchel and Cyffylliog (two small villages and rural districts near Ruthin) in Dyffryn Clwyd/ the Vale of Clwyd, north-east Wales.

3 My account of selling cattle at the Ruthin Farmers' Auction is constructed from my observations during several visits to the market in March and April 1995. On these visits I took photos, collected written texts and made audio recordings. I also discussed this data with Stan, farmers like Dewi Wilkinson and the auctioneers.

4 Other auction staff dealt with the farmers selling other kinds of cattle: heifers or steers, etc.

5 I recorded Stan's interaction with farmers and his auction staff colleagues with a tape recorder that I carried in a bag on my shoulder. I followed Stan about in the cattle section as he did his work. I did not photograph this encounter between Stan and Farmer 3 because I felt it would be intrusive and disrupt their interaction given that I was standing so close to them. After they had finished, I had a chat with the farmer about my research at the auction as well as exchanging news about mutual friends.

6 The notion of a 'discourse order' or 'discourse formation' comes originally from the work of French discourse analysts, Michel Foucault (1972) and later Michel Pêcheux (1982), who conceptualised social order as comprising a complex network of interconnected discourse formations. Norman Fairclough (1989, 1992) also uses these concepts in his theory and methodology of Textually Orientated Discourse Analysis.

7 The point I am making here is close to the general point Dorothy Smith makes that: 'The process of inscription is of special significance at the boundaries of organization or discourse where "environing" actualities are converted into the conceptual and categorical order of organizational or discursive courses of action' (1993, p. 216).

8 Other accounts of bureaucratic mediation by Mike Baynham (1993) and Liezl Malan (1996) describe encounters between 'lay people' who have little understanding of the bureaucratic discourse of the bureaucratic system they are dealing with and have to depend upon literacy mediators or cultural brokers to interpret and explain for them.

References

Bannister, N. (1997) 'Dishing Up a Brighter Future', *Guardian*, Saturday 10 May, p. 26.

Baynham, M. (1993) 'Code Switching and Mode Switching: Community Interpreters and Mediators of Literacy', in B. Street (ed.) *Cross-Cultural Approaches to Literacy*, Cambridge: Cambridge University Press.

The Council of the European Communities (1992) 'Council Regulation (EEC) No. 3508/92 of 27 November 1992 Establishing an Integrated Administration and Control System for Certain Community Aid Schemes', *Official Journal of the European Communities* L355: 1–5.

Davies, P. (1994) 'Long-term Unemployment and Literacy: A Case-study of the Restart Interview', in M. Hamilton, D. Barton and R. Ivanič (eds) *Worlds of Literacy*, Clevedon: Multilingual Matters.

Fairclough, N. (1989) *Language and Power*, London: Longman.

Fairclough, N. (1992) *Discourse and Social Change*, Cambridge: Polity Press.

Foucault, M. (1972) *The Archaeology of Knowledge*, trans. by A. Sheridan-Smith, London: Tavistock Publications.

Garfinkel, H., Lynch, M. and Livingston, E. (1981) 'The Work of a Discovering Science Construed with Materials from the Optically Discovered Pulsar', *Philosophy of the Social Sciences* 11: 131–58.

Giddens, A. (1990) *The Consequences of Modernity*, Cambridge: Polity Press.

Goody, J. (ed.) (1977) *The Domestication of the Savage Mind*, Cambridge: Cambridge University Press.

Halliday, M. (1985) *An Introduction to Functional Grammar*, London: Edward Arnold.

HMSO (1993) *Welsh Language Act 1993*, London: HMSO.

HMSO (1995) No. 12 *The Bovine Animals (Records, Identification and Movement) Order*, London: HMSO.

McArthur, T. (1986) *Worlds of Reference: Lexicography, Learning and Language from the Clay Tablet to the Computer*, Cambridge: Cambridge University Press.

Malan, L. (1996) 'Literacy Mediation and Social Identity in Newtown, Eastern Cape', in M. Prinsloo and M. Breier (eds) *The Social Uses of Literacy: Theory and Practice in Contemporary South Africa*, Amsterdam: John Benjamins Publishing Co.

Ministry of Agriculture Fisheries and Food (1995) *The Integrated Administration and Control System 1995*, London: Ministry of Agriculture Fisheries and Food.

Pêcheux, M. (1982) *Language, Semantics and Ideology: Stating the Obvious*, trans. by H. Nagpal, London: Macmillan.

Sarangi, S. and Slembrouck, S. (1996) *Language, Bureaucracy and Social Control*, London and New York: Longman.

Smith, D. (1993) *Texts, Facts, and Femininity: Exploring the Relations of Ruling*, London and New York: Routledge.

Weber, M. (1978) *Economy and Society*, 2 vols, London: University of California Press.

6

TEXTS IN PRACTICES

Interpreting the physical characteristics of children's project work

Fiona Ormerod and Roz Ivanič

In this chapter we claim that literacy practices can be inferred not only from events but also from characteristics of the 'text' itself. By viewing a text not just as a form of visual and verbal representation, but also as a material object with distinct physical features, we can locate the meanings it is conveying within the physical, technological and social practices associated with its construction and use.

We first describe some of the physical characteristics of a 'project' produced by one 9-year-old child as part of independent topic work set by his teacher and undertaken mainly at home. In the main part of the chapter we extrapolate from our study of the physical characteristics of over forty projects, to suggest a framework for studying a literacy artifact as a 'material' object, reflecting practices associated with its physical production and anticipated future use. We end by discussing the sociocultural nature of the literacy practices we are identifying, showing how they are rooted in the children's experiences in and out of school, as individuals and as members of different social groups. We see the specific activities of these individual children as instantiations of culturally recognisable and historically situated practices, embedded in broader patterns of social change.

We begin with an overview of the research in which this study of physical characteristics is located, in order to place it in the context of a more broadly based study of literacy practices.

Overview of the research[1]

The research is a longitudinal study of 37 children, in one year group at primary school, from year 4 to year 6. The children live in a predominantly middle-class neighbourhood, in a small town in the north-west of England, and the majority have been in the same class together since they started school. We are interested in the changes over time in the literacy practices and products associated with independent 'project work', when they are given a completely free choice of subject matter or a broad field, such as 'animals', from which to select a topic to study. They are expected to work in their own way, over a set period, often in their own time at home as well as at school, and to produce a 'written' outcome: a 'project', which demonstrates not only what they have learned about the topic, but also what they have learned about 'project work'. In developing their understanding of what it means to 'do a project', children bring with them values, attitudes and ways of working rooted in both individual personal histories and shared school learning experiences. While the school and the teacher are to some extent shapers of these activities, as the initiators and ultimate readers of the children's work, they do not exercise as much control over it as they do over many other forms of school work.

We find 'project work' particularly interesting because it seems to engage the children's own interests and enthusiasm, spans the divide between home and school, puts the children more in control of their own work, and allows for a greater variety of approach than more traditional school work. The 'project' as an artefact is very important, in our view, since it embodies, in textual and material form, the whole complex constellation of decisions, actions, feelings, beliefs and processes concerned with focusing on, investigating, studying, engaging with and re-presenting the chosen topic. Choice of semiotic resources (verbal, visual or other modes of representation), materials (surfaces, substances and tools) and technologies results in distinctive characteristics, making each project both similar to and different from others by the same writer and those by other children: a multi-modal literacy artefact, situated textually and materially in the life of the child.

In our research we are carrying out detailed textual analysis which pays attention to the linguistic, visual and physical features of the children's projects. Our observations provide a starting point for text-based interviews with individual children in which we find out more about their work. Each page reveals traces of many different moments in the life of the project, drawing us in and leading us to ask further questions about the surrounding context, and the actors, actions and decisions involved. A single feature pointed out by the researcher can bring to mind specific events, purposes, problems, thoughts and feelings to do with the construction of a particular page, and the project as a whole. This can be particularly rewarding in cases where the child may be fairly quiet and not appear to be recalling anything that they feel is worth mentioning to the researcher. We feel that these two research approaches (multi-modal textual analysis and text-based interview) complement each other, in helping us to understand the relationship between the children's texts and the practices in which they are situated. We are using our data to draw comparisons between the children, and to record how their individual and group practices change over time.

Our focus in this chapter is on the ways in which the *physical characteristics* of the projects – what Kress and van Leeuwen (1996) and van Leeuwen (1998) call the 'materiality' of texts – contribute to our understanding of the children's practices. To illustrate more clearly what we mean by the term 'physical', here is a brief description of one of the projects which we have studied.

One text and its story: Ray's 'Bats' project

The project we have chosen to describe was completed by Ray Abercrombie in Year 5, when he was 9. His teacher set the general topic of 'animals' and the children were free to choose a particular animal, and to work alone or in pairs. Ray decided to work alone and to do his project on bats.

The project takes the form of a small, slim booklet (8 pages, A5 size), hand-produced by the child, using a range of materials. It appears to have been constructed by placing two pieces of thin, plain white A4 card and two pieces of plain white A4 paper in alternating layers, one on top of the other, then folding these together down the centre and securing them with three staples along the fold at top, centre and bottom, so that the first layer of card forms the front and back cover and the other sheets form the enclosed pages. The edges of the sheets appear slightly jagged, suggesting that they have been roughly cut or trimmed, with scissors, to the required size (see Figures 6.1–6.4). These alternating card and paper pages form the surfaces on which Ray works, using different substances and tools. On one page he has added a small, glossy 'batman' sticker, but everything else has been created by him.

Most pages contain a mixture of words and drawings. Ray has used a wider range of materials and techniques for the drawings than for the words. The drawing on the front cover has been densely shaded in pencil and felt tip, with the words written over the picture, in felt tip and biro, creating layers of substances (see Figure 6.1). Inside the booklet, he has produced a map, finely outlined in pencil and shaded in with felt tip and crayon (see Figure 6.3), a chart, drawn in a mixture of biro and felt tip, with Tipp-Ex used to make alterations (see Figure 6.2), and several detailed pencil drawings, constructed using a range of strokes: for example, three small drawings showing the characteristics of different types of bats (see Figure 6.4). In some drawings, indentations on the surface indicate where lines of earlier drafts have been erased.[2]

Most of the words have been written in black biro, in small letters. They are packed closely together in the available space. Many pages bear the imprint of the letters on the reverse surface, indicating the heavy pressure that Ray has applied. He has used Tipp-Ex throughout the project to make alterations to single words (see Figure 6.2) and to whole lines (see Figure 6.4), spreading it thinly in a few places but very thickly elsewhere, creating

Figure 6.1

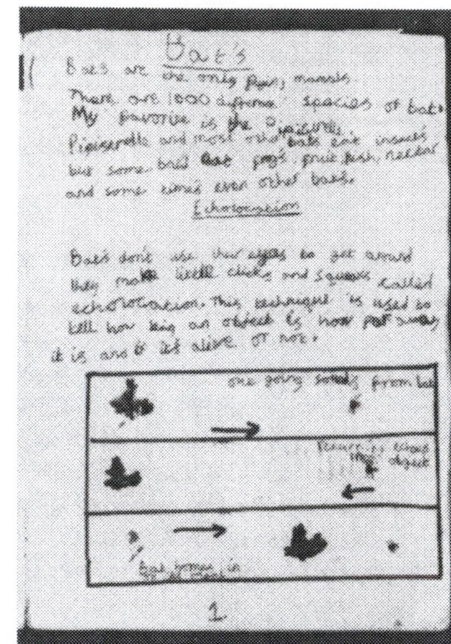

Figure 6.2

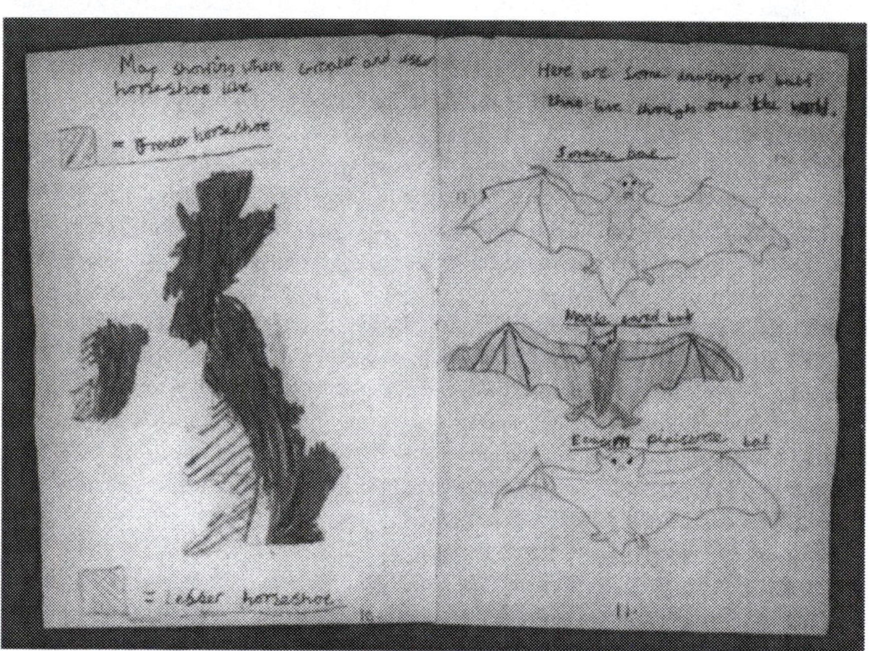

Figure 6.3

Figure 6.4

Figures 6.1–6.4 Ray's 'Bats' project

a raised, rough surface; words are written in biro, on top of the Tipp-Ex, and smudging of the two substances suggests that the Tipp-Ex may not have been completely dry when he started to write over it, making the task difficult.

There is a very strong 'textural' feel to the project, giving a clear impression of the different ways in which Ray has used his materials, in constructing the booklet and communicating his message. We can imagine him carefully choosing his tools, bending over the page, moving his hand in a particular manner. The pages are fairly crumpled and creased, suggesting that the project has received a good deal of handling. Small spots on the front and back cover suggest that some kind of liquid has been splashed on it, by accident, at some point. It appears to have had an eventful life.

These details illustrate what we mean by 'physical characteristics': that is, those features which indicate the types of materials used, the ways in which the materials have been used and the ways in which the project has been handled. They show that Ray was very much involved physically, as well as mentally, in the process of producing this little book. They provide a glimpse of some of the kinds of things that matter to him: he is not just telling us what he knows about bats; he is also expressing his understanding of what kind of physical object a project is, what it means to read a project, and what it means to do 'project work'.

Through our interview with Ray, and informal conversations with his teacher and parents, we have built on what we learned from our observations. Ray's teacher worries about him because he doesn't express much interest in classwork; she seems surprised that he puts so much effort into his projects. Ray explains that he is interested in anything to do with physics but finds schoolwork frustrating as it offers him no opportunity to develop this interest, except through project work; he is looking forward to going to secondary school where he will be able to 'do more science'. His parents support this interest, and help, where they feel they can. They expressed the difficulties they experienced in helping with the diagram on echolocation (see Figure 6.2), saying he had 'really wanted to understand it, how it worked' but they had found it hard to explain in a way that made sense to him. His mother also told us that he always becomes 'totally absorbed' in what he is doing and 'really frustrated when things don't go the way he wants them to'. Such comments help us to make more sense of our observations of the physical characteristics of Ray's project, leading to a richer understanding of his work and the context in which it is situated.

Studying literacy artefacts as material objects

The physical characteristics of literacy artefacts rarely attract much conscious attention from researchers or teachers, but we believe that they convey many messages. Ray's project can be seen as a multi-modal semiotic object which, through its verbal, visual *and physical* features, carries not only meaning about a particular topic, but signs of how it came to be as it is and of how it is expected to be handled. We suggest that a literacy artefact can be examined 'physically' in two ways associated with these types of meaning: first as a *textual object, carrying meaning about a topic and reflecting meaning-making processes* and second as a *material object, reflecting and anticipating physical processes.*[3]

We have discussed elsewhere the first of these two types of meaning (Ormerod and Ivanič 1998). In this chapter we discuss the second type of meaning: the ways in which physical characteristics of literacy artefacts carry traces of literacy practices associated with their *production and life experience so far* and their *anticipated future use.* Figure 6.5 provides a summary of aspects of literacy which we have inferred from the physical characteristics of the texts we have been studying. We suggest that this list might provide a useful starting-point for studying how the physical characteristics of other types of text also reveal traces of the literacy practices associated with them.

In the next two sections we illustrate and subcategorise these points, using examples of several projects from our research to show how physical characteristics point backwards, to processes of production, and forwards, to anticipated future use, providing insights into the children's beliefs about the nature of project work and contributing to our understanding of their literacy practices.

PAST: reflecting practices associated with the physical production of a text
The use of materials and technologies
The material and technological contributions of other people
The impact of time on literacy work
Accidental damage

FUTURE: anticipating practices associated with the physical use of the text
How the author expects the text to be 'read' in a physical sense
How the author expects the text to be treated as a material object

Figure 6.5 Some aspects of literacy which can be inferred from the physical characteristics of texts

How physical characteristics carry meaning about the production of the text

The use of materials and technologies

The physical characteristics of the projects we have studied show the children gaining experience in using different materials and technologies, and at the same time, through trial and error, learning lessons for the future about the strengths and limitations of particular ways of working.

Range of materials and technologies

Physical characteristics indicate the different kinds of materials and technologies that have been used in the project's construction. First, it is made up of materials which are present and visible in the final product: surfaces and 'containers' (such as plastic ring binders, transparent plastic sleeves, card envelopes, lined file paper or coloured card); textual objects (such as leaflets, tickets, photographs, photocopies or CD-ROM printouts); 'natural' objects (such as feathers, twigs or eggshell); substances (such as ink, paint, Tipp-Ex, grease or glue); and tools (such as Sellotape, staples or string).

Second, the physical form of the project is the result of processes of research and construction involving a variety of tools and equipment which are not a part of the finished object: small hand-held, non-electronic tools (such as pencils, fountain pens, biros, erasers, stencils, scissors or hole punchers); small hand-held electronic tools (such as cameras and tape-recorders); larger non-electronic equipment (such as typewriters and guillotines); or large electronic equipment (such as photocopiers and word-processors). As a class, the children select from a wide range of materials and technologies considered suitable for use in project work.

Ways in which they are used

Physical characteristics can tell us something of the specific ways in which materials have been used during the process of production, carrying traces of the actions associated with them. First, they can point to different aspects of the project's construction as a solid three-dimensional object. It may be created almost completely from scratch, from paper and other materials (as in Ray's case) or may incorporate 'ready-made' artefacts such as a ring binder. Physical characteristics often indicate how, within book-like objects, the pages have been brought together, for example, by punching holes in the sides of the sheets or slipping them into transparent sleeves and inserting them into a ring binder.

Second, physical characteristics may show how individual pages have been constructed using different layers of surface materials which have been roughly or carefully cut out, and attached, loosely or firmly, using different kinds of tools, to the background surface. For example, on one page of Denise's project on fish, she has constructed a very detailed key to a map, using layers of tiny pieces of paper and strips of Sellotape, which gives the impression that it must have been an awkward and time-consuming process involving both manual dexterity and a good deal of patience. The construction of the project as a solid object can involve the physical manipulation of materials and tools in a variety of ways.

Third, physical characteristics can work, together with the visual, to provide evidence of the ways in which different tools and materials are used in the inscription of words, drawings and other graphic elements. In Ray's writing, for example, the physical quality of the biro line, producing an indentation on the page, suggests a tight, rigid control of the pen, whereas the words in Denise's bird project appear to have been produced using a much looser hold and a more fluid stroke. The character of a line can also indicate the quality of the tool (for example, a blunt pencil, or a dried up felt-tip pen), or may provide evidence of the use of other tools such as pencil sharpeners, erasers or rulers; for example, Ray used a sharpened pencil and an upturned bowl to draw the moon (see Figure 6.1). Children vary greatly in their selection and control of small hand-held tools used for the purpose of inscription.

Where a child has produced a 'perfect' final draft, the non-existence of 'blemishes' points to other aspects of the process of production, such as the tearing or screwing up and throwing out of earlier drafts. A word-processed text points to other kinds of physical activity: the tapping of fingers on a keyboard, the actions involved in the control of a mouse, a distinct bodily position, the head held at a particular angle, a different kind of eye contact with the text. The layout and graphic variation can also reflect the effort and concentration that has gone into the electronic production of these visual effects. While 'writing' is always a physical act, it can take very different forms, leaving different kinds of physical evidence.

Understandings, attitudes and decision-making associated with materials and technologies

The project's physical form appears to reflect its author's understanding of what kind of material object a project 'is'. Some children have stapled or strung pages together and talked in the interviews about wanting to make their work 'look more like a book'. Many have used ready-made school exercise books or ring binders, making it more of a 'school-situated' literacy object. Projects produced using word-processors share more of the characteristics of published texts. Occasionally a project consists of texts on loose sheets of paper, placed in a cardboard folder, like a set of documents. Posters, models, and other objects such as leaves, or football memorabilia, carry something of the quality of a museum display. In deciding what form their project should take, the children appear to be drawing on their knowledge of the physical features of different kinds of literacy artefacts in the surrounding world, sometimes demonstrating unexpectedly fluid ideas of the boundaries between them.

Physical features can point to a child's preference for certain materials and technologies. In the interviews, the children often express confidence and enjoyment in using a particular means of expression. Bob's projects reflect her particular preference for communicating meaning through the construction of three-dimensional forms. In a drawing of a tiger, she carefully cut out and attached a circular piece of paper with the word 'hello' on it, to the animal's mouth, using a hand-made paper 'spring'. She explained, 'I like making springy things out of paper'.

Physical characteristics can also provide evidence of technical problems. We have already pointed out how the very thick Tipp-Ex in Ray's project looks as if it was difficult to write over, and Edward expressed disappointment about the erased pencil marks showing on the front of his tiger project, because the eraser 'wasn't very good'. Technological problems may not be visible in word-processed texts but are sometimes mentioned in interviews; for example, Jim explained the difficulty he had faced in working out the layout of his text so that it would be printed in the right position on the CD-ROM printout.

At the same time, physical characteristics can show how children make use of their awareness of the particular strengths and weaknesses of different materials, in deliberately selecting specific materials and methods that they consider appropriate for their purpose. For example, Ray explained that he used pencil for the drawing of the three bats (see Figure 6.4) because it made the shading 'easier'. Many children are keen to use a word-processor because it enables them to leave no traces of corrected mistakes, or because they think the print looks better than their own handwriting.

Such characteristics also draw attention to differences between the children, in their individual concerns. For example, Ray's careful attention to linguistic and visual accuracy indicates that for him it is worth bothering about the presentation of meaning, but this does not mean that he has to start again from scratch on a new version every time he realises that he has made a mistake; it is acceptable, in his view, to make corrections over an earlier version, while for others, it is important for their work to appear neat, tidy and 'unblemished'.

The examples in this section on the use of materials and technologies show that the children tend not to select materials and methods at random but make informed decisions on the basis of their concept of the project as a literacy artefact, their own preferences for particular ways of working, their perceptions of the importance of visual presentation, and their views on the appropriacy and exploitability of available materials and technologies, for a particular purpose. Some tend to stick to the same tried and tested methods, whereas others are more adventurous in their willingness to try out different techniques.

The material and technological contributions of other people

We have found that project work is embedded, in many interesting and often unexpected ways, in social interaction, and the immediate physical and social environment out of which the text is born can cross domains beyond the boundaries of home and school. Physical characteristics reflect differences in networks of support (as described in Barton 1994 and Barton and Hamilton 1998), the social and material resources available to the children, as well as the ways in which such resources are exploited.

Providing access to resources

Physical characteristics can tell us about the immediate material environment within which the project is produced. For example, some children have used large sheets of rough grey paper supplied by the school. Denise's work reflects access to a wide range of home resources, including a computer (her father paints, and her mother writes academic papers). Some children have their own materials, others have to share: when interviewed about his project on birds, Scott explained that he used wax crayon even though he doesn't particularly like using it; he prefers to use felt-tip, but his brother had taken these to school, so he couldn't use them. Some children use new materials, others use second-hand parts; for example, some projects are enclosed in shiny, new ring binders, others in well worn, older ones. Scott explained that his old, green card envelope-folder, which has all sorts of other bits of writing all over it which have nothing to do with the subject of his project, came from his father, who had used it previously for purposes relating to his taxi business.

Imported textual components often indicate use of material and technological resources in the wider environment. Edward explained that he found a map in an atlas at school, took it home, then gave it to his father, who took it to work and made several photocopies in different sizes for him to choose from; Jim explains that he acquired his CD-ROM printout from Currys' computer shop, because his father has a friend who works there. Several children included letters, leaflets and posters from organisations or individuals, received in response to their phoned or written requests for information, and many included photos taken on family trips, and items picked up on these visits.

The material, geographical and social environment in which their work is situated is different for each child: resources may be individually owned and controlled, or shared between family members; some families are able and happy to buy new items, while others make a habit of recycling; some go on trips to places of interest further afield, while others remain in the local area. Given family circumstances, children make use of those materials and technologies which are available to them, although these may not always be those which they would, ideally, prefer.

Providing ideas for material presentation

Physical characteristics can draw attention to the ways in which children get ideas for the material presentation of their work from the people around them. The teacher may suggest particular materials; children are also influenced by the work of their friends and others in the class; older siblings and other people outside school may also provide models and offer advice: for example, Elizabeth's mother suggested using cling-film to cover her project. We have noticed that, as the children move through school, experimenting with new ideas, discarding some approaches and retaining others, their projects are generally becoming more uniform in their physical features. By the end of year 6, the majority are using ring binders, A4 paper and word-processors. These physical similarities reflect shared ideas about the shape of the project-as-academic-artefact, which have their origins both in and out of school.

Providing direct physical help with production

A change in physical features (the materials themselves or the manner of construction) can indicate where another person has been directly involved physically in the process of production. Lisa explained that having 'jotted down the facts' from one of her father's books, and put it into her 'own words', she then gave the text to her brother to type out because 'he doesn't like me messing around on his computer'; Bob's father coloured in her pencil drawing of a lion because she was still busy working on another part of the project, and time was running out. These examples show how people help the children in dealing with problems associated with unfamiliar technologies, or in helping them to complete the project by the stipulated deadline. We have noticed that the projects vary enormously in the extent to which, and ways in which, their physical form reflects collaboration of this kind.

The examples in this section on contributions of other people draw attention to differences in the ways in which people provide support. Children vary in the type and amount of help that they feel they need and in their responses to offers of assistance. The support available can affect their attitude towards project work. Some children enjoy working at home, making their own decisions, accepting some offers of help and rejecting others. Others feel less confident and express a need for more support; they may prefer working at school because of the range of available resources or because, as Edwin put it, 'school is where you learn'. Physical characteristics can therefore raise questions concerning the relationship between social and environmental resources, and attitudes to literacy learning.

The impact of time on literacy work

Apart from a few timetabled slots in school, the children are free to organise their work in any way they wish, over a given period. The physical characteristics of the projects may indicate points at which home or school events, or the final deadline, have imposed themselves upon it, breaking into the physical process in some way.

The relationship between literacy work and other aspects of life

Physical characteristics such as a sudden change of substance (a different coloured ink, for example) can indicate a point at which other everyday life events have intruded in some way upon the project – where, for example, a meal, or bedtime, or the arrival of other people in the room have taken priority, drawing the child away from their work. The children have talked about how project work fits in with the rest of their lives. For some, it is something they enjoy doing to fill the time; for others it is difficult to fit it into their very busy schedules. Physical characteristics can reflect these differences in the shape of the children's everyday lives and in the value that they place on project work, as one activity amongst others.

The effect of deadlines

Physical characteristics may also indicate the arrival of the deadline set by the teacher. In Kyrah's project one page contains what appears to be a half completed drawing of a buddleia bush, outlined in pencil, and partly coloured in with felt-tip, but with large parts left uncoloured; Kyrah explained that she ran out of time, as she was in the middle of the drawing when she reached the project deadline. Deadlines often cause considerable worry and from the children's perspective can be seen as a limiting factor, affecting the physical structure of the final product. However, not all children view the project, or deadline, in this way. The structure of Edward's project reflects a different approach. He explained that he is continuing to expand the newspaper cuttings section, which he calls his 'update file'. Whenever he or his parents read a newspaper they note any articles about tigers and he cuts them out and slips them in. He says, 'I'm always going to be updating this': his project remains in the process of construction. Physical features can therefore point to differences in the children's attitudes towards time limits, and the extent to which they feel able to manage their time in relation to this kind of work. They also raise questions about their understanding of what it means for a piece of work to be 'complete', and their perceptions of project work (and perhaps learning in general) as a limited or ongoing process.

The examples in this section on the impact of time illustrate how interruptions to the physical process can remain permanently visible in a project, providing evidence of the ways in which this kind of work is situated in time, between other activities and commitments in home and school life, and raising questions concerning its author's attitude and approach towards this kind of work.

Accidental damage

The physical condition of a project always tells us something of its life experience as a material object. It may display evidence of damage caused through the action of construction; for example, the pages may be creased, or torn, or the surface roughened by repeated use of an eraser or Tipp-Ex. It may have been damaged through unintentional contact with other bodies in the surrounding environment; the spotting on the cover of Ray's project would fall into this category. Individual components may have experienced other uses; indentations on a surface, for example, might indicate its use to support another text in the process of being written. Second-hand parts often carry evidence of damage. Some projects show substantial evidence of handling; others appear pretty much 'untouched', or to have been touched extremely carefully. The absence or existence of traces of 'accidental damage' gives a possible insight into the author's attitude towards the physical condition of their work, suggesting that the projects may be valued in different ways as material artefacts.

How physical characteristics carry meaning about the anticipated use of the text

Just as there is an interpersonal dimension to the linguistic and visual communication of a text, creating a particular relationship between the writer and the reader, in which the words, pictures and other visual elements invite the reader to interact visually and cognitively with the written text, so the physical characteristics of a textual object attempt to involve the reader in a physical way. For example, a poster may require the reader to stand and look at it, or glance at it in passing; a book requests that we hold it and turn over the pages with our hands; a text on a computer screen demands that we tap buttons on a keyboard; a map invites us to unfold it carefully, run our fingers over it, and point to particular bits of it. There are two aspects to this interactive process: one concerning physical actions to do with *reading*, and the other concerning the *treatment* of the text as a material object. The physical characteristics of a literacy artefact carry both these types of meaning.

How the author expects the project to be 'read', in a physical sense

The physical characteristics of the children's work suggest that there are different ways of reading projects, in terms of the type and amount of physical interaction expected. For example, Kyrah's poster instructs the reader to open 'windows' in the picture of the wood, to find out where the birds live; Lucie's little cakes were made to be tasted; Robbie expects his reader to hold the project up close to their nose, or to bend down towards the page, in order to sniff the blackcurrant scented rollerblade grease which he has smeared on to the page (to make this absolutely clear, he has added a written explanation and instruction: 'Some wax; please smell'). These examples demonstrate the children's understanding that reading is a physical activity involving more than just visual, linguistic and cognitive abilities. Hands are not necessarily limited simply to turning pages, and the nose or mouth may be as useful as the eye; 'reading' can be a multisensory experience resulting from different kinds of physical responses to different kinds of textual objects.

How the author expects the project to be 'treated' as a material object

As we explained in the section on 'Accidental damage', a project may be handled in different ways. The ways in which it is treated can affect its condition and its life expectancy. Some children use special materials to protect certain parts of the project. For example, they may carefully stick protective rings around the holes punched in the side of the page, to stop the paper from being torn, or enclose their pages in transparent plastic sleeves. Some have gone to great lengths to protect the cover; Paul laminated his and Elizabeth used cling film so that it 'wouldn't get ruined'. The use of protective materials shows an awareness of possible damage that can be done by readers through physical interaction with the text, and of those specific areas which are most susceptible to damage.

Such features also signify a serious concern for the physical condition of the project, suggesting that it is highly valued as a material artefact, embodying the hard work put into its construction. They appear to reflect a sense of achievement and pride in the finished product, on the part of either the child or the person whose idea it was to protect it in this way. A project which exhibits little evidence of any physical 'damage' can give the impression of being almost 'untouchable', a valued material object which deserves to be treated with great respect. A piece of work in less pristine condition can appear more 'inviting', suggesting that it may be valued differently. For example, while Ray's project appears to have been handcrafted with care and pride, the smudges, crumpled pages, creased corners, and spots on the surface of the paper communicate the message that it does not expect to be handled with special reverence.

The examples in this section show the children's awareness of the ways in which readers can be invited to interact physically with a literacy artefact, as text and object, and also the value that they place on the materiality of their own work.

Conclusion

Physical characteristics tell us about the ways in which a text is located within practices in its surrounding social and physical environment. They reveal something of the position of the child as a writer within that environment and of their attitude towards project work, as a demanding activity taking up time and energy within everyday life. Our research has led us to five observations regarding situated literacy practices.

First, *physical characteristics reflect attitudes, beliefs and approaches.* These concern the types of materials that are appropriate to draw on, the ways in which they can or should be read and handled, and the role and value of project work in the life of the child. We have noticed similarities between the children in the physical characteristics of their work, which situate it within a recognisable, shared area of literacy activity, and at the same time, we have noticed differences suggesting that project work means different things to different children.

These *practices and beliefs are rooted in the children's experiences in and out of school, as individuals and as members of different social groups.* Projects experience very different lives as material objects, and children experience different lives as writers: texts and practices are both rooted and intertwined in the individual and shared contexts of people's everyday lives (see Clark and Ivanič 1997, Chapters 3 and 4).

In relation to this, *project work flows between different social and geographical domains, involving a wide range of people* (see Barton 1994; Barton and Hamilton 1998). From the germ of an idea for a topic, through the processes of research and construction, to the project's final completion, different people (not just teachers and parents, but other relatives, friends, neighbours, parents' colleagues, and representatives of organisations), provide support in many different ways (see Hannon 1995; Barton and Hamilton 1998). In this chapter we have focused, very briefly, on only one aspect of this: how people contribute, with resources, ideas and practical assistance, to the construction of the project as a material artefact.

Importantly, *physical characteristics draw attention to the complexity and significance of the 'physical dimension' to literacy learning.* The verbal and visual elements of a text are inextricably bound up with the physical, and writers and readers interact physically with a text during its production and use. Literacy does not simply involve knowledge about conventions of grammar, phonics, punctuation, graphics and layout; it also involves a great deal of knowledge about physical and social ways of getting different types of literacy work done. In learning to do project work children have to manage their time, learn how to access, select and manipulate different kinds of materials, become familiar with new technologies, learn how others can help them with these tasks, and develop their understanding of the kinds of physical involvement that can be expected of their readers. Children respond in very different ways to the challenges of this kind of work.

This leads to our final point: *the processes we have observed are not static, but constantly changing, both in the lives of individuals and as cultural resources.* In the many varied situations which the children describe to us, we get a sense of the ways in which project work involves them in a continuing process of informal sense-making, in learning about the kinds of practices which are relevant to the production of this kind of literacy artefact. As they learn about different kinds of texts, as they observe the practices of other people, as new materials and technologies become available to them, and as they study their chosen subjects in greater depth and perceive the need to find new ways of expressing their new-found knowledge and understanding, their literacy practices change (see Kress 1997). Their experience of engaging in this kind of work has consequences for their identity as writers, changing the meaning-making resources and literacy practices available to them for future use (see Ivanič 1998; Kress 1996).

Besides observing changes in individual ways of working, we are noticing changes in the group as a whole, from Year 4 to Year 6. Situating these observations of a specific group of children within their macro-sociological context, we may be observing more generalisable changes and capturing some practices which are dying out. We do not have data for explaining these changes, but can speculate about the effects of the technologisation of communication in the wider social context, of changing concepts of time, and changing relationships between the body and the environment.

This leads us to ask about the future of the kinds of texts that we have been examining. We wonder whether primary school children in the future are likely to continue to produce texts of this type, or whether new technologies will sweep aside the varied physical characteristics we see here, leading to standardisation at an ever earlier age. If this is the case, then what material characteristics will such texts share, what physical processes will they embody and how might they be valued as literacy artefacts?

In conclusion, the similarities and differences between the children's projects draw attention to culturally and historically situated values and practices surrounding the production and use of different texts. The kinds of literacy practices that we have observed are fluid, dynamic and ever-changing, both for the individual children themselves and for the sociocultural environment that sustains them, representing a fast-changing period in the development of technologies of literacy.

Notes

1 We are grateful to The Leverhulme Trust for funding the current phase of the research, entitled *A multi-media corpus-based longitudinal study of children's writing* (Grant No.F/185/AG).

2 It is important to recognise that the reproductions of his work here are on a different surface, using different technology, and cannot capture the materiality of the original.

3 This distinction is similar to the one made by Martinec (1998, forthcoming) between 'representing action' which serves to represent some ideational content, and 'presenting action' which carries messages about the social context in which the action is performed, but does not necessarily attempt to represent some other content.

References

Barton, D. (1994) *Literacy: An introduction to the Ecology of Written Language*, Oxford: Blackwell.

Barton, D. and Hamilton, M. (1998) *Local Literacies*, London: Routledge.

Clark, R. and Ivanič, R. (1997) *The Politics of Writing*, London: Routledge.

Hannon, P. (1995) *Literacy, Home and School: Research and Practice in Teaching Literacy with Parents*, Brighton: Falmer Press.

Ivanič, R. (1998) *Writing and Identity: The Discoursal Construction of Identity in Academic Writing*. Amsterdam: John Benjamins.

Kress, G. (1996) 'Representational Resources and the Production of Subjectivity', in C.R. Caldas-Coulthard and M. Coulthard (eds) *Texts and Practices*, London: Routledge.

Kress, G. (1997) *Before Writing*, London: Routledge.

Kress, G. and van Leeuwen, T. (1996) *Reading Images: The Grammar of Visual Design*, London: Routledge.

Martinec, R. (1998) 'Action and Language as Part of an Intersemiotic System', draft manuscript, London College of Printing.

Martinec, R. (forthcoming) 'Towards a Semiotics of Action', in J. Martin and R. Iedema (eds) *Multimodal Communication*, the proceedings of the Sydney workshop (December 1997), Sydney: Routledge.

Ormerod, F. and Ivanič, R. (1998) 'Children's Use of Material Resources for Meaning-Making in Topic Writing', Sociolinguistics Symposium 12, March.

van Leeuwen, T. (1998) 'Taste in the Framework of a Semiotics of Materiality', in A. Piroelle (ed.) *La Representation Sociale du Gout*, University de Bourgogne, Dijon: PRISM.

7

FAMILY LITERACY

A pedagogy for the future?

Kathy Pitt

> *'In the outside world you'd have a bender-building exam. Here you just get on with it. That's what I liked'.*
>
> (Animal)[1]

Family literacy programmes are a recent form of literacy pedagogy in this country, introduced by the Basic Skills Agency (BSA) in 1993 and spreading rapidly throughout the country with the help of government and other forms of funding, so they offer a new site to explore the struggles over changing understandings and uses of language and literacy near the turn of this century. In this chapter I will explore the connections between one representation of this new form of literacy education and the makings of a more egalitarian society. As a new century begins, can these new programmes help the participants to respond to changes in the way language is used, to changing demands in the workplace, to increasing complexity of life in the public and private domains?

The BSA model of family literacy brings together the literacy practices of three domains; the private domain of the home and family, and the public domains of the school and education and the workplace. To create a new literacy pedagogy which can cover these domains, the model draws on established and sometimes conflicting discourses and pedagogic practices. Voices from these different origins can be heard in the language and images of the BSA's television programmes for teachers on *Developing Family Literacy* (BSA 1995a); they show the hybrid nature of this new vision of literacy education. Identifying these voices and seeing which voices are stronger and dominate, is part of my process of understanding the cultural and social contexts of this literacy pedagogy and one way to consider the contributions to literacy education this model offers. In the critical discourse analysis that follows (see Fairclough 1992a), I trace these voices back to the fields of the school, Adult Basic Education (ABE) and the New Literacy Studies (NLS) and I consider the contributions to literacy education this new pedagogy offers.

The television texts at the centre of this discussion are four 30-minute programmes put out by BBC Select in 1995, to be recorded and used for literacy education training purposes. They draw mainly on pilot demonstration programmes in England and Wales, funded by the BSA. The television programmes are made up of edited interviews with students, teachers, headteachers and other educational experts involved with the demonstration projects, interspersed with scenes of activities actually taking place on these courses, the cohesion being provided by a female voice-over who introduces, provides links and summarises key points, with the aid of graphics. The intended audience are teachers and other experts who are, or will be, involved in this type of literacy education. As such, these television texts cannot be regarded as a representation of the reality of any one particular course in progress. Their aim, as stated in a leaflet about them, is *'to increase knowledge and understanding of constructive approaches to family literacy'* (BSA 1995a).

I focus on these television programmes because they are '*enactive*' texts, (a term I take from Gee, Hull and Lankshear 1996); that is they have been produced to give the BSA's vision of this type of literacy programme and to influence the shape and content of any existing or future family literacy projects, alongside the BSA's control over funding. Therefore, they offer a detailed picture of this national agency's ideal conception of the meanings and roles of basic literacy education, a picture carved out of a multiplicity of interviews and activities collected from actual ongoing practice; a pedagogy which they claim to be a *'foundation for reading and writing which can last a lifetime'* (BSA 1995b). I argue in this chapter that this foundation is a somewhat wobbly one for a future democratic society. To do this I first list and discuss the texts that are part of literacy events involving the parents we see in the programmes. I then analyse the practices surrounding these texts and the sometimes contradictory voices I find within them. In the last section I consider the texts and practices both present and absent in this representation in the light of a new century and new texts and practices in the work and public domains.

What do the parents get to read?[2]

The model of family literacy being recommended in these television programmes is three-tiered; *'separate work with parents, separate work with children, joint activities'*, as the voice-over explains in the introduction to each programme. To start this analysis I will look at the reading featured in the adult literacy strand, and the texts involved.

As can be seen from the list in Figure 7.1, the texts read by the parents that we are shown on these programmes fall mainly into three categories; texts involved in learning about emergent literacy and their children's school experiences (1.1, 1.2, 1.4, 1.5, 2.3, 3.1, 4.2, 4.3); texts involved with

Programme 1: Developing reading with parents and children

1.1 Parents read and discuss the instructions of educational games for young children and identify the elements of emergent literacy practised in these games with an itemised list of early literacy skills that has been given to them.
1.2 Parents watch a video about children's early reading skills, and take notes on a handout prepared by the teacher.
1.3 Parents read a flipchart in the classroom which tells them what the aims are of the session they have participated in and how different parts connect to the Wordpower accreditation scheme they are taking.
1.4 Parents read and discuss two letters addressed to an agony aunt, asking for advice about reading with their young children. The letters do not appear in the format of a magazine column and seem to have been written especially for this classroom session as a way of revising knowledge about early reading.
1.5 Parents look at, discuss and assess a range of children's books brought in by the teacher.

Programme 2: Developing writing with parents and children

2.1 Some parents write sentences in Urdu about photographs of the family they had brought in, and then read and copy out translations of the sentences by the teacher.
2.2 Parents read and fill in a typed record sheet at the end of each session, about their achievements and feelings in that session.
2.3 Parents read a flipchart, written by the teacher, with notes about 'I can do' books they are going to make for their children. These notes include references to this activity serving also as revision of knowledge '*we will evaluate the early literacy skills PACT has tried to encourage throughout the course. We will analyse how these skills can be broken down into small achievable goals with our children.*'
2.4 Parents read and use the written and iconic instructions of word-processing and computer graphics software to produce books for their children.

Programme 3: Developing listening and talking with parents and children

3.1 Parents explore educational software for children.
3.2 Parents read and complete a questionnaire about their television viewing and discuss the use of television in the home.

Programme 4: Structures, assessment and evaluation

4.1 A parent shows us a printed record sheet with a list of activities accomplished by the parents on the course.
4.2 A parent 'reads' a selection of her child's drawings, in terms of the progress that can be seen in them.
4.3 A parent refers to doing science experiments in the classroom and at home, so presumably reading instructions were involved here.

Figure 7.1 Adult reading in the BSA 'Developing Family Literacy' television programmes for teachers

being a student in Britain today, (1.2, 1.3, 1.4, 2.2, 2.3, 4.1) and those involved in developing and using computer, and possibly television literacy (2.4, 3.1, 3.2).[3] The first two categories dominate, and often overlap as can be seen in 1.2 where parents watch and discuss a video about early reading, thus learning about this subject through an electronic text, and also take notes on what it says about the topic on a prepared handout while watching; a use of literacy which is very common in educational practices for the transmission of knowledge, and presented as part of student and certification practices by the voice-over in programme 2: '*whilst children are involved in early writing, their parents practise note taking and letter writing, which can lead to accreditation*'.

The texts about early literacy seem to be mainly secondary sources, except for the children's books and games. We see one electronic text being used, a video entitled 'Leading to reading'. It is not possible to ascertain if this was made for teachers or specifically for parents on this type of course. Apart from this, the only texts we see that indicate how the parents learn about this topic are notes written by teachers on flipcharts and prepared handouts. There are references to texts on school policies in programme 2: '*family literacy teachers are able to introduce parents to topics like this through their detailed knowledge of the school's policy*' and a teacher says '*I also make a point of reading the school reading policy and writing policy*'; we see a teacher telling parents about handwriting policy, but there is no indication that these texts are made available to the parents to read and discuss.

Turning to the other main category of texts, those connected with learning and accreditation, these are texts written by teachers which the parents can use to chart and record their learning within the discourse of accreditation. For example, in 1.3 part of the flip chart reads as follows; '*By the end of this session you should: 1. understand how to encourage a child's early reading skills. 2. be able to: a) take notes from a video 12.2 b) take part in a discussion 10.1/10.2*'. Here the numbers refer to units in the Wordpower accreditation scheme and the learning outcome is predetermined by the teachers. In 2.2 a teacher explains the practice of recognising and recording achievements as part of the learning process:

> *the parents have a record sheet which they fill in at the end of each session and they record what they have achieved during the time they've spent with us and they also write down their comments, how they felt about the activities that they'd accomplished.*

As this use of text is being explained the camera focuses on a specific record sheet and one of the entries reads '*the next day we all had a diary to write in our skills we have to do each day*'. This illustrates one parent beginning to construct their activity on the course within a specific understanding of literacy within an educational discourse in which literacy is translated into classroom tasks and can be broken down and measured and assessed.

One reason for the dominance of this kind of text could be a pragmatic one. The pilot courses are intensive, but short, so the dominant position of learning and accreditation may be a way of justifying the claim to be a foundation for learning. As a teacher says in programme 2 '*I know twelve weeks isn't long enough to fix all of the problems. We can identify them, we can show them where to go next*'. Setting the parents on the learning journey is one aim of the BSA model of family literacy and provides a reason for reading and writing done on the course. Supporting their children's literacy is another aim of family literacy, and explains the large amount of texts about early literacy. But other texts that adults may have to, or want to read when not in the role of literacy student or parent, are nowhere to be seen.

The parent as learner: the voices of school and adult education

What about the literacy practices these texts are situated within? As Hamilton and Barton point out *'(literacy) practices are not observable units of behaviour since they also involve values, attitudes, feelings and social relationships'* (1998). Nevertheless, some information can be gathered about the literacy practices involved in the events we see in the television programmes because we can actually see the physical contexts, what texts they are using, who does what. In addition, when the parents and teachers talk to the camera about what they are doing and how they feel, this gives an indication about their attitudes towards the reading and writing they do on the courses. Their contributions are subject to editing, and only parts of what they say are available to the viewer, so these indications can only be partial and refer to their experiences in specific courses, the totality of which the viewer cannot see. What the editors have chosen to present from these interviews, however, is, I would suggest, indicative of the attitudes and feelings which they considered as appropriate for this particular vision of literacy education.

To begin with environment, the cultural and physical context of nearly all the adult literacy events shown in these programmes is that of the school classroom. Except for one project which takes place at a family centre, all the courses are situated in primary or nursery school buildings. Literacy events take place with the parents sitting round tables put together and filled with ring binders and texts prepared for the classes. There is usually a flipchart and often we see the teacher standing at this flipchart talking, and the parents sitting around the tables, listening. We also often see them working in smaller groups discussing various texts or making things. This behaviour and the artefacts that can be seen in these television texts belong to the institutional practices of formal education.

Another school practice, referred to by Animal in the quotation at the beginning of this chapter, is also present in this new literacy pedagogy.

Animal, at the time of being interviewed by the *Guardian* newspaper (Vidal 1997), had recently left school with ten GCSEs, and so had plenty of experience of contemporary school practices. As she had joined the group of people commonly called eco-protesters by the media, she was speaking as an insider of a world of makeshift camps, tunnels, direct action and alternative discourses, and, looking out of it, could articulate how knowledge needed in the public domain, such as building benders, is recontextualised and turned into a simulation or evaluation task by school practices: '*in the outside world, you'd have a bender-building exam*'. There is an illustration of this practice in 1.4, where the genre of letter to an agony aunt is simulated; reading and discussing 'real' advice column letters may be part of some parents' practices, but replying to them, in the role of agony aunt, in order to rehearse formal letter writing, is a specific school literacy practice. Another illustration of thinking about literacy in terms of how it is used in schools can be seen in this extract from an interview with a parent in programme 2, '*we done a writing piece on memories and I done three pages full, and I was so proud of it, and I couldn't wait to hand it in, you know, like a school kid would with the homework*'. Here, an expressive piece of writing is addressed to the teacher for evaluation and described in the terms of school literacy.

Family literacy programmes, however, draw from more than one field of education, and this is reflected in the hybridity of the practices visible in the television texts. Among the artefacts on the tables, for example, as well as ring binders there are often mugs, presumably of tea and coffee. These would not be present if the classroom participants were schoolchildren, and, in my experience, are part of the way ABE tutors try to establish a different working relationship with adults in a school context. Another ABE practice whose voice is present in these programmes is that of individualised work plans. There are references, by some teachers, to the use of these, and consultation with the parents to decide on course content and literacy focus:

> *at the beginning of the course as well the parents have the chance to talk to me and they make individual work plans and . . . I bear in mind what sort of things people want to work on.*
>
> (programme 2)

And in programme 4, when talking about creating a syllabus one teacher says '*the absolutely essential factor in all of this is to listen very carefully to, in this context, to the parents [.], to what they really want from a situation, be sufficiently flexible*'. Half of the teachers in these programmes come from the ABE sector, so drawing on ABE practices of negotiated learning plans,[4] may be expected to be one of the dominant practices in the adult strand of family literacy.

Although some teachers talk about individualised learning however, what we actually see on the screen, and overhear as the camera shows us ongoing activities, are teacher-centred practices: teacher initiating an activity, introducing a text, or texts, and the parents addressing these texts as instructed by the teacher. I will take just a few examples from the list of literacy events in Figure 7.1, to illustrate this. In 1.5 the teacher introduces the activity with '*I brought in as many children's books as we can muster for us to have a look at today*'. The use of pronouns here suggest the parents were not invited to contribute books for this activity. In 1.4 we do not see how the activity of reading two letters to an agony aunt is set up, but in programme 2, we are shown how it leads to a writing task, and we can see on screen a printed sheet carrying the instructions '*early reading: writing a letter. Choose a letter and imagine you are an agony aunt*' again any trace of student participation in initiation and design is absent. In 2.3 the activity is initiated and introduced by the teacher '*this morning I think it would be nice if we could produce some "I can do" books which we can take home and use with our children*'. The school practice of teacher initiations of literacy events can be found throughout the programmes.

The practices and settings presented in these television programmes are, as I have shown above, mainly school practices and one of the outcomes presented is the parents taking up the social identity of students, as can be seen in some of the edited extracts of interviews with parents and teachers:

> *before this course I wasn't doing nothing, (it's helped give?) more encouragement to go to another course when this one finishes.*
>
> (parent, programme 1)

> *I thought about an English course, GCSE or something cos I always liked English at school.*
>
> (parent, programme 1)

In programme 2 a teacher describes parents as people '*who've emerged from the course as an adult who's a learner, a potential student for all sorts of things*'. In programme 3 a teacher says '*some of the women have actually gone on to other courses because in XXX there are a lot of bilingual courses going on, and after having done this they felt they could go on to other courses*', and in programme 2 a teacher says '*they have seen me for what I am which is simply a stepping stone to further education, and it was nice to see a hundred percent of the parents in the last course all going on to further education*'.

The emphasis in these practices and texts concerned with learning and accreditation, is on the construction of specific types of students, well versed in self-evaluation and recording practices. Accreditation schemes and standardised core curricula have already colonised the practices of ABE in the last decade (see Hamilton 1996), prioritising the economic function of literacy. This colonisation, and the dominance in these programmes of these texts reflects the contemporary political and economic contexts in which this new literacy pedagogy has been formed, in which the emphasis is also on the need for literacy for '*lifelong learning*' for work-place needs. As Gee *et al.* say, language, literacy and learning are situated in, and shaped by '*the work order*', as well as by liberal philosophies of education (1996, p. 1). They argue that change in this order has been so fast that 'old' capitalist ways of organising the work-place are under challenge. They draw attention to management theorists who argue that, in a lifetime's work, all employees will have to cope with change and new knowledge and new ways of working and the authors argue that these theorists are shaping the demand in the work-place for lifelong, flexible learners as employees. That these expectations of education have entered political discourse can be seen in the Labour manifesto for the 1997 general election where '*Lifelong learning*' is defined as '*We must learn throughout life, to retain employment through new and improved skills*' (Labour Party 1997, p. 9), in a section labelled '*lifetime learning*' in the Conservative manifesto (Conservative Party 1997, p. 24) and in the following description of contemporary life in a section on education in a regional Labour Party newsletter '*Successful modern economies demand a flexible, highly trained and multi skilled workforce*' (Smith 1997). The BSA television texts, representation of texts and practices reflect this situating of literacy as a vehicle for learning and skill acquisition for work-place needs.

The parent as teacher: voices from school and the New Literacy Studies (NLS)

In the parent and child strand of this family literacy model, there is also a mixture of voices and the literacy crosses the public and private domains, rather than public and work domains, as above. The context for most of the literacy events we see in this strand is again the classroom, and events seem to be initiated and guided by teachers. The viewer does see parents and children enacting literacy events in the home, but in each one of these scenes the mother and children sit on the floor facing the camera and act in a similar way to how we see them together in the classrooms; the home setting acts only as a kind of backdrop. It is used symbolically, to show the intended destination of the behaviour and literacy practised in the joint activity strand; the events filmed are not situated within the flow of activities and practices that usually take place in the home domain.

One of the focuses of the joint activity session is the teaching and mastering of early literacy, and is shown to be the practical application of the parents' knowledge acquisition in the adult strand. Helping children to become successful users of literacy in school is one of the motivations behind this new literacy education, because schools are failing to produce children who can reach standardised literacy levels. According to this line of reasoning, what the schools are doing is right but they need more help, and one of the aims of family literacy is to harness the support of the parents for the schools. So, family literacy programmes are explained, at the beginning of each programme, as courses where '*parents . . . learn about ways of helping their children and . . . try these out in a supportive environment*' and '*family literacy gives children extra learning opportunities*'.

There is a dominance here of an educational discourse in which reading is something that is explicitly taught to children. One parent highlights this aspect in programme 1 by saying '*what I've got out of the course is I've learnt how to teach my own, my daughter how to read*'. When talking about the choice of a book for their child the following extracts from two parents' discussion are selected; '*it's got repetitive noises where she could follow along with her finger and pick the words out*' and '*it's got nice big words he could read a couple of times in bed cos he can see them ok*' (programme 1). What we are shown in these clips from the classroom is the parents' acquisition of knowledge about the mechanics of reading rather than how the story might stimulate the child's imagination, or help the child make sense of the world. This emphasis on teaching also occurs when a teacher explains a session on the uses of television and computers in the home, '*during the session we hope to look at the important role that television, video and computers can play in the home as educational tools*' (programme 3). What the voice is encouraging here is the transfer of practices in the teaching of early literacy from school to home. '*Parents are their children's first teachers*' and '*taking the view that parents are an important teacher of their own children*' are utterances repeated in the introduction to all four programmes.

Trying to close the home/school gap by changing the practices of the home belongs to a well-established tradition. In America where family literacy programmes were started in the 1980s, they emerged partly out of compensatory education programmes in poor areas, such as Headstart. In the UK, too, the BSA model of family literacy is aimed at city and rural areas where there is unemployment and school failure, and it is stated at the beginning of each programme that '*all the programmes are in areas where involving parents so as to prevent underachievement is a priority*'. This statement is accompanied by an image of a typical inner city shabby street. From this perspective, the changes needed are seen to be one-way; from school to home (see Auerbach 1995; Taylor 1997; Vincent and Tomlinson 1997).

Talking about literacy as something that is to be taught and measured can background the sheer pleasure that reading and writing can bring. However, what the viewer sees on the television screen is not only the parent as school teacher, but also the parent absorbed in literacy events with their young children. Research into literacy practices outside the school, forming part of the knowledge of literacy practices built up under the name of the New Literacy Studies, also has a voice in this model of family literacy. This view that literacy can be bound up with fun, creativity and play, which is also part of contemporary primary school practices, clashes with the school literacy the parents may remember from their childhoods (a parent in programme 1 says '*I hated reading, couldn't stand it*'), or their experiences of literacy as potential students. These contrasting attitudes to literacy are illustrated in an observation by a teacher in programme 2; '*we're encouraging the parents to sit down at home and do fun activities which promote literacy. I think very often parents think unless they're doing some kind of formal teaching, it isn't worthwhile*'. In learning about emergent literacy, and in the joint activity where parents make books and games for their children, and share books and songs, the viewer sees the adults using reading and writing creatively: the energy and enjoyment this gives rise to vibrates throughout the television texts in classroom scenes of women absorbed in making books and games. This pleasure and creativity is referred to in some of the interviews:

> *last night when I went to bed I kept thinking, my brain was ticking over, thinking of other ideas for games that I could do with him.*
>
> (a parent, programme 1)

> *bedtime is different now, Emma will go to bed five or ten minutes earlier, and we spend that time reading together, singing songs, talking about the day.*
>
> (a parent, programme 1)

> *I think in making books that parents have developed their own creativity . . . and what they are able to do has really helped their own sense of self worth, I think.*
>
> (a headteacher, programme 3)

In these events the viewer can see the parents finding pleasure in using literacy and, as some of the above quotations suggest, changing their practices in the home and increasing their self-esteem.

Through this experience of reading for pleasure the parents in these programmes also encounter literacy in practices very different from those seen in the adult strand of family literacy. A general education adviser says, in programme 3, that stories are vehicles to a '*fantasy world*' and '*story helps children to make sense of their world*', and the television texts are full of scenes of parents and children sharing stories together. The pleasure that reading children's fiction can bring is represented in parent interviews:

> *I've never been very confident with reading, but when it's a child's book, I don't know why, all your apprehension seems to go out the window because you know it's a child's book and you know it's fun, it's supposed to be fun.*
>
> (a parent, programme 1)

Where literacy equals pleasure, reading is not a problem, and another parent shows how a changed reading practice can inspire imagination:

> *I take a lot more time to read a book with them now and I'm a lot happier to break the book down and not to just read the lines on the page, but to actually explore the sides of the story, and even go off at a tangent sometimes.*
>
> (programme 1)

Here is one of the paradoxes in this representation of family literacy. The focus on children's reading, and parents' support and interaction with them in literacy events, is on pleasure, creativity; we see storytents and storysacks and personalised games and books. But this dimension of literacy is absent from the adult strand. Can literacy only be pleasurable and inspiring when you are a young child, or a parent of one? What happens to this making sense of the world through story as these children grow older?

Looking at children's learning of literacy outside the school is one of the focuses of the NLS approach and research has also been carried out, in the US and Britain, into the connections between home literacy practices and success in literacy at school (see, for example Taylor 1983; Wells 1985). This research carried the message that children's literacy practices and subsequent success at school, could be shaped by the practices in their home environment; that children can learn the values and meanings of literacy from home environments where reading and writing form part of multiple daily practices. For example, Taylor studied six American families where there was at least one child learning to read successfully, and found that the children participated in and learnt from their family's daily uses of literacy, rather than through any formal teaching by the parent. She concluded that *'in families participating in this study, literacy is deeply embedded in the social processes of family life'* (1983, p. 92).[5] This way of understanding the role of reading and writing in the home as part of the environment of children's acquisition of early literacy also has a voice in the television programmes. For example, after watching a video about early reading a parent observes '*if you are sitting here reading a paper or a book, if the child's watching you read, it wants to always copy what you're doing*' (programme 1), and in programme 2 the voice-over introduces a section on writing toolboxes by saying, '*family literacy shows parents how and why what they already do at home with their children helps develop their reading and writing. It suggests ways of building on this*'.

Even more fundamental is the way this research has been interpreted and how it influences the overall design of this family literacy model. If good parenting practices to provide an environment for naturally emerging literacy before school were the only aim of this pedagogy, then knowledge about early literacy and how to support it would be sufficient, and, indeed, there are many home/school projects that aim to do this. But the BSA take the findings of this approach to research and turn it around to a possible negative face, to explain the rationale of the three stranded model; '*the second strong research finding is that in families where the parents' own literacy is low, the children's literacy attainment tends to be low as well*', Greg Brooks, National Foundation for Educational Research, programme 4). Consequently, they have a strand devoted to the literacy development of the parents. Thus, they seem to be agreeing with research that says the parents' use of literacy in the home is significant. Yet, as we have seen in the literacy events around adults' personal reading, there is no inclusion in this television model of family literacy of the reading that might go on in homes other than that involved in study and replicating school literacy events. The parent's reference above, to reading a paper or a book, is the only indication in these programmes that other kinds of reading may go on in the home. As a result of a longitudinal study of children in Bristol, Wells argued that '*it was through the place and value given to literacy in the everyday activities of the family that we considered social and educational inequality to be transmitted from one generation to the next*' (1985, p. 234), and yet, the television programmes give space to a very narrow range of reading practices as a foundation for facilitating parents' uses of literacy in the home. One of the absences is any reference to adults reading for pleasure or inspiration.

Family literacy: literacy for life in the next century?

I will now consider how this analysis of some of the texts and practices of the BSA's vision of family literacy pedagogy, and the voices within them, contributes to answering the questions I asked at the outset. First I will consider the question of providing greater equality of access to education and the work-place. The evidence presented, in these programmes, of changed practices in the home as a result of the parents' new knowledge of the acquisition of literacy, and their involvement in creative and fun literacy activities, would indeed seem to indicate a better start in education for the children, as early literacy activities are extended in the home domain. The parents too, by sharing in some of the teachers' expert knowledge about early literacy, and learning more about school practices, are at less of a disadvantage in their interactions with the children's teachers and other professionals, an outcome noted in research findings in programme 4, '*the parents are also very clear that they have made improvements in . . . their approach to their children's schools and their teachers*'; this can increase their ability to advocate on behalf of their children and generally may reduce the gap between home and school practices, at least at primary school level.

As well as giving the children more support, this new knowledge of the parents and the opportunity for their reading and writing to be accredited, and publicly acknowledged, can help women[6] who look after young children in the home, and who do not have paid work or qualifications, have more of a sense of their own worth, as this interview extract illustrates; '*I haven't actually achieved very much in my life, and to actually be able to see that I have a City and Guilds certificate, well that gives me more confidence in myself*' (mother, programme 1). Parents who feel good about themselves and their literacy have more emotional space for their parenting role, as another mother observes, '*I think if we gain confidence, then we can pass the confidence over to the children. They feel more confident if we are*' (programme 3). The symbiotic relationship between a person's use and feelings about their own literacy, and how they feel about their own social identity is evident here, and emphasis on increased self-esteem is highlighted in the extracts of interviews with parents and teachers. Bringing these families inside the educational field, and encouraging them to continue within it can be seen as a step towards equality of access to wealth and power for them, and the limited range of text types presented as relevant for adult literacy in these television programmes may be opened up by the new experiences of literacy for those who do continue within the field. Equally, opportunities to develop computer literacy, alongside print literacy, will enhance their value in the work-place and their remuneration prospects, where employment opportunities exist.

Reaching into the home to change the practices in it, can, however, be viewed from another perspective which is absent from the surface of these television programmes. Institutional intervention is seen by some social theorists as part of contemporary power practices; enabling the power of the state to reach into and exert control over our daily lives. Both Giddens (1991) and Rose (1989) highlight the socialisation of children in the home as an example of this. Rose argues from a Foucauldian perspective that intervention programmes are part of the internalisation of discipline process in which mothering practices beneficial to the state become '*pedagogic norms within the mother's own desires and fantasies, for them to form an inescapable and pervasive grid for calculating and judging her own behaviour and that of her child*' (1989, p. 196). Giddens argues that professional knowledge is taking over the role of intergenerational or social group knowledge in the formation of the self; '*The early socialization of children, for example, tends increasingly to depend on the advice and instruction of experts (pediatricians and educators), rather than on the direct initiation of one generation by another*' (1991, p. 33). The increasing significance of the expert in practices in the home domain may work to maintain a hierarchical social system if expertise remains the preserve of specific social classes. BSA family literacy pedagogy would fit into these theories of contemporary power practices and identity formation, in that the joint activity strand of the model guides parents towards early literacy activities and behaviour seen as appropriate by educational professionals. The emphasis is on parenting practices based on expert knowledge, to support institutional practices. There is no space given to questioning the appropriacy of these institutional practices as well as questioning parenting practices. And in the adult strand we see parents learning how to talk about and monitor their literacy achievements and progress in specific ways, which also fosters contemporary hierarchical social practices.

The domination of school practices in the television texts positions the student as subjected to and the teacher as agent of literacy practices on the courses; good study practice is represented as listening and following instructions, writing down information received; discussion and questioning of texts is not represented and the texts are controlled by the teacher. ABE practices, in which the student initiates, explores and uses literacy in collaboration with fellow students, and the teacher acts as facilitator, are backgrounded. Gee *et al.*, in their analysis of new developments in business organisation and expectations, cite Reich's prediction of the development of two distinct categories of workers in the global economy; the elite symbolic-analytic and the more widespread routine production services and in-person services. They describe the second category as follows; *'beyond demands for basic numeracy and the ability to read, such work tends to call primarily for reliability, loyalty, and the capacity to take direction and, in the case of in-person service workers, "a pleasant demeanour"'* (1996, pp. 46–7). The adult literacy practices visible in BSA's television texts are more likely to encourage the following of direction than the problem-identifying and solving and knowledge work expected of the symbolic-analytical worker. The energy and creative possibilities of literacy needed by the symbolic-analytical worker, or by the increasing emphasis on team work, quality circles, etc. in many contemporary work-place practices, is present in the BSA's model of family literacy, but, as I argue above, restricted to pleasure and the exploration of imaginary worlds through the reading of children's fiction and the making of games.

The parents taking part in these television programmes are participants in a society increasingly invaded by *'mass media culture, global commodity culture and communications and information networks'* (New London Group 1996).The narrow range of text types and the reading practices of the adult literacy strand do not reflect this social change. The role of television in the home is given space in programme 3, but the focus is on the young child and the use of video as text in the adult literacy strand (1.2) is treated as unproblematically information-giving. Mass media texts are part of the public domain and contribute to decision-making by these adults on issues such the single European currency, whether to buy beef for their children, the meaning of school league tables. The literacy they need to read such texts is another absence from the texts and practices of the BSA model of family literacy. Texts are represented as autonomous objects to be decoded, rather than produced in specific economic and cultural contexts.[7]

Conclusion

This analysis traces the construction of the BSA vision of family literacy from various existing literacy pedagogies and intervention practices. The adult literacy strand draws on the conflicting voices of ABE, where student-centred practices compete with accreditation schemes situated in economic and political motivations for literacy, and established school practices. The parent and child strand is the site where intervention programmes advocating the extension of school educational practices into the home meets with NLS research into emergent literacy and the everyday uses of literacy in the home domain. I argue that the texts and practices that the BSA choose to represent as a model of family literacy education provide a somewhat uneven '*foundation for reading and writing which can last a lifetime*' (BSA 1995b). The creative and problem-solving potential of literacy is restricted to the adults' identity as parent; success in reading and writing as student is fenced in by school practices which control access to and ownership of texts and practices, and the adult as citizen and user of literacy in a pluralistic, '*information*' society, is not part of the vision. The parents' lives outside the classroom are marginalised in the texts and classroom practices of the television programmes, and this reduces the opportunities to exploit the diversity of literacy practices which can be found in the home, and, I would argue, decreases the potential of this model of education to contribute towards a less hierarchical society. Changes in the literacy demands of work and public domains calls for a pedagogy which draws on a wider range of texts and literacy practices and understandings of language and literacy use, if the goal is a society where access is open to all.

However, bringing the lifeworld texts and practices of the adult into the classroom will not necessarily be sufficient to open up this model, as they run the risk of being recontextualised into a school literacy task, another 'bender-building exam', and so become a different text and practice. Similarly, increasing knowledge about language use has been exploited in language engineering practices that work in favour of present power relations.[8] The situating of literacy education within school practices needs to be open to discussion and critique by all the participants in family literacy, as they have been in many ABE practices. This is not an easy task in a literacy education where the schools are hosts and partners in the projects, and is not attempted in the BSA model. The BSA vision of family literacy does represent reading and writing, and the acquisition of new knowledge as powerful and potentially emancipating forces in the formation of specific social identities, but marginalises social identities and perspectives on texts and practices that have their origin outside of school practices. Within this construction of a literacy pedagogy, the use of literacy as a means of control lies uneasily alongside the power of literacy and knowledge to cross domains and transform practices.

Notes

1 Animal is a 17-year-old protester against road-building, and she was quoted as saying this in a newspaper article about her and other eco-protesters by John Vidal 1997. At the time of the interview she was living in camp and involved in direct action against motorway construction, with a community of protesters.
2 I am concentrating on reading because of the space requirements of this chapter, although it is not always possible to separate out reading from writing.
3 I think it is important to keep in mind, when discussing the texts and practices that can be seen in these television texts, that they do not represent the actuality of the students' experiences on any one of these courses, and that what may be missing from these programmes may well form part of any one of the courses drawn on.
4 See Hamilton 1998; Mace 1992; or Thompson 1980 for description and discussion of ABE practices.
5 More detail of this research, and the development of family literacy programmes in America and Britain can be found in Barton and Pitt 1996.
6 Although I generally use the word 'parents' to describe the adult students of the BSA model of family literacy, in line with the usage in the television texts, in fact, nearly all those in the programmes are women, and all the quoted interview extracts are from women. Here I refer specifically to women as it is still very rare in our society for men to stay at home, do the unpaid work of looking after young children, or take on this role publicly if unemployed.
7 See Fairclough 1992b, for detailed discussions of pedagogies to promote critical practices.
8 See Fairclough 1996 for an argument on the technologisation of discourse.

References

Auerbach, E. (1995) 'Which way for Family Literacy: Intervention or Empowerment?', in L. Morrow (ed.) *Family Literacy: Connections in Schools and Communities*, Newark, DE: International Reading Association.

Barton, D. and Pitt, K. (1996) 'Family Literacy Campaigns', in *Literacy Practices and Education Unit 3*, YMCA George Williams College.

Basic Skills Agency (1995a) *Developing Family Literacy*: TV programmes for teachers, and leaflet, London: Basic Skills Unit.

Basic Skills Agency (1995b) *Read and Write Together Leaflet*, London: Basic Skills Unit.

Conservative Party (1997) *The Conservative Manifesto*, London: Conservative Central Office.

Fairclough, N. (1992a) *Discourse and Social Change*, Cambridge: Polity Press.

Fairclough, N. (ed.) (1992b) *Critical Language Awareness*, London: Longman.

Fairclough, N. (1996) 'Technologisation of Discourse', in C. Caldas-Coulthard and M. Coulthard (eds) *Texts and Practices: Readings in Critical Discourse Analysis*, London: Routledge.

Gee, J.P., Hull, G. and Lankshear, C. (1996) *The New Work Order: Behind the Language of the New Capitalism*, NSW, Australia: Allen & Unwin.

Giddens, A. (1991) *Modernity and Self-Identity*, Cambridge: Polity Press.

Hamilton, M. (1996) 'Literacy and Adult Basic Education', in R. Fieldhouse (ed.) *A History of Modern Adult Education*, London: National Institute for Adult Continuing Education.

Hamilton, M. (1998) 'Keeping Alive Alternative Visions', *RaPAL* 36: 4–16.

Hamilton, M. and Barton, D. (1998) *Local Literacies*, Routledge, London.

Labour Party (1997) *New Labour: Because Britain Deserves Better*, London: The Labour Party.

Mace, J. (1992) *Talking about Literacy: Principles and Practice of Adult Literacy Education*, London: Routledge.

New London Group (1996) 'A Pedagogy of Multiliteracies: Designing Social Futures,' *Harvard Educational Review* 66(1) 60–92.

Rose, N. (1989) *Governing the Soul: The Shaping of the Private Self*, London: Routledge.

Smith, G. (1997) 'Better Chances for Children', *The Morecambe and Lunesdale Rose*, Warrington: North West Labour Party.

Taylor, D. (1983) *Family Literacy: Young Children Learning to Read and Write*, Portsmouth, NH: Heinemann.

Taylor, D. (ed.) (1997) *Many Families, Many Literacies: An International Declaration of Principles*, Portsmouth, NH: Heinemann.

Thompson, J. (ed.) (1980) *Adult Education for a Change*, London: Hutchinson.

Vidal, J. (1997) 'Gone to Ground', *The Guardian Weekend* February.

Vincent, C. and Tomlinson, S. (1997) 'Home–School Relationships: "The Swarming of Disciplinary Mechanisms"?', *British Educational Research Association* 23(3): 361–77.

Wells, G. (1985) 'Preschool Literacy-related Activites and Success at school', in D. Olson, N. Torrance and A. Hildyard (eds) *Literacy, Language and Learning*, Cambridge: Cambridge University Press.

8

EMERGENT LITERACY PRACTICES IN AN ELECTRONIC COMMUNITY

Renata de Pourbaix

Given a virtual space – an electronic newsgroup[1] – for discussion purposes, how will a newly formed community of university language learners approach communication within that space? What external influences will impact upon that communication? What internal practices will emerge? Could an analysis of emergent discourse practices assist in understanding students' perceptions, assumptions, or expectations of communication and communities? Could this knowledge be used to assist students in locating their current practices and their approach to communication in a constantly changing world? These were some of the questions leading to a study of language learners' computer conferences at an academic institution.

This chapter will introduce the situation under study, then discuss three main elements in the study of this situated literacy – first, the evolution of theoretical concepts in approaching this study, specifically, a consideration of the concepts of academic literacy, information literacy and computer literacy, in light of the theory of literacy as a social practice; second, the multiplicity of overlapping communities and domains of practice potentially impacting upon the emergence of discourse practices in a newly formed community; and finally, actual practices which emerged, considering both observable aspects and participants' retrospective views of their development.

Viewing the electronic discussion group from a social practices viewpoint, it will be seen that a specific set of practices emerged over time. These practices were not necessarily based on 'standard' skills and techniques as originally conceptualised by participants in their role of second-language learners, but rather practices which came to be found appropriate in a given context (the electronic discussion group) as decided by the participants, and not by an external authority (for instance university administration or course teacher), although external validation was an influencing factor.

It will be seen that students aspired to academic literacy, in relation to their changing perceptions over time of the meaning of the term. Academic literacy was understood by participants to include the ability to find information (information literacy in terms of research required for posting[2] and interaction, as well as suitable use of resources, although not necessarily evaluation of information except in terms of interest or suitability for specific use), to carry on sustained interaction (not only to react or to answer on a one-time basis), to use appropriate language and technology (computer/technological literacy in terms of practice in electronic discussions, and of suitable program command use), and less obviously, to be identified as members of an academic community, although not necessarily the one in which the electronic discussion was being held.

The situation

This chapter is based on a longitudinal study of Canadian university students engaged in course-based student-moderated asynchronous computer conferencing. The students were enrolled in on-campus credit level courses of 'English as a Second Language for Academic Purposes' (EAP) – courses required for those students applying for entrance to degree programmes at the university, but unable to demonstrate the level of language proficiency required by the university. Thus the physical 'community' formed by membership in a specific course was artificial in origin, composed of members working towards externally imposed goals, and with a life-span of only twelve weeks (the duration of the course). Within this community, however, a somewhat less artificial sub-community was formed, based on participation in an electronic discussion group established for course members. This will be referred to as an electronic or a virtual community, rather than merely an additional mode of communication available to course members, since the basis of interaction departed from the course norm in terms of responsibility (student, rather than teacher, initiated, organised and moderated discussions), content (student choice of topic and topic development), membership (established for course members but open to public access both in terms of reading and posting messages), location (physical presence in a classroom not required), and time (class time limits irrelevant). Rheingold's definition of virtual communities (1994, p. 5) as 'social aggregations that emerge from the Net when enough people carry on . . . public discussions long enough, with sufficient human feeling, to form webs of personal relationships in cyberspace' could be applied to the situation under study.

Although a number of virtual communities based on electronic discussion groups were studied over a 2-year period, this chapter will draw upon material from the electronic discussions of one specific community, and one set of student logs[3] related to those discussions,[4] for a more consistent view of the development of practices. Student logs should be considered not merely as research data, but more importantly as the comments of members of an emergent community, reflecting on their situation and experiences during the development of the community. As such, logs constitute a vital dimension of this chapter, and should be read as an integral part of the text, rather than viewed only as illustrative examples.

> *STUDENT LOG – EXCERPT A*[5]
> *Electronic communication is a new medium of communication and has been used commonly in the public recently. It has been very effective and advantageous means in academic purposes in schools. One part of this kind of communication is electronic discussion. Electronic discussion is somehow similar to oral discussion but is also very different from it. Both kind of discussion provide people chances to preresent their thoughts, suggestions, or arguments about a topic. Both oral and electronic helps people obtain knowledge about the topic from others opinions. However, unlike oral discussion, which is organized as a meeting, electronic discussion is introduced through screen of a computer; in this kind of discussion, people contribute their ideas to each other without seeing each other. In oral discussion, the contribution of one's ideas is affected by many factors such as mood, emotion, and expression of his or her own and of other members. Meanwhile, in electronic discussion, people usually introduced their ideas in a comfortable and relax states.*

While not everyone may agree with the presence of a state of relaxation in electronic communication, it cannot be denied that the use of electronic communication is on the increase, with modes of electronic communication and the number and types of individuals and groups which have access to those modes, increasing over time.

In the academic world, as elsewhere, there is a growing tendency for the physical and the virtual to merge. Activities previously carried out in one specific physical location may now be carried out from a number of different locations, and possibly in different ways. For instance, lectures may be delivered by a professor in a campus lecture hall to a group of students, or they may be delivered as television broadcasts, viewed by individuals in their own homes. Course seminars may be conducted in a classroom, on a conference phone, or online through an electronic discussion (newsgroup). To the office location of a professor, may have been added a telephone number, followed by a fax number, an e-mail address and possibly a URL.[6] Course assignments may be posted on a Web page rather than circulated as paper handouts. These modes of electronic communication are not merely available modes but, increasingly, expected modes of communication. As discussed by Knobel *et al.* (1998) second language education reflects the larger educational context in technologisation of teaching and learning.

In September 1994 at Carleton University, Canada, an electronic communication system known as CHAT[7] became available to all students, offering access to electronic mail, newsgroups and Internet services. By September 1995, over 65 per cent of the student population had computer accounts, available through self-registration, and 400 courses had a course newsgroup, available through instructor request.[8]

Access to the computer system was available on campus in computer laboratories, or by remote access through a modem.[9] These facilities and technologies, including e-mail for office hours and assignments, course newsgroups for announcements, assignments and discussions, and Internet/ Web resources for research projects, are increasingly used by university course instructors, with, in most cases, no direct instruction in their use being provided to students.

At the time of the study, three main categories of newsgroups were accessible through the campus system – Internet, Carleton (university focused), and course newsgroups. In the category of course newsgroups, two types could be requested by course instructors – materials newsgroups, on which course assignments and information could be posted, and discussion newsgroups, designated as virtual spaces for student discussion on course topics. It is the latter category of newsgroup which forms the basis of the electronic community under discussion.

In response to feedback from participants in the previous 2 years of electronic discussions, the discussion under study was organized within a loose framework which provided a basic structure, but left responsibility for the discussion with students. Over a 12-week period, ten student groups of four to five members each led the electronic discussion of specific topics, each topic discussion lasting for approximately 2 weeks, with an overlap of 1 week with the following topic. Each student was a member of two different groups during a 12-week span. In some cases the two groups were composed of similar members. It was the responsibility of each group to decide upon a topic, post an initial message on the discussion newsgroup, and to 'be responsible' for the topic, a phrase with a meaning which altered over time as the perception of communication altered over time, and practices emerged within the electronic community.

Evolution of theoretical concepts

STUDENT LOG – EXCERPT B

When we use computer discussion, we not only learning language, but also knowing the technology. This is one of the preparation for our academic purpose. There are many possibility to use these kind of discussion in future.

Although the community under discussion was artificially created, with an externally imposed goal, in fact that goal – achievement of the required level of language proficiency – was not surprisingly accepted as a shared goal of the community, although perceptions of what that goal actually consisted of in detail, and how to achieve it, varied considerably. In general, however, participants commented upon the importance of language (communication, skills, strategies and academic appropriateness), information (knowledge and research), and technology (computer use). The electronic discussion was seen by participants as providing access to, and experience with, those elements, and as such, not as much the simulation of reality in an educational context of which Bigum and Green (1992) are critical, but rather a relatively risk-free introduction to an increasingly technologically oriented academic culture – itself a potentially problematic issue in the assumed acceptance of the dominant paradigm.

The basic premise underlying this study was that of literacy as a set of social practices mediated by texts (Street 1995). Situated literacies take account of the context and the importance of practices and events. How apparent are these practices, however, to participants? Individuals may not be overtly aware of practices in which they engage, or the relationship of practices to context, even in situations in which such knowledge would be of great value.

Students, instructors, and administrators may often view literacy as a set of taught skills rather than as practices which emerge and change over time and with context. A skills approach to literacy seems problematic in its static nature, while a practices approach, on the other hand, allows for the flexibility necessary to deal with change. The increasingly interdisciplinary nature of academic communication is one aspect of change that would be poorly served in a skills approach which equated specifically delineated skills with specific disciplines. A practices approach, however, would allow for the consideration of practices which emerge over time in a new discipline, or set of interrelated disciplines, and which might change as a discipline expands or alters its area of concern.

Three main areas of importance identified by course participants in their logs and newsgroup postings, and referred to in this work as academic, computer and information literacy, will receive attention. An overlap among these three areas is suggested, considering a situation in which academic literacy, which is the somewhat ambiguous goal of the participants, includes some form of information literacy, which in turn includes some form of computer or technological literacy. The term 'some form' is used deliberately, since definitions of each item vary widely.

The following discussion will focus on a suggested evolution of theoretical conceptualisation, and to some extent an evolution in student understanding. Figure 8.1 illustrates a move from decontextualised skills (information skills, academic skills, computer skills, etc.) to overlapping literacies, with definitions of such varying from a focus on competencies, to a consideration of discoursal practices, but nevertheless largely dependent upon external validation. At the other extreme of the diagram, a move is suggested from rigidly defined, isolated physical communities or locales (home, academic, work, etc.) to overlapping domains, or spheres of activity (Fishman 1972). In the centre of the diagram, communities, domains and literacy practices are seen as overlapping, evolving over time, and considered to have permeable, rather than strictly defined, boundaries. This study focuses on the resulting community practices within those situated literacies. This evolution of concepts must be considered, since many students and educators are still operating at the level of decontextualised skills and literacies, or considering physical communities and possibly domains of practice, but not yet considering the relevance of internally situated practices. As will be seen, conceptions of student needs and performance by participants in the electronic discussion group evolved within this framework.

Academic literacy

> *STUDENT LOG – EXCERPT C*
> *I regard it [electronic discussion] as my ladder to English academic communication. By participating in this activity, I become familiar with and active in the electronically academic communication with my peers.*

Street's (1995) use of the term 'dominant literacies' is of profound relevance to students enrolled in a university language course which has been designated as a requirement for entrance to a degree programme. Whatever students' actual literacy practices may be, they are in a sense required to conform to the surface level practices of an academic institution, as defined by an evaluating academic body. Student assumptions of what is being evaluated, of what academic language and behaviour consist of, and thus of what their goals should be in academic language learning and practice,[10] play an important role in any activity that is part of a language course. Many students involved in electronic discussion felt that the discussion provided an opportunity to become acquainted with or to practise the observable elements of a dominant literacy – that of the electronic academic community.

Academic literacy for students may be considered from at least two distinct perspectives. One focuses on skills required for academic success, often presented as a list of items required for functional competence. This perspective may be the most familiar to students and educational institutions. A more useful perspective is one which focuses on an understanding of the discoursal practices of an academic community, keeping in

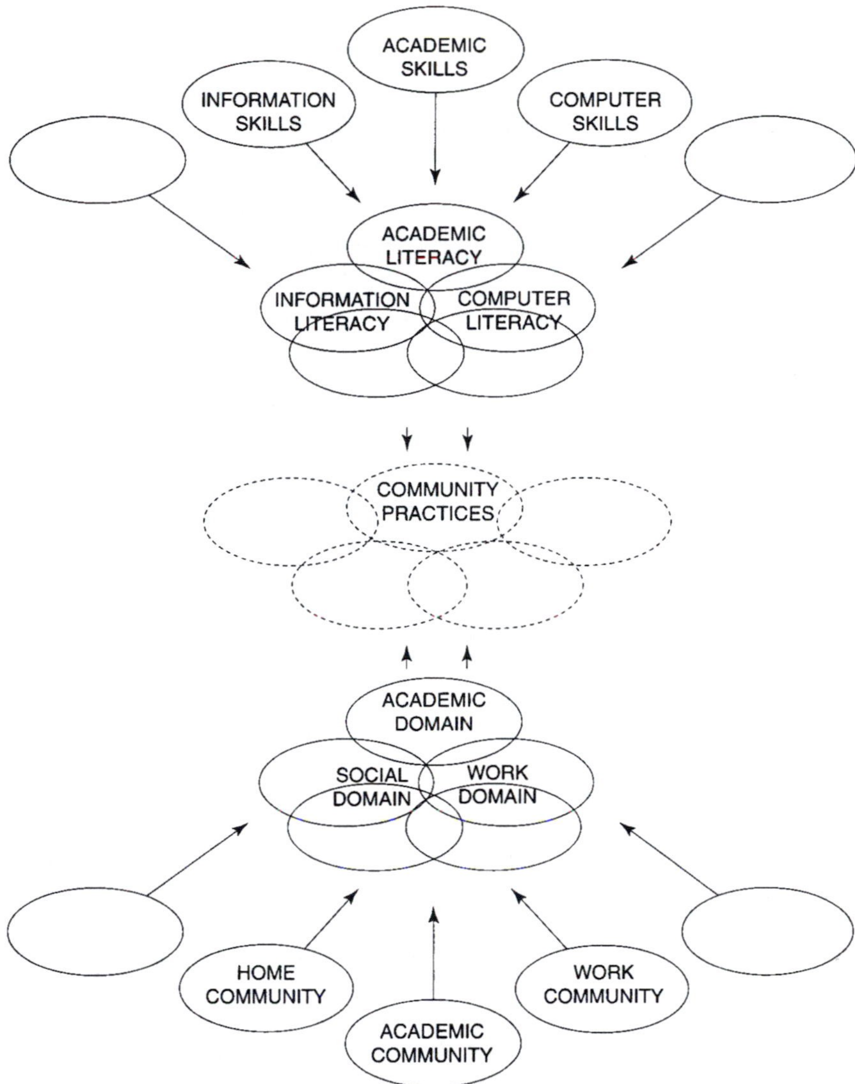

Figure 8.1 Evolution of theoretical concepts

mind the fact that there exist a multiplicity of academic communities, sharing some aspects, but distinct in others. These distinctions may not always be apparent to students, although awareness may develop over time with exposure to specific disciplines. Student conceptions of academic literacy tend to reflect their past experiences and present concerns.

Information literacy

> *STUDENT LOG – EXCERPT D*
> *CNTD*[11] *has help not only in my course work but also other areas such as writing, finding information, analysing people ideas . . . The effects of CNTD are helping me to explore other material not only library but also the internet.*

Information literacy, which in earlier definitions often focused on bibliographic reference use, is now more likely to include computer literacy, and to focus on electronic information. Behrens' historical overview of information literacy illustrates the move from using information, to locating and using, and finally to evaluating, understanding the power of information, and differentiating between knowledge and information, culminating in what is considered to be 'an evolving concept, its meaning dependent on the social and individual requirements of a specific society' (Behrens 1994, p. 318). Shapiro and Hughes (1996) identify information literacy as an ambiguous concept, and suggest an extended view which includes seven dimensions: tool, resource, social-structural, research, publishing, emerging technology and critical literacy. Common definitions currently include reference to the ability to access, use and evaluate information (Bruce 1995; Clark 1995; Vision Committee, AASL/AECT 1997). In general, there is a trend towards linking of technical skills with understanding of information and being 'concerned with the strategic use of information' (George and Luke 1996, p. 207). George and Luke further state that information literacy is 'embedded within particular discourses of the field under consideration and is focused on engaging with those discourses in purposeful and meaningful ways'. Demo (1986, cited in Behrens 1994, p. 312), 'observed that the meaning of information literacy could be explained from different perspectives, depending on whether librarians, educators, or communication experts define the term'. To this list should be added students, who will also bring different perspectives to bear, strongly related to their needs at any given time. Certainly, it was noticeable that students involved in electronic discussion displayed an increasing concern over time about locating and including relevant information in their postings.

Computer literacy

> *STUDENT LOG – EXCERPT E*
> *In 21th century, people don't have to go to the office, what they need is a computer. They can do their job inside the house, any time they want. The CNTD does do this kind of fuction. We learn how to addapt new technology.*

Goodson and Magnan (1996) believe that the term computer literacy is ambiguous, resulting from its state as an ideological concept; not a neutral entity, but rather one closely linked to the agendas of its proponents. Mackay (1992, p. 125) suggests that 'understanding the social nature of technology' is a prerequisite to understanding the nature of computer literacy, mentioning the change in definition from mastery of technique, through awareness of context, to focus on access to tools, while McMillan (1996, p. 165) suggests that the term is simply inappropriate, since 'at one level [it] refers to the use of computers and at another to the social and economic effects of computers on society'. The definition thus has been used to span a continuum ranging from the operational level with its focus on programming skills, to the level of social effects and beyond. The majority of studies, however, still equate computer literacy with technical skill prior to involvement in some form of electronic communication such as an electronic discussion group. Participants in the electronic discussion showed an evolution of views, from a focus on the importance of technical information, to the suitable application of technical knowledge; from a concern for physical access to on-campus computer laboratories, to a discussion of the need for more efficient modem access from home and the desire for a graphical user interface; from immediate usage concerns to a consideration of possible uses in the future.

A multiplicity of communities and identities

EAP classes at Carleton University are heterogeneous in terms of students' native language, ethnicity, and field of proposed study. Classes are usually composed of a mixture of visa (foreign) students, recent immigrants, those with refugee status, and Canadian citizens. Some have family responsibilities, some have part-time or full-time jobs, and some may be taking additional courses at another university, college, or secondary school, usually in the hope that such courses will speed up the completion of their degree programme. Students may belong to ethnic, religious, recreational, sports, or study-related societies or associations, both on-campus and off-campus, both physical and virtual. In other words, students have the potential for very full, very complex lives in terms of their simultaneous membership in a number of communities, both academic and non-academic, and thus also a multiplicity of identities. In a number of cases, communities or domains may overlap, for instance in the situation of friends, or members of an ethnic association, who are also classmates in one or more course.

Wilbur (1997) raises the question of whether virtual communities are structured around communal or personal identity. It is possible not only that the answer may vary dependent upon the specific community, but that structure and identity may evolve over time. Certainly evidence of student identification with specific communities was most noticeable in the choice of information included in newsgroup message closings (elaborated in the section on 'Signatures'). Personal information was included, which indicated connections to physical communities (street address, city, country) and virtual communities (NCFreenet address, Web home page), as well as some information on overlapping communities (membership in university ethnic associations). More limited reference to identity within other communities (such as family, friends or country of origin) was found within the content of some postings, however on the whole identification focused on the academic context. While shared 'academic' identity seemed to be a stronger influencing factor in the community's structure, personal identity became more evident over time, and it is entirely possible that it may have influenced the community more strongly if the opportunity (longer duration of the electronic discussion group) had existed.

More specifically, from an academic viewpoint, most students are associated with a specific faculty and department, whether by registration in a degree programme, or a desire to register in one. They are also members of specific courses within departments, and possibly specific sections or seminar groups within those courses. Overt identification with a specific academic community was evident in the inclusion of such academically related information as the name of the university, faculty or department, year of study, and course name, number or section in electronic signatures created by students, as well as in references within postings to the shared general identity of 'student' or more specifically 'ESL student' or 'language learner' (see the sections on 'Evaluative comments' and 'Moderation').

Whilst members of a specific EAP course, students were also more specifically members of a virtual community within that course – the electronic discussion community. Overlap existed between the electronic discussion group and the class in a number of ways, but in others they were distinct. Within the electronic community, students were also members of sub-communities with different roles, as for instance when they were members of a topic-posting group. Message openings and closings were used to identify membership, with message content also including references to individual roles (illustrated in the sections on 'Interaction' and 'Expectations').

A student should be seen as a person whose identities may vary over time, even within one term of study – a person who has multiple identities simultaneously (student, family member, friend, etc.), the importance of each of which may vary with context and situation within the context. Academic interaction may increase the rate of change within what has previously been considered a static, stable identity, that of 'student', to include an increased awareness of the multiplicity of student communities and identities.

Emergent practices

Changing awareness of community and identity was reflected in the emergent practices of the electronic newsgroup. Nine practices will be mentioned, expanded upon by participants' comments and reflections, both from newsgroup postings and logs. Practices were not static, as evidenced by participants' descriptions of the differences in their own postings over time. Practices emerged and changed in response to individual perceptions, and in response to more direct comments and discussions, both within the electronic community, and externally.

In the electronic community, emerging practices seemed to be based on a feeling for the importance of academic, information and technological skills within a given context of attaining both externally imposed goals (university language requirements), and an increasing awareness of the possibilities and importance of effective communication.

Interaction

> *STUDENT LOG – EXCERPT F*
> *My performance were different during several periods. When I started doing the CNTD, I did it in the same way as I wrote an essay. Every time when I post my response, I just read the questions given by a CNTD group and wrote my answers. In that period, I did not pay much attention to the responses given by the rest of the class, and I considered the CNTD activity as a burden. Little by little, I learned to communicate with others and began to enjoy the CNTD. When I was a host in a CNTD, I read other's responses on a regular base, answered their questions, and reacted to their comments after our group's initial post. When I was a guest in a CNTD, I tried to be the first person to response. If I was not, I read the previous responses carefully and gave my opinion based on both the questions given by the host group and the previous responses. After my posting, I kept a eye on the later responses. If they had questions or comments on my responses, I tried to do my additional responses as soon as possible. Also, I asked questions and gave comments on the later responses. By the end of this course, I have built the confidence and felt comfortable in electronic communication with my peers.*

The most noticeable emergence was that of dialogic, or possibly multilogic[12] posting, also referred to by Argyle and Shields (1996) as 'many-voiced', rather than monologic posting. Initial essay type postings, possibly written to display skills, and directed, even if obliquely, at the course teacher under the guise of answering a topic-posting group's questions, evolved into meaningful interaction among community members. The upper portion of Figure 8.2 illustrates the initial posting pattern, that of a

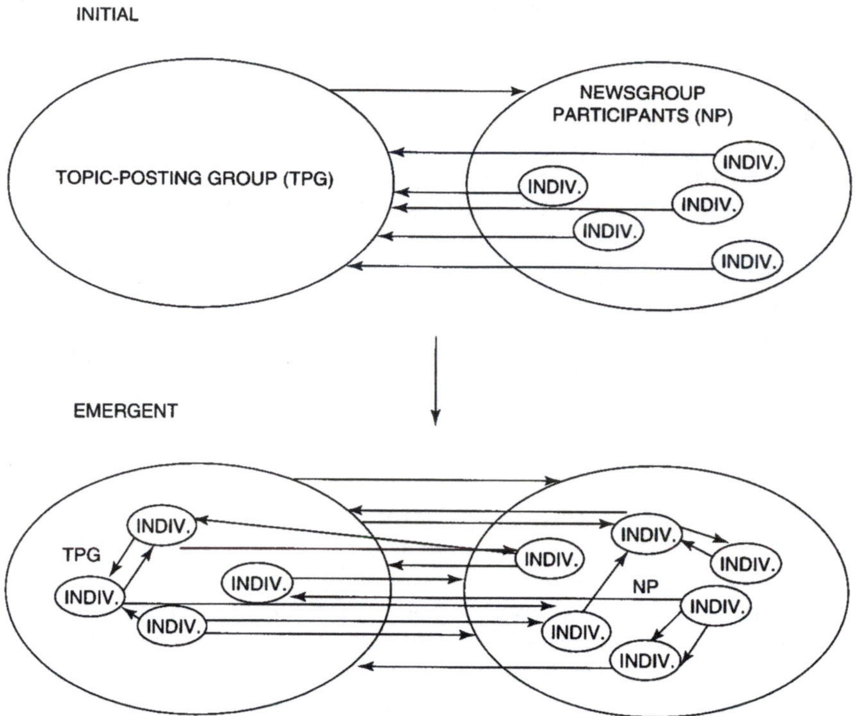

Figure 8.2 Patterns of interaction

topic-posting group (TPG) initiating a discussion through the posting of a single message composed by group members, followed by a series of individual responses (INDIV.) posted by newsgroup participants (NP) who were not members of the topic-posting group. Each of those individual replies was posted in response to the original message. Over time, multiple, complex patterns of interaction emerged, as seen in the lower portion of Figure 8.2, in which individual newsgroup participants might respond to a topic-posting group as a whole, to one or more of the individuals in a topic-posting group, or to individuals outside of the topic-posting group, not limiting their postings to one response, but rather responding, commenting, or reacting as suitable for a given situation, any number of times. In addition, topic-posting group members might post further messages as a group, or as individuals, in response to other messages.

During the process of electronic discussion, expectations and standards – acceptable practices – evolved in terms of what was considered to be suitable content and format in postings. Role changes occurred, with corresponding changes in responsibility, both in group and individual identities.

Expectations

One factor in the evolution of practices was an altering perception of responsibility, both of the topic-posting group, and class members responding to the topic, in terms of content and type of posting expected. Newsgroup posting – Excerpt A, illustrates a typical emergent situation, in which student Axxx[13] posted a message, directed to the topic-posting group, commenting on that group's lack of sufficient information in the original topic message. This student expected the topic-posting group to provide a specific level of information about their topic, in this case, writing skills. Student Bxxx responded on behalf of the group, indicating that this was not a suitable expectation, and elaborating on the group's expectations, that is, that individuals not in the topic-posting group would provide information and discuss that information, while topic-posting group members would guide the discussion. Such metalinguistic comments, related to elements of the discussion other than the actual topic, became increasingly common over time.

NEWSGROUP POSTING – EXCERPT A[14]

Axxx (Axx@chat.carleton.ca) wrote:
> Your group didn't provide too much information and methods on
> writing skills. Could you give us more information on how to write
> well or what kind of methods are good for us to achieve our goal
> on writing well.

This is Bxxx and I am a member of this group.

Hi Axxx,

Thank you for making comments on our topic. Our group is responsible for guide this discussion in the right direction. From this topic, we decided to discuss on writing skill. From this discussion, our group expect good informations and methods from all of you. In this way, we are also learning and getting advantages from your comments. As group members, we are responsible for happening this discussion.

In the end of the discussion, we will provide a summary, which will conclude all the ideas that you had provide for us. Then, it would be easy to learn more on writing skill.

From this discussion, we not only expect more information from you. We also expect you to make comments on others opinion, which they had posted for our discussion. Therefore, lets focus on their comments.
[signed by Bxxx]

Evaluative comments

Another emergent practice, and stimulus for change, took the form of evaluative comments. Newsgroup posting – Excerpt E provides one student's comment on the quality of postings. In this case, not only were other postings evaluated in terms of quality, but the topic under discussion was evaluated – 'academic' and therefore 'hard to discuss'.

NEWSGROUP POSTING – EXCERPT B

Hi Friends,
This is Cxxxx and thank you for your wonderful jobs. In this discussion, I was wondered that all of your responses provided excellent ideas including well explanations. I really surprised about it, because I thought that it is a academic topic and it would be hard to discuss. However, you all proved that you are advanced ESL students. . . .
[signed by Cxxx]

Community netiquette

Over time, an increasing number of postings dealt more specifically with the method of posting, or with netiquette (network etiquette). Students commented on what was and was not acceptable and community standards were seen to develop. Some of these dealt with elements such as spelling (Newsgroup posting – Excerpt C), in which student standards moved towards those of general newsgroup netiquette practices. The first newsgroup participant to comment on spelling errors was criticised, and quickly agreed that spelling errors should not be a point of discussion.

NEWSGROUP POSTING – EXCERPT C[15]

Gxxx wrote:
>Dear Fxxx,
>[. . .] I just read your response to Dxxx and your name
>in a new version. I nearly laughed out. But you, don't pick other's
>mistakes too much. Please read how you write Exxx's name.

I would like to say sorry to both Dxxx and Exxx!
I will never peck our international names again. Spelling mistakes are permitted, please!! Sincere thanks to Gxxx.
[signed by Fxxx]

Other comments focused on technical aspects of posting (Newsgroup posting – Excerpt D), with newsgroup participants identifying features of posting methods which they found to be irritating or unacceptable, and providing descriptions of alternative, acceptable methods.

NEWSGROUP POSTING – EXCERPT D

. . . electronic discussion is an excellent idea for our improvement. We can not only gain opportunities to write, but also learn different ways to write in the same topic through reading others' responses. However, reading on a computer is easier to get tired. In order to keep someone's interest to read your article, please enter 'F' instead of 'f' while posting a follow up.[16]

[signed by Hxxx]

Experimentation – adjustment

Students experimented with communication, not always successfully. When one student used a fairly standard element of electronic communication, a capitalised word to denote a physical state or gesture ('SMILE'), the reaction was strong and unexpected. The counter reaction was to retreat, and to declare that only 'academic' writing would be used in future, since that seemed to be the acceptable form within the discussion (see Newsgroup posting – Excerpt E). Thus it can be seen that practices which developed were not always those of other newsgroups, but rather those which were viable within the community.

NEWSGROUP POSTING – EXCERPT E

Ixxx (Ixxx@chat.carleton.ca) wrote:
> Dear Jxxx
> [. . .] what's with the 'SMILE' that you wrote, is that suppose to be
> an insult or friendly talk. I don't understand that, I think it is a insult
> and so does some of my friend think when I asked for the opinion.

In my knowledge, 'insult' is a very bad word. I have never thought that I could make people have such feeling, being insulted by ME? The misunderstand between us is due to our different cultures. . . . Unfortunately, I can see that you and your friends feel very uncomfortable. Please accept my apologize! I am very sorry about that. What you will read later are pure academic writings. . . .

[signed by Jxxx]

Moderation

Increasingly, participants began to act as moderators – of both the content and the approach to the discussion – whether or not they were members of the topic-posting group. Students had no technical moderation power; that is, they could not delete other students' postings, but could and did discuss the appropriateness of those postings, both directly, and indirectly, as seen in Newsgroup posting – Excerpt F.

NEWSGROUP POSTING – EXCERPT F

Dear Kxxx and Lxxx,
I was quite excited to read the responses in this topic. It is really like a face-to-face discussion.. All of our mother languages are not English. Because of different culture, we might have different ways of expression in communication. Although we are all discussing in English, we will misunderstand or mislead the meaning. It is because we are now a language learner. . . . I like this topic to be discussed continuously and peacefully.[17]
[signed by Mxxx]

Time and location

A notable change, both in terms of actual and potential impact on classroom pedagogy and community relations, is illustrated in Figure 8.3. This change consisted of a move from initial posting exclusively from one physical location (a campus computer laboratory) and during one particular time (scheduled class time), to posting from a number of different locations, at any convenient time of day or night. Initially, students considered newsgroup participation as simply an additional course activity, to be dealt with during the physical presence of a course instructor. This approach evolved over time as participants became more familiar with the technology involved, as they came to understand that learning was not limited to time- and place-specific activities, and above all, as a sense of community emerged, both within the course, and within the electronic discussion group. As this latter intensified, electronic messages were increasingly posted outside of class time, and from various locations. While some newsgroup participants continued posting during scheduled computer laboratory times, others began posting from their place of residence (whether on-campus student dormitory, or off-campus) or from another person's residence (that of a family member or a friend, again possibly on or off campus). Those participants with jobs used their office computers to participate, and messages could even be read and sent from other cities (or countries),

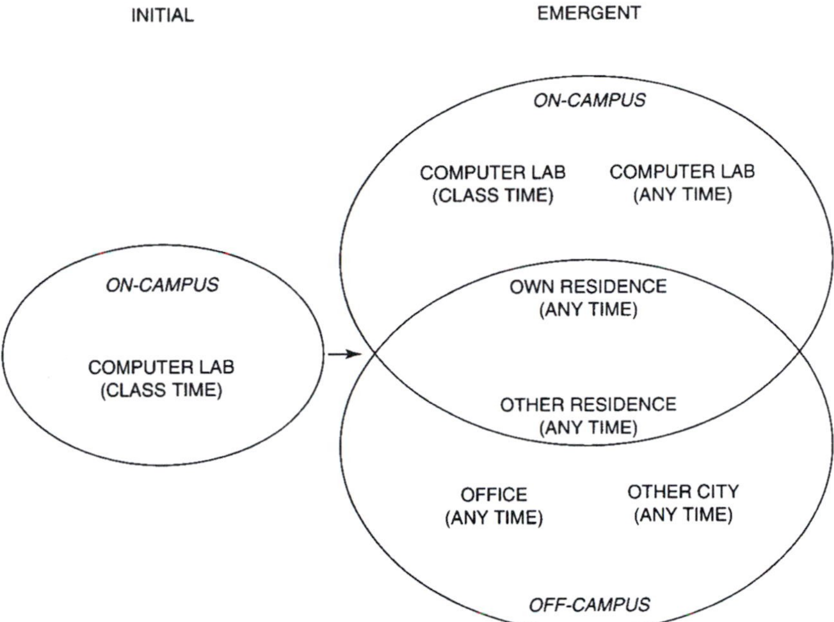

Figure 8.3 Posting time and location

when a computer was available. Computer access thus supplanted time of participation as a consideration. The complexity and expanded possibilities – the achieved flexibility – of posting time and location strengthened the distinction between what students considered to be 'regular' course activities (temporally and spatially limited) and participation in what became, over time, an electronic community, in the sense that its origin and focus were electronic.

Modes of communication

> *STUDENT LOG – EXCERPT G*
> *Communication between other students did not stop at the newsgroup, but some people communicated with me through phone and e-mail asking questions about the topic that I and my group posted in the newsgroup. Xxxx called me asking about how to set up netscape in her computer at home after the CNTD #X was posted. Also someone else sent me an e-mail asking how Internet could be helpful for his law studies.*

While spatial and temporal limitations decreased, active modes of communication increased. Figure 8.4 illustrates the change from an initial

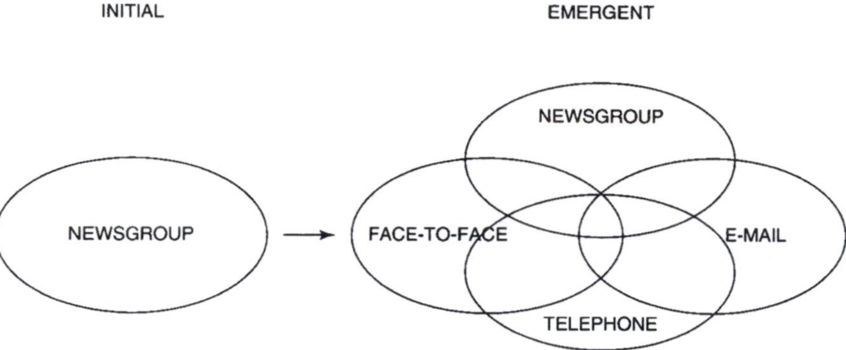

Figure 8.4 Modes of communication

reliance upon newsgroup posting for communication, to an expanded view of possibilities. Participants in the electronic discussion certainly continued to post newsgroup messages, but supplemented those messages with other forms of communication. E-mail messages were utilised for private discussion of potentially controversial topics and for discussion of side issues related to newsgroup topics, especially when discussants were not acquainted with each other personally, that is, when they were unable to match names or logons to faces. Discussions sometimes led to face-to-face meetings, and to exchange of information or views by telephone both with members of the electronic community, and with non-members. This latter category included those with whom newsgroup participants exchanged information about newsgroup topics, and often, but not always, consisted of members of the larger academic community.

Signatures

A final emergent practice which will be discussed is one strongly related to individual and community identity – that of signatures.[18] In newsgroup postings, individual identity often seemed to be subsumed by that of 'EAP student' identity, or specific course member or even group member identity, however signatures indicated a more complex situation. In particular, the change in signatures over time was indicative of the emergence of an understanding on the part of individual students of practices of the newly formed community. There was an indication of change that seemed to relate to what was considered acceptable, standard, and relevant at any given point in time, while still allowing freedom to express individual identity.

The computer program in use by participants included a standard signature feature. Theoretically, upon registering for a computer account,

```
-----------------------------------
Full Name
Carleton University

Email address: xxxxxx@chat.carleton.ca
-----------------------------------
```

Figure 8.5 Basic signature

a signature file was automatically generated. This signature consisted of the account holder's full name, followed by the university's name, then a blank line, and finally the holder's e-mail address, this information being printed between two horizontal lines, as illustrated in Figure 8.5.

In actual fact, this signature was not automatically generated for all students, so that some students encountered it when they started to use their computer account, while others did not. A facility existed by which all users could either create a new signature, or alter an existing one. It is interesting to note that over the course of the term, a number of participants altered their signatures, and although it is not within the scope of this chapter to conduct an in-depth analysis of those alterations, the form taken by some of them will be discussed, since that form seemed to be a reflection of the overlapping communities that participants were members of, and the changing importance of those communities over time, as well, possibly, as the changing understanding of the practices of those communities.

Considering signatures of the most recently studied group of students, a large majority used signatures that were different in some way from the automatically generated signature, even when those differences were minor. As seen in Figure 8.6, a common alteration to the standard signature was the addition of faculty or departmental affiliation, and possibly elaboration of the signature borders.

Of those students who altered their signatures, a majority made additional changes throughout the term, one participant alone moving through seven different versions. Changes varied from elaboration through the inclusion of borders or ASCII art,[19] to alterations in the form of the name used and inclusion of additional information, such as an additional e-mail address, department, faculty, URL for a personal web page,

```
************************************
* Full Name                        *
* Faculty or Department            *
* Carleton University              *
* Email address: xxxxxx@chat.carleton.ca *
************************************
```

Figure 8.6 Altered signature

city/province/country, or in some cases, deletion of information or of elaboration. Figure 8.7 presents a signature which was customised over time to include a combination of academic and non-academic identity. In general, there seemed to be an indication that participants were presenting themselves less as private individuals or as members of one specific course and more as members of a department or faculty. The academic identity was moving to the fore, and that final academic identity was not of the electronic discussion group, but rather that of the community individuals aspired to in relation to their degree programs.

```
                                          '~'
                                         (o o)
#--------------------------------- oooO--(_)--Oooo---------------------------------#
|                                      Full Name                                   |
| Xxxxxx Dept.                                                        ### Street   |
| Carleton University,                                            Ottawa, Ontario |
| Ottawa, Canada                  oooO         Oooo                  Post Code     |
|                                 (   )        (   )            Ph #(xxx)xxx xxxx |
#----------------------------------\__)--------(__/--------------------------------#
email: xxx@chat.carleton.ca OR xxx@freenet.xxx.xx
Visit 'xxx' at http://www.xxx.xxx.xx/xxx
```

Figure 8.7 Customised signature

Discussion

A view of literacy should be considered which moves beyond skills and considers the constantly evolving nature of communication needs, events and practices, the overlapping of communities and domains, and the inclusion in educational practice of a recognition of the multiplicity of communities, domains and literacies which constitute everyday life, both from internal (community member) and external (non-member) viewpoints.

Participants in the electronic discussion group seemed to view computer literacy in terms of electronic communication skills required for the future, and information literacy in terms of the ability to access information from a variety of sources. They considered academic literacy to be a combination of computer and information literacy, in addition to content knowledge and skills required for study. This was a change from their previous unquestioning acceptance of largely undefined 'academic' language requirements, and an incomplete knowledge of 'academic practices' and their changing nature, which may have excluded them from full participation in those practices. In addition to this altered view of academic literacy, there seemed to be an emerging understanding of the evolution of communication, and of the multiplicity of literacies involved.

From externally defined skills (university language requirements) which students felt were required, there was a move to internally defined practices, that is, those practices which were accepted by the community as appropriate for the context, as well as a recognition of this change. Could this recognition be taken further to assist students in analysing practices of the communities to which they aspire, communities in which lack of knowledge of the appropriate practices might be an obstacle to full membership or even to entrance? Could it be applied in determining a suitable approach to course design for language learners, including consideration of attitude and understanding versus skills, of the identities and goals of students, and of cross disciplinary networks and support systems? Should it not then, in fact, be taken even further to include a consideration of critical practice, in which learners would be encouraged to 'explore the social implications, for various individuals and groups, of (particular) discursive practices and values being the way they are, and to consider how different forms of practice and different values might produce different outcomes' (Lankshear and Knobel 1997, p. 156).

This chapter has focused largely on change – an important element for consideration. Certainly change has always been in evidence in all aspects of our lives, but it is currently occurring with great speed, in many contexts simultaneously, and with possibly hidden expectations in tandem with those changes. The emergence of a set of discourse practices in a community – a network of people joined by common overall goals, though with individual specific goals – is one illustration of an adaptation to change within an academic community. The speed with which practices emerged, altered, and were adapted as suitable for community needs mirrors the speed of change in our current world.

Notes

1 Electronic newsgroups are known by various names – asynchronous computer conferences, electronic bulletin boards, electronic discussion groups, special interest groups or on-line interest groups. They refer to many-to-many written (typed) electronic communication, in which all messages posted by one person on a central server are available for a set time period for reading by all others who access the conference. Such conferences are not to be confused with electronic mail 'conferences', which offer only one-to-one communication, or with synchronous electronic communication (IRC, talk or chat), which offers real-time electronic conferencing facilities.

2 The term 'posting' refers to newsgroup messages. While e-mail is more commonly 'sent', newsgroup messages are more commonly 'posted'.

3 The term 'student logs' refers to student written summative notes, reflections on course related activities and topics, and responses to language and communication related questions, sent to the course instructor via e-mail for response to any questions or concerns raised. Logs have been presented here anonymously, identified only by excerpt number.

4 Permission was obtained from all participants for the use of electronic discussion postings and logs. Although postings might be considered by some to be in the public domain, with permission not required for their use, the sense of authorship and ownership among student posters was an issue that could not be ignored, thus informed, written consent was obtained for use of these materials. Due to the nature of the electronic discussion (anonymous postings not permitted by the university, and access available to the public) anonymity and confidentiality were not possible, nor was privacy in usual terms, but rather in the choice of posters to communicate by e-mail rather than to participate in the electronic discussion, or to limit the extent of their participation on a particular topic.

5 Excerpts have been taken from the logs of various students who were participants in one newsgroup. All logs are presented in the students' own words, with no corrections of grammar or spelling.

6 URL – Universal Resource Locator – refers to the address or location of information on the World Wide Web.

7 CHAT (Carleton Hotline for Administration and Teaching) is distinct from 'chat', which refers to synchronous electronic discussion, also known as IRC (Internet Relay Chat).

8 Details about the CHAT system are available at http://chat.carleton.ca/index/history.html

9 Almost 80 per cent of participants in the newsgroup reported modem use for access, usually from their homes. At the time of the study, access to university course newsgroups was also available through the local community freenet (NCFreenet – National Capital Freenet), and for those students with computer accounts on this network, access was also possible through NCFreenet dedicated terminals at some public libraries.

10 When referring to their language-learning goals, students often related those goals to the context of the university in general or to that of specific courses, with a focus on skills the students believed to be necessary to be competitive with native-English speakers, or to attain a desired or required course grade.

11 CNTD refers to the course-specific name of the electronic discussion – Course Newsgroup Thematic Discussion.

12 Gary Shank (1993) suggests use of the term 'multiloguing' to indicate a number of participants, with the initial sender no longer retaining control of the exchange.

13 Xxxx has been used in place of specific names and logons to provide post-newsgroup anonymity.

14 All newsgroup excerpts are presented in the students' own words, with no corrections of grammar or spelling, however format may vary somewhat from the original, with any changes made for the sake of clarity.

15 This posting illustrates the potential complexity of a single newsgroup message. 1) Student D posted a newsgroup message. 2) Student F commented on D's message, including E's name. 3) Student G sent F an e-mail comment on F's newsgroup message about D and E. 4) In the newsgroup message seen here, Student F has included a portion of G's e-mail message, and responded to the content, including reference to students D and E.

16 The command F generated a follow-up message to the posting being read – a follow-up that did not include a copy of the original posting. The command f generated a follow-up that included a copy of the original posting at the beginning of the reply. There was a feeling that either the command F should be used, or, if the command f was used, then the copy of the original posting

should be edited to include only relevant content so that participants would not be required to re-read the same original message multiple times (as part of each follow-up message).

17 This message was posted in response to the one flame (emotional argument) which occurred during the discussion. Although the general feeling seemed to be that the flame was inappropriate, there was also quite a strong reaction in terms of interest at the level of intensity that had been possible in what some had seen as an emotionless mode of communication.

18 A standard signature is an automatically generated closing which is appended to the end of an electronic message sent from an account, whether e-mail or newsgroup posting. It usually includes the user's name and e-mail address, but is often extensively customised both in content and form. Not all programs include a signature feature.

19 ASCII art refers to a drawing composed of the standard characters of a keyboard. A graphical user interface was not available for use by participants at the time research was conducted.

References

Argyle, K. and Shields, R. (1996) 'Is There a Body in the Net?', in R. Shields (ed.) *Cultures of Internet*, London: Sage.

Behrens, S.J. (1994) 'A Conceptual Analysis and Historical Overview of Information Literacy', *College and Research Libraries* 55(4): 309–22.

Bigum, C. and Green, B. (1992) 'Technologizing Literacy: The Dark Side of the Dreaming', *The Australian Journal of Discourse* 12(2): 4–28.

Bruce, C.S. (1995) 'Information Literacy: A Framework for Higher Education', *The Australian Library Journal* 44(3): 158–70.

Clark, I. (1995) 'Information Literacy and the Writing Center', *Computers and Composition* 12(2): 203–9.

Demo, W. (1986) *The Idea of 'Information Literacy' in the Age of High-Tech*, New York: Tompkins Cortland Community College (cited in Behrens 1994).

Fishman, J.A. (1972) 'Domains and the Relationship between Micro- and Macro-sociolinguistics', in J. Gumperz and D. Hymes (eds) *Directions in Sociolinguistics*, New York: Holt, Rinehart & Winston.

George, R. and Luke, R. (1996) 'The Critical Place of Information Literacy in the Trend towards Flexible Delivery in Higher Education Contexts', *Australian Academic and Research Libraries* 27(3): 204–12.

Goodson, I.F. and Magnan, J.M. (1996) 'Computer Literacy as Ideology', *British Journal of Sociology of Education* 17(1): 65–79.

Knobel, M., Lankshear, C. Honan, E. and Crawford, J. (1998) 'The Wired World of Second-Language Education', in I. Snyder (ed.) *Page to Screen – Taking Literacy Into the Electronic Era*, London: Routledge.

Lankshear, C. and Knobel, M. (1997) 'Literacies, Texts and Difference in the Electronic Age', in C. Lankshear (ed.) *Changing Literacies*, Buckingham: Open University Press.

Mackay, H. (1992) 'From Computer Literacy to Technology Literacy', in J. Beynon and H. Mackay (eds) *Technological Literacy and the Curriculum*, London: Faber.

McMillan, S. (1996) 'Literacy and Computer Literacy: Definitions and Comparisons', *Computers and Education* 27(3/4): 161–70.

Rheingold, H. (1994) *The Virtual Community: Homesteading on the Electronic Frontier*, New York: HarperCollins.

Shank, G. (1993) 'Abductive Multiloguing – The Semiotic Dynamics of Navigating the Net', *The Archanet Electronic Journal on Virtual Culture* 1(1): Online at <LIST-SERV@KENTVM.KENT.EDU> <GET SHANK V1N1>

Shapiro, J.J. and Hughes, S.K. (1996) 'Information Technology as a Liberal Art', *Educom Review* 31(2): 31–5.

Street, B. (1995) *Social Literacies: Critical Approaches to Literacy in Development, Ethnography and Education*, London: Longman.

Vision Committee, AASL/AECT (1997) 'Information Literacy Standards for Student Learning', *Techtrends – For Leaders in Education and Training* 42(1): 52–3.

Wilbur, S.P. (1997) 'An Archaeology of Cyberspaces: Virtuality, Community, Identity', in D. Porter (ed.) *Internet Culture*, London: Routledge.

9

RESPECT AND THE PURSUIT OF 'SYMMETRY' IN RESEARCHING LITERACY AND STUDENT WRITING

Simon Pardoe

Introduction

In this chapter I contribute a further way of articulating some of the key methodological principles which are fundamental both to New Literacy Studies (NLS) and to related research of work-place literacy and of student writing. My suggestion is that as researchers with an interest in understanding marginalised literacy practices and unsuccessful student and employee writing, we could benefit from explicitly employing and developing a methodological principle known as 'symmetry'. This has been developed within the field of Science Studies, and powerfully taken up within recent research of the public understanding of science.

Symmetry is an issue of the *repertoires of explanation* that the researcher draws on (and fails to draw on) in their research. In the context of researching literacy and student writing, it is an issue of whether we draw on say, psychological or social, single or multiple, universal or contingent *repertoires of explanation* when trying to understand and to explain literacy practices, and the successful and unsuccessful writing of our students. This focus may seem rather abstract, but the notion of symmetry actually offers a very practical guide in the process of research and analysis, as well as a tool for reflexivity and critique in such research. It offers a powerful means of explaining the strength of the kind of research advocated by NLS, and a potential clarification of what it means in NLS to 'relativise literacy practices at an analytic level' (Street 1996, p. 5). Significantly, it offers a further challenge to the pervasive *deficit* accounts of public literacy and student writing within popular and political discourse, and even within much research.

Researching marginalised literacies and unsuccessful student writing

Literacy and student writing are interesting and difficult areas of social practice to research. They present us with the challenge of understanding practices that are already very firmly divided up as either 'right' or 'wrong', adequate or inadequate, successful or unsuccessful, dominant or marginal. A fundamental issue in such research, and the focus of this chapter, is therefore *why* and *how* it might be useful to research the understanding, rationale and skill involved not only in literacy practices and student writing that are viewed as successful, but also those viewed as 'wrong', inadequate, unsuccessful, and marginal. This is a central focus of NLS and much research of student writing. But it is easily misunderstood.

Many people might argue that literacy and writing research should instead confine its focus solely to developing our understanding of the knowledge, expertise and practices of *successful* expert writers, and of the standardised forms and dominant discourses and genres they use. This can be argued not only from the 'right wing' perspective of increasing conformity to the standard forms, but also from the 'left wing' perspective of empowering people by teaching them to use the powerful forms of written language. The priority and urgency of such a focus is seemingly affirmed by large scale literacy tests or surveys, which apparently reveal the *inadequacy* of people's knowledge of standardised spellings and grammar, and their *lack* of competence to use the powerful genres.

Yet implicit in this argument is a *deficit view,* in which low-status writing practices, and unsuccessful student writing, are viewed simply 'as failed attempts to access the dominant, standard form' (Street 1996, p. 4). In responding to this view, it is of course important to acknowledge that some instances of low status and unsuccessful writing may actually *be* (in one sense) failed attempts to access the dominant, standard form – on the basis that this was intended or demanded. But they are not *only* this. The problem is that if research adopts this deficit view, it fails to offer any further insight into such writing practices. In other words, to describe such writing in terms of absence and deficit is not to offer an understanding of it. Such an account does not tell us what implicitly and explicitly guided the writers. Therefore, by focusing on what is *not* there, rather than what *is* there, such research fails even to recognise the existing understandings and practices that are the basis for any further development (see Shaughnessy 1977, p. 5). It therefore cannot inform the process of developing people's literacy even towards what would be viewed as more successful forms. It cannot inform pedagogies or policies for literacy development, but can only reiterate the 'pedagogically empty' (ibid.) criticisms and assertions that 'something must be done'.

A second implicit element of this argument is a view of the qualities of successful texts as describable in terms a monolithic system of rules, rather than being both highly *under*determined by rules, and highly varied within the complex and subtle conventions of established genres. This is a view of successful texts as inherently and uniquely rational, rather than conventional and embedded in dominant social practices. As a consequence, it prompts a view of learning to write as an issue of developing technical skill and conformity, rather than of developing understanding of the social practices, of the functions of texts, and of *how* these functions are conventionally achieved. In a broader sociological sense, the assumption that literacy is somehow singular not only fails to acknowledge the diversity and complexity of successful writing, but also fails to offer insight into the ways in which *non-standard* and *low-status* literacy practices may also be highly functional, and even highly rational, in different social contexts.

My own interest in understanding unsuccessful writing has been prompted by experiencing the inadequacy of deficit views of unsuccessful writing, even in practical pedagogic terms. As a teacher of 'second chance' and access courses in an inner London Further Education college, I worked closely with highly articulate and experienced students who were evidently unable to show this in writing, or at least within the written genres of education. Interacting with them was a constant challenge to the easy deficit descriptions of such students that can be inferred from their unsuccessful texts. I realised that a pedagogy based, however subtly, on an 'autonomous' view of educated literacy as an asocial, technological 'skill' (Barton 1994; Street 1995, 1996), ignores the multiple cultural assumptions, and the familiarity with particular ways of talking and relating (Bartholomae 1985), that are required of a successful text. It makes inevitable the deficit view of student's existing low-status literacy practices, as failed attempts at this. It therefore simply reinforces the students' own sense of their learning of writing as somehow 'remedial' (Hull and Rose 1989; Swales 1990, p. 2). Crucially it makes teaching and learning an issue of *replacing* the students' existing repertoire of literacy practices rather than *refining* and *adding to* these. And it does so even when the students' existing practices are clearly central to their sense of identity, and to their successful functioning in other contexts.

Such a pedagogy therefore does not empower students, but emphasises their exclusion, and makes this an issue of their personal failure. Rather than encouraging them to learn the standardised forms and dominant discourses, it simply encourages their hostility and resistance. It fails to recognise and address students' already highly reflexive ambivalence (or love–hate relationship – Ivanič 1990, p. 128)) with Standard English, Received Pronunciation and high status discourses and genres. It therefore fails to help them ever to move beyond this hostility and resistance. Most fundamentally, it fails to recognise the enormity of the cultural and textual understanding and skill that the students are already drawing on in their writing (compared with that which needs to be learned), and therefore effectively ignores the foundations for further development (see Shaughnessy 1977).

Relativism, romanticism, (ir)relevance . . . and respect

In response to this, and in order to develop our understanding of literacy practices viewed as marginal and unsuccessful, a key element of research within NLS is to 'suspend judgement' (Street 1996, p. 2). The intention is to suspend the judgement about unsuccessful writing, in order to be able to pursue an understanding of it. By this I mean that in order to understand marginal and unsuccessful practices and texts, we must first refuse to dismiss (or 'explain away') these in deficit terms, as misunderstanding, or as dysfunctional, irrational, incoherent or inconsistent. This is how Street explains the point:

> Instead of privileging the particular practices familiar in their own culture [or subculture], researchers now *suspend judgement* as to what constitutes literacy among the people they are working with until they are able to understand what it means to the people themselves, and from which social contexts reading and writing derive their meaning.
>
> (1996, pp. 2–3, emphasis added)

Inevitably perhaps, this opens research in NLS to criticism and misunderstanding. First, it can be criticised for being apparently *relativist* about what counts as literacy, as if suggesting 'anything goes'. Second, it can be criticised for appearing to *romanticise* low status literacies and unsuccessful writing, with the effect of maintaining the status quo (Street 1996). Third, it can therefore be criticised for being apparently *irrelevant* to the main task of improving literacy standards and empowering people with the dominant discourses and genres. Street calls these critiques the three Rs:

> 'three areas of criticism to which NLS in general is subject . . . Relativism, Romanticism and Relevance – the three Rs.
>
> (1996, p. 2)

Street's response is that, far from being *relativist,* NLS recognises and addresses the issue that some literacies hold greater power and status in society, which is ignored in the monolithic view of literacy as merely 'correct' or 'appropriate', and merely an issue of technical skill. The relativism of NLS, he argues, is only 'at an analytic level' (1996, p. 5); it is the issue of '*suspending judgement*' in order to pursue understanding. (I will explore this more fully later.) Equally his response is that, far from *romanticising* low-status literacies so as to maintain the status-quo, NLS seeks to inform and pursue social change. He argues that, far from being *irrelevant*, NLS research is actually far more effective in informing understanding, policy and pedagogy than research based on a monolithic view of literacy, for all the reasons I have identified.

Yet, as Street acknowledges, these critiques nevertheless provide a major challenge for researchers who are seeking to convince the funding body, practitioner, critic, research user or policy maker of the value and significance of NLS research. My own interest in this was prompted by the difficulty of explaining and justifying a study of student writing which deliberately involved suspending judgement. Echoing the work of Shaughnessy (1977), Bartholomae (1985) Hull and Rose (1989) Ivanič (1996, 1997) and others, I wanted to research the understandings and practices that the students were drawing on to guide their writing, including those understandings and practices that appeared to guide them in directions which were seen as unsuccessful by the tutor (further explanation below). The difficulty of explaining such research was made apparent to me when it was described as a '*charitable reading of student writing*'. I realised that the notion of '*charitable*' made the central issue of suspending judgement into one of merely 'being nice or generous to the writers'. It thereby made suspending judgement a potentially laudable principle, but separate from issues that promote theoretically and empirically rigorous and useful research. It also implied that I would be pursuing a '*charitable reading*' of what I really viewed all along as the students' mistakes. In other words, the deficit view remained intact.

The challenge to explain the methodology of suspending judgement is therefore particularly acute when *proposing* research. While the evidently relevant and useful insight from previous research in NLS can retrospectively validate the approach taken, the difficulty comes in proposing a new study. This is when the misunderstanding and criticisms around the three Rs (Street 1996, p. 2) are potentially at their most powerful and their most difficult to counter. Moreover, while the well-established researcher may be able to gain funding in order to build on previous research recognised as valuable, the less-established researcher and the practitioner-researcher have to rely on convincing explanation within the proposal.

For those with a background in qualitative, anthropological and ethnographic research of literacy practices and student writing, or familiar with the findings, the challenge is more acute. The case for this kind of research can appear so powerful that it can seem almost self-evident, and therefore difficult to articulate. As Street argues:

> it is not always easy for the epistemological innovators themselves to recall where they have come from and what assumptions their readers and critics will bring to the new accounts.
>
> (1996, p. 2)

Indeed it is partly the *affective* experience and learning offered by such research (of being faced with the evident diversity, complexity and sophistication of people's literacy practices) that imparts a profound relativism towards what 'counts' as literacy. Such research prompts a profound *respect* towards the writers and their literacy practices, which guides both the view of literacy and the research methodology.

Yet while I believe this underlying notion of *respect* is crucial, I suggest that it is inadequate for explaining the rationale for such research within a research proposal. First, *respect* can be seen as deriving simply from an affective experience; it can therefore be regarded as irrational, rather than rational, and therefore as an unaccountable and 'unscientific' basis for a research methodology. It is difficult to argue that respect is actually essential. Second, an explanation based on *respect* doesn't address the basic problem that to respect something that is known to be 'wrong' or unsuccessful can seem perverse or naïve, and to suspend or resist the labels *wrong* and *unsuccessful* can seem simply relativist. We need some further way of separating the practice of *suspending judgement* from the suggestion that 'anything goes'. Third, respect can be *heard* as just an *ethical* issue (in the limited sense that Cameron *et al.* (1992) identify) as an issue of politeness, or of how those being researched are 'treated'. Like the notion of '*charitable reading*' this misses the more fundamental issue of *respect* within research – that we have something to learn from the texts and practices of unsuccessful writers, and have something to learn even from their own accounts of these.[1]

Researching unsuccessful student writing – an example

I will briefly describe the study of student writing (Pardoe 1997) which I found so difficult to explain in the proposal, and which prompted my interest in symmetry. This illustrates the issue of suspending judgement, and will help in illustrating the practical implications of symmetry for literacy and writing research.

The research was carried out with the active interest and participation of the course tutor, who wanted to understand why his students, year after year, found the writing on his course particularly difficult, and frequently produced very inadequate texts, despite his having provided tutorial support within the course.

The course was a vocationally oriented unit of an MSc in Environmental Management. The students were learning about professional practice in *Environmental Impact Assessment* (EIA). (UK and EU law require an assessment of the likely environmental impact to be carried out when a new development is proposed, such as a road, supermarket or quarry. The requirements of the EIA text are set out in government guidelines.) The students' learning was through researching a local environment and producing an EIA, in response to a proposed local development. They wrote this collaboratively in a team as they would in the professional setting. All students were previously successful at degree level in the natural sciences.

My research was an ethnographic study of the students' writing, focusing particularly on their talk around their writing. I attended the course with the students, and recorded the lectures, tutorials and field trips. I joined and recorded the students meetings around their collaborative writing of the Environmental Statement, and interviewed both them and the tutor about the writing during the course, and after the assessment of their texts. An important experience of being a participant observer was that while the instructions and task seemed initially clear to me as a passive observer, when I joined the students' meetings I found that I could not resolve the questions they faced in my own mind. I therefore researched their discussions about their texts, and the understandings and practices they drew on, always unsure of what might in the end be seen as successful or unsuccessful.

In the analysis, I took the tutor's critique of the students' final texts, and explored the textual features he seemed to be identifying as unsuccessful. I then pursued the origins of these. Going back to the recordings, I analysed the students' earlier discussions, and their accounts of their texts to me, to explore the ways in which their understandings of the task and of EIA, and their decisions about the text, had developed in directions that the tutor saw as unsuccessful. (See Pardoe 1997 and 1999.)

Initially I had expected to analyse the ways in which the students' unsuccessful decisions and assumptions about their texts might have involved drawing on understandings and practices from other areas of their lives. This had been my finding in a previous study (Pardoe 1994). Yet here, I found that their *un*successful understandings and practices, also drew very directly on ways of thinking about science, and writing, and EIA, that had been made available to them within the course, within the EIA literature and legislation, and from their past science education. In other words, the students' difficulties needed to be explained in terms of their *un*derstanding of science, the lectures and the legislation, rather than their *mis*understandings. Their difficulties therefore offered insights beyond their own background, practices and understandings. Specifically they offered insight into the ambiguities and tensions within the available accounts of EIA. More broadly, they offered insight into the ways in which the students' unsuccessful texts were guided by familiar views of writing and texts, and by dominant discourses within science and education.

Symmetry as a methodological principle in science studies

In the process of this research, I increasingly drew on research within Science Studies. Initially this was as a means of trying to understand the issues of science within the students' talk and writing. But I found the methodological debate and principles within Science Studies to be also potentially valuable for this research of writing.

There are certain important parallels between Science Studies and research of literacy and student writing. First, both face the challenge of studying practices and understandings that are already divided up into 'right' and 'wrong': science like literacy is usually seen as simply 'right' or 'wrong'. Second, Science Studies shares with NLS an anthropological tradition, and an ethnographic focus on understanding multiple, complex and contingent causality. This is part of what John Law calls a 'modest sociology': like research in NLS, the starting point of research in Science Studies is usually the small-scale and detailed anthropological research of people, things, actions and accounts, from which the researcher gains insight into the big issues – society, science and power (see Law 1994; Myers 1996). Third, research in Science Studies has similarly shifted in focus from analysing the product (i.e. scientific knowledge and texts) to exploring the social practices that produced these (i.e. the practices of scientists involved in producing scientific knowledge). Bruno Latour describes the focus as being on 'science in the making' rather than 'ready-made science' (1987). Fourth, Science Studies shares with NLS and research of student writing an interest in the potential insight from researching those who are on the periphery of a set of dominant understandings and practices, or excluded by them .

Symmetry has been a central methodological principle within Science Studies since the late 1970s (Pinch 1993). It is actually a defining principle for the particular fields of research known as the Sociology of Scientific Knowledge and Actor Network Theory. To explain symmetry, Latour (1993) describes how traditional anthropology could study the knowledges and practices of other 'primitive' cultures, and even the knowledge and practices of low status groups within 'western' societies. Yet significantly, such research was not applied to 'our own' respected and accepted knowledges. In particular, it was not applied to the practices and findings of western science. Here, the production of 'facts' and knowledge was regarded as beyond sociological and cultural analysis: these were simply 'true' (Latour 1993, p. 92). Therefore, while traditional sociological studies of science (e.g. Merton 1973) developed interesting sociological explanations of scientific *error*, they shared the assumption of empiricist science, that the accepted 'truths' of science were determined by 'nature' itself: they could therefore be explained only in terms of nature.

The fundamental shift was to apply anthropological research also to the accepted 'truths' and knowledge of western science. It was to view even 'hard science' as socially and discursively constructed, and as an object for empirical sociological study. The principle of *symmetry* is central to this. Symmetry constitutes a rejection of the traditional practice of explaining accepted 'truths' and 'errors' in science by reference to different *repertoires of explanation.* By this I mean that a currently accepted truth had been explained by recourse to nature, while errors and rejected theories of science had been explained by recourse to discourse and society.

The problem is that in such studies, as in the natural sciences, when an accepted 'truth' is found to be erroneous, the repertoire of explanation may shift: it is no longer explained in terms of nature, but in terms of social and discursive causes, such as the lack of skill or the misguided loyalties of the scientists, the contingency of the experiment, or their misguided trust in previous research articles. In addition, during a scientific controversy, different scientists may draw on different repertoires to explain or dismiss competing scientific claims, explaining those they believe by reference solely to nature, and explaining away those they reject by reference to social factors.[2]

The principle of *symmetry* therefore suggests that when studying the practices of scientists, we should be equally interested in the social and discursive processes of producing knowledge claims, whether these are currently accepted as 'fact' or rejected as 'error', whether they are currently seen as success or failure. Specifically, David Bloor ([1976] 1991) proposed that research be impartial with respect to truth and falsity, rationality or irrationality, success or failure: both sides of these dichotomies require explanation. Moreover, he proposed that research should be *symmetrical* in its style of explanation: the same types of cause should be pursued to explain truth and falsity, rationality or irrationality, success or failure.

From anthropological research of the processes of producing scientific knowledge, researchers in Science Studies have argued that even the 'facts' in science were not simply *determined* by nature, but depended on the questions asked, the avenues pursued, the skill and judgement of the scientists, their interpretations of evidence, the theoretical perspectives adopted, the relations of dialogue, trust and/or scepticism between researchers, the funding allocated, whether claims got noticed and taken up, and so on. During the processes of developing, testing and asserting scientific claims, these social and discursive elements are central. They are therefore important areas for research, in order to understand the development of scientific knowledge. However, they are usually omitted from the formal and retrospective accounts of science: the research article and textbook traditionally adopt a scientific discourse of empirical determinacy, in which scientific claims are apparently determined by nature, and controversies resolved by recourse only to nature.

Researchers in Science Studies have pursued social and discursive explanations of scientific knowledge as a counter to this dominant scientific discourse of empirical determinacy. In fact, many researchers have pursued social explanations of science practice and scientific claims, as if nature took no part in scientific fact.

However, Bruno Latour and others argue that this involves a further asymmetry: it takes a constructivist view of nature, while taking a realist view of society to *explain* our scientific knowledge of it (1993, p. 94). This effectively demands that sociology should become the source of explanation of, for example, the whole of physics, and our knowledge of the ozone hole. They therefore refuse to rule out nature as a source of explanation. (Indeed they reject the practice of separating and reifying 'nature' and 'society', arguing that each is implicated in the other. To understand society, we need to explore the ways in which it has enrolled say, metals, animals, rivers and radio waves.) In studying science, we should be interested in the ways in which scientific claims actively enrol both elements of nature, such as rocks, atoms or cells, and technologies, such as microscopes and silicon chips: we should refuse to view the construction of a scientific claim as somehow a purely 'social' process. More broadly, their argument is that anthropological research should involve pursuing the often complex and multiple sources of explanation, rather than selecting these a priori along the lines of conventional academic disciplines. Their intention is once again to point to, and to reject, the conventional and often implicit preselection of *repertoires of explanation* within research.

This more recent shift has been particularly important in guiding recent studies of the public understanding of science (PUS) (see Wynne 1995). Rather than pursuing only social explanations for public (mis)-understandings of science and technology, researchers have explored the ways in which these understandings may actually be highly functional (they may work), may be based on experience and evidence, and may be linked to understandings of science otherwise viewed as 'rational' and 'true'. This has been a major counter to the dominant research and discourse of PUS, which has traditionally researched the public *ignorance* of science. In this way the work of Wynne and others therefore echoes research in NLS, in challenging the dominant research and discourse of public *deficit*.

The implications of pursuing symmetry within research of literacy and student writing

I now want to reformulate the methodological principle of symmetry in order to apply it directly to research of literacy and student writing. In doing so it is clear that symmetry embraces what many researchers of literacy and student writing already do. But it usefully clarifies and elaborates this, and offers a way of explaining research methodology. As

I have explained, we can embrace three components within the principle of symmetry:[3]

1 That our research be impartial with respect to whether literacy practices are currently dominant or marginal, or regarded as successful or unsuccessful: both require explanation. We need to view all literacy practices as of research interest, and thereby avoid the view that some practices and some texts are simply 'correct' or 'rational', and therefore beyond social explanation.
2 That our research be symmetrical in its style of explanation: we pursue the same sources of explanation to explain literacy practices whether these are currently dominant or marginal, or regarded as successful or unsuccessful.
3 That in our research we do not rule out, a priori, certain sources of explanation: in keeping with an anthropological tradition, we should pursue the often complex and multiple sources of explanation, rather than selecting these a priori along the lines of traditional academic disciplines. In particular, when researching marginalised and unsuccessful writing we should not rule out an analysis of the ways in which these may also be guided by rules, be highly functional and rational in particular contexts, and be guided by practices and understandings that we otherwise regard as 'true' or 'correct'.

I will now elaborate on some of the implications of symmetry for research of literacy and student writing, by pursuing four themes.

Symmetry offers a framework for critique and reflexivity in research

It is important to emphasise that, as in Science Studies, the value of symmetry is not as a kind of *recipe* for good research, but as a conceptual tool and methodological *principle*. In the widest sense, symmetry has an important function simply in focusing attention on the repertoires of explanation being drawn on in accounts of literacy and student writing. The choice of explanatory repertoire can no longer be simply left implicit or assumed to be 'natural', but requires justification. This does not mean that every study of writing should try to pursue every possible repertoire of explanation. Rather, it means that the often implicit preselection of repertoires of explanation in research, and the asymmetries in their use, should be the focus of reflexivity and critique.

In this way the principle of symmetry very powerfully foregrounds and problematises the *a*symmetry inherent within traditional *deficit* accounts of public literacy and student writing, which are both prevalent in political and media debate, and sustained by some traditional research. On the one hand, the monolithic and 'autonomous' literacy that is construed as the goal of education and literacy programmes, is explained as uniquely determined by rules, rationality and clarity. The accounts are asocial because this literacy is seen as not requiring social explanation. The social histories of dominant literacies and the diversity of successful writing are both ignored, together with the very particular cultural knowledge and assumptions they require. On the other hand, the (il)literacy of the public, and the unsuccessful writing of students, is explained in terms of social and psychological factors, including individual lack of skill or ability, social deprivation or deviance, and so on. The possibility that unsuccessful writing and marginal literacy practices may also be guided by rules, and be highly functional, effective and rational in some contexts, is ignored. In other words, the two accounts draw on very different repertoires of explanation to account for discourses and practices depending on whether these are dominant or marginalised, respected or stigmatised, successful or unsuccessful.

In the light of the concept of symmetry, the accusations of being 'perverse' or 'politically committed' can be redirected away from NLS and towards this traditional research. This can now appear as prematurely selective in its repertoire of explanations, and as making unwarranted deficit accounts of writers whose texts in education or work are seen as unsuccessful, while naïvely accepting of the dominant and target practices as not needing further explanation.

The power of traditional asymmetrical research of literacy and student writing is that it has become so usual, so automatic, so obvious and apparently 'natural', that the asymmetrical explanations come to be seen as having an empirical legitimacy (i.e. as reflecting a reality) rather than representing the shifting explanatory repertoires of the researcher. Symmetry is therefore a powerful tool for critique. It is a way of foregrounding the way in which research constructs explanation. It is therefore a means of addressing and critiquing the potentially implicit and self-affirming cycle between explanation and research methodology, in which an often implicit, a priori selection of explanatory repertoire may be embedded even within the initial questions and methodology of research.

Within our own research, the symmetry constitutes a demand at least to reflect on the repertoires of explanation we pursue, and those we may have implicitly put aside. It is a demand to account for the asymmetries in research, if not to remedy them. If, for reasons of a disciplinary tradition, our research is confined say, to offering cognitive and individualistic repertoires of explanation, or to grand explanations from social theory, then it is important to make this explicit, rather than claiming (or implicitly suggesting) that this is the only form of explanation that might be suggested by the evidence. Echoing John Law (see p. 156), symmetry is therefore a call for modest claims for literacy research, in which findings are located not only within the context of the people's writing, but also within the disciplinary traditions of the research. It is a demand for some reflexivity about the methodology and the production of research knowledge. Contrary to setting up any universal methodology, symmetry comes from within the anthropological tradition in Science Studies (informed by Wittgenstein and Kuhn) which is precisely about the *indeterminacy* of rules and method, and the *situated, provisional* and *contingent* nature of explanation. Any dogmatic claim to have *achieved* symmetrical explanation should be met with the same sceptical critique as a claim to have *achieved* comprehensive explanation or the final word on a subject. Symmetry may be one source of legitimacy for the findings of research, but it is not a route to categorical or autonomous knowledge.

Similarly, it is important not to confuse this with neutrality. Faced with say, contrasting views of a student's text by the student and tutor, or more broadly, faced with the political debate around public literacy, symmetry is not the same as neutrality. Neutrality refers to the notion of 'balance': it is an issue of whether the analyst holds the prior conclusions or perspectives of a particular protagonist, or refrains from providing an analysis which may support either side. As Wynne argues (1996, p. 360), neutrality refers to a position within a controversy in which the 'sides' are taken for granted. By contrast, symmetry is an issue of the explanatory resources drawn on: it is a basis for engaging in critique of competing accounts, for contributing insight which may have been missed by the protagonists on both sides in their own competing repertoires of explanation. It is a basis for contributing to a debate, rather than avoiding it, a demand for more equivalent forms of explanation and enquiry, and a demand for both 'sides' to account for the asymmetries and shifts in the repertoires of explanation they employ. Rather than assuming or affirming either side, the contribution of symmetry is likely to be in challenging simple categories of true and false, successful and unsuccessful.

The same repertoires of explanation are used for texts and practices which are successful and unsuccessful

The practical implications of actually *pursuing* the methodological principle of symmetry within our research, are that we analyse marginal and dominant literacy practices, and successful and unsuccessful student texts similarly, pursuing the same potential repertoires of explanation. For instance, in a study of student writing we avoid the prior judgement that the accounts from the tutor and in the literature can be explained in terms of their functionality, rationality, coherence and truth, while the students' accounts of their unsuccessful texts must be ill-informed, illogical and potentially misguided, to be uniquely explained in terms of cognitive and social factors. We don't look for coherence in one, and incoherence in the other. We don't assume precision in one and ambiguity in the other. Above all, we don't resort to 'explaining' students' unsuccessful writing in terms of their cognitive deficit, or lack of skills, ability, knowledge and understanding, until we have at least pursued the functional nature of their text, its potential coherence and 'rationality', and the links the writers themselves seem to make to conventions, dominant practices and the task they were aiming to achieve. Only then can we understand what guided their text, and in a pedagogic context, understand what more they might need to know to make their writing more successful.

Successful writing (as well as unsuccessful writing) requires social explanation

One side of this symmetry is that successful writing, as well as unsuccessful writing, requires social explanation. As Street (1996, p. 1) and others have argued, dominant and successful literacy practices need to be researched (as well as those viewed as marginal and unsuccessful) in terms of the ways in which they are 'embedded in specific contexts, discourses and positions'. Echoing the principle of symmetry, part of the focus of research in NLS is precisely to develop a contextual understanding of dominant and successful literacy practices, as well as marginal and unsuccessful ones.

Within academic and professional settings, the field of genre analysis has pursued a social explanation of dominant and successful literacy practices, albeit with a focus often confined to the written text. The genre analysis of John Swales (1990) and others has shown the complex and conventional functions and rhetorical organisation in successful texts. This kind of analysis has shown the ways in which both form and function are conventional and subtly varied, rather than 'autonomous' or monolithic. It has affirmed the view that genres or literacy practices cannot be simply reinvented by students through 'skill' or 'intelligence', but need to be learned. This in turn powerfully challenges both deficit views of unsuccessful student writing, and the 'remedial' view of teaching writing, as having 'nothing to teach but that which should have been learnt before' (ibid., p. 2).

The challenge symmetry poses for any analysis of dominant and successful literacy practices and genres, is that we should not assume that these are necessarily coherent, homogeneous, purposeful, functional or rational, while therefore assuming that the unsuccessful texts of the novice or 'outsider' are uniquely varied, inconsistent and lacking in a single coherent purpose. This is a danger in accounts of high status genres, but also in reports of writing research, which typically give the reader a simple coherent account of the task or the genre, and then explore the students' uncertainties, difficulties and misunderstandings in their writing. The simple coherent account gives the reader, as passive observer, the misleading impression of *knowing* the task and the demands, so that they can only see the students' difficulties in terms of their misunderstanding. The apparent coherence obscures the possible ambiguities and tensions in what is required, and the potential diversity of texts produced by successful writers. It is exactly these that the student may be struggling with, when trying to work out what is required of them.

More generally, it is inevitable that any official account of a genre within a discipline or profession will seek to construct unity and coherence: this is after all its function. For instance, in my research of student writing in Environmental Impact Assessment (Pardoe 1997), it became clear that the accounts of EIA within the legislation and guidelines did not respond to the particular questions and doubts experienced by the students. These accounts achieved a unity for the profession precisely by backgrounding or omitting the sources of diversity in EIA texts and practice.[4] While they may seem adequate to the passive observer or experienced assessor, the questions raised by the students made the omissions and ambiguities apparent. The students could actually use these available accounts to affirm understandings of EIA, and actions in their texts, that were later criticised by the tutor.

Researching unsuccessful writing involves keeping open the repertoires of explanation

The other side of pursuing the principle of symmetry is therefore that researching *un*successful writing involves keeping open the repertoires of explanation. In particular, symmetry in researching marginal and unsuccessful literacy practices means that we should avoid pursuing only social or psychological explanation. For example, we should avoid looking for explanation of students' unsuccessful writing *only* in terms of their social experiences beyond education, the social factors in their own social worlds. It is important that we also explore the implicit and explicit links between their practices and understandings and those that we regard as successful, rational or 'true'. In other words, we explore the ways in which they may also be drawing on dominant practices, on the available accounts of what they should be doing, on the examples available to them, and on linguistic forms that are regarded as 'correct' and successful elsewhere.

Contrary to the notion of '*a charitable reading of student writing*' symmetry does not involve patronising the students with a charitable reading of what we really view all along as *their* mistakes. Instead, suspending judgement involves simply suspending the premature explanation of an unsuccessful text, in order to pursue an understanding of it through research.

Contrary to the criticisms of relativism, romanticism and irrelevance, discussed above, this does not mean pretending that successful and unsuccessful texts are equally 'right', nor suggesting that 'anything goes' in a kind of naïve relativist view that loses touch with generic conventions and 'standards'. In contrast with absolute relativism, the point of this methodological relativism is precisely to research the ways in which unsuccessful writers may actually draw (whether implicitly and explicitly) on conventional practices, established knowledges, evidence, information and so on. It is to research the crucial links between a student's text and the accepted truths, dominant forms of rationality, powerful discourses, genres and practices, and previously published texts that are available to them. The intention is not to say that these do not matter. They matter to the student in their learning: they are what guide the writing, and eventually make it successful or not. It is precisely these links that the tutor is looking for (however implicitly) when judging whether a student has learned and used the conventions, rational forms of argument, accepted knowledge and established tenets of the discipline, drawn on appropriate evidence and other sources, and identified the significance of their claims. In a broader sociological sense, it is these links that make some texts and some discourse practices successful and powerful, and others less so. Researching these links is part of both developing our sociological understanding, and informing our pedagogy.

The challenge is not only to employ principles of symmetry or suspending judgement when researching students' understanding of complex issues of genre, but also to employ these when researching the more *apparently* clear cut and 'rule bound' issues in writing, such as punctuation. Roz Ivanič's study of the use of punctuation, by mature students with no formal qualifications, is important in doing exactly this. Through exploratory discussion with the student writers about a text they had written, she asked about their choices of punctuation. She wanted to gain an understanding of their reasons for their use of punctuation. In so doing, she effectively suspended her potential judgement of their punctuation as 'wrong'. She recognised that grammatical rules leave some room for negotiation in context, and used her linguistic understanding to analyse and question the students' own actions and understandings. She found that rather than being ignorant of 'the rules of punctuation', they were often applying (or over-applying) these in ways that were unsuccessful. She therefore gained a richer insight into the students' understandings of texts and punctuation, and into the degree of guidance offered to them by the available rules. In a broader sense, she was able to explore the complex, often implicit, issues at stake, not only for learners but also for experienced writers, when making decisions about punctuation. As all good teachers know from experience, we can learn from exploring the difficulties of our students, and from becoming aware of the understandings and practices they draw on. We can learn not only what more we might need to explain if we are to enable them to produce writing that will be seen as successful, but also something about our own implicit knowledge and practices.

Notes

1 Learning from their own accounts of their writing does not involve an uncritical acceptance of the writers' own insights, which is incidentally pervasive in the research of successful writing (for example in Bhatia 1993, pp. 34–6)). Instead it means questioning practitioner accounts, and analysing the understandings practices and discursive resources that they draw on implicitly as well as explicitly. It does not mean assuming their accounts are comprehensive, but exploring the potential shifts and ambiguity of these accounts when they are used to guide and explain practices in writing.

2 Analysis in Gilbert and Mulkay (1984), summarised in Chapter 7 of Potter and Wetherell (1987).

3 I am using the term symmetry in the broader sense, to embrace the three principles that I outlined in the previous section. This is more useful than limiting it strictly to the original usage by David Bloor, which referred only to the second of these. As I have explained, the first (impartiality) is in some ways a prerequisite of symmetry and is always cited with it, and the third is an important development of it, in the pursuit of further symmetry.

4 These included the relation of the environmental assessment to the development proposal (written sequentially or alongside), the relation of the environmental assessor to the developer (employed or independent), and the inevitable uncertainty of both the data and methods involved in predicting future changes in a local environment.

References

Bartholomae, David (1985) 'Inventing the University', in Mike Rose (ed.) *When a Writer Can't Write: Studies in Writers' Block and Other Composing-process Problems*', New York: The Guildford Press.

Barton, David (1994) *Literacy: An Introduction to the Ecology of Written Language*, Oxford: Blackwell.

Bhatia, Vijay K. (1993) *Analysing Genre: Language Use in Professional Settings*, London: Longman.

Bloor, David ([1976] 1991) *Knowledge and Social Imagery*, 2nd edn, Chicago: University of Chicago Press.

Cameron, Deborah, Frazer, Elizabeth, Harvey, Penelope, Rampton, M.B.H. and Richardson, Kay (1992) *Researching Language: Issues of Power and Method*, London: Routledge.

Gilbert, G. Nigel and Mulkay, Michael (1984) *Opening Pandora's Box: A Sociological Analysis of Scientists' Discourse*, Cambridge: Cambridge University Press.

Hull, Glynda and Rose, Mike (1989) 'Rethinking Remediation: Toward a Social-cognitive Understanding of Problematic Reading and Writing', *Written Communication* 6(2): 139–54.

Ivanič, Roz (1990) 'Critical Language Awareness in Action', in Ronald Carter (ed.) *Knowledge about Language and the Curriculum: The LINC Reader*, London: Hodder & Stoughton.

Ivanič, Roz (1996) 'Linguistics and the Logic of Non-Standard Punctuation', in Nigel Hall and Anne Robinson (eds) *Learning About Punctuation*, Clevedon: Multilingual Matters.

Ivanič, Roz (1997) *Writing and Identity: The Discourse Construction of Identity in Academic Writing*, Amsterdam: Benjamins.

Latour, Bruno (1987) *Science in Action: How to Follow Scientists and Engineers through Society*, Cambridge, MA: Harvard University Press.

Latour, Bruno (1993) *We Have Never Been Modern*, Hemel Hempstead: Harvester Wheatsheaf.

Law, John (1994) *Organising Modernity*, Oxford: Blackwell.

Merton, Robert (1973) *The Sociology of Science*, Chicago: University of Chicago Press.

Myers, Greg (1996) 'Out of the Laboratory and Down to the Bay: Writing Science and Technology Studies', *Written Communication*, January.

Pardoe, Simon (1994) 'Writing in Another Culture: The Value of Students' KAL in Writing Pedagogy', in David Graddol and Joan Swann (eds) *Evaluating Language*, Clevedon: British Association for Applied Linguistics/Multilingual Matters.

Pardoe, Simon (1997) 'Writing Professional Science: Genre, Recontextualization and Empiricism in the Learning of Professional and Scientific Writing within an MSc Course in Environmental Impact Assessment', PhD thesis, Lancaster University.

Pardoe, Simon (1999) 'A Question of Attribution: The Indeterminacy of "learning from experience" ', in Mary Lea and Barry Stierer (eds) *New Contexts for Student Writing in Higher Education*, Buckingham: Open University Press.

Pinch, Trevor (1993) 'Generations of SSK', *Social Studies of Science* 23: 363–73.

Potter, Jonathan and Wetherall, Margaret (1987) *Discourse and Social Psychology: Beyond Attitudes and Behaviour*, London: Sage Publications.

Shaughnessy, Mina P. (1977) *Errors and Expectations: A Guide for the Teacher of Basic Writing*, New York: Oxford University Press.

Street, Brian (1995) *Social Literacies: Critical Approaches to Literacy in Development, Ethnography and Education*, New York: Longman.

Street, Brian (1996) 'Preface', in Mastin Prinsloo and Mignonne Breier (eds) *The Social Uses of Literacy: Theory and Practice in Contemporary South Africa*, Cape Town: Sached Books.

Swales, John M. (1990) *Genre Analysis: English in Academic and Research Settings*, Cambridge: Cambridge University Press.

Wynne, Brian (1995) 'Public Understanding of Science', in Sheila Jasanoff, Gerald E. Markle, James C. Petersen and Trevor Pinch (eds) *Handbook of Science and Technology Studies*, Thousand Oaks, CA: Sage Publications.

Wynne, Brian (1996) 'SSK's Identity Parade: Signing-Up, Off-and-On', *Social Studies of Science* 26: 357–91.

10

RESEARCHING LITERACY PRACTICES

Learning from activities with teachers and students

David Barton

One of the best ways for students and others to increase their understanding of literacy is for them to reflect upon their own practices and the everyday practices around them. They can do this by carrying out research on literacy. With colleagues I have been developing ways of encouraging this on university courses and in-service training. I have become very aware of the parallels between these activities and the research I do which studies literacy in people's everyday lives. In this chapter I give examples of how students and others can be encouraged to research their own practices, and I explore the links between teaching and research, and between education and everyday life, examining how the research process can be a pedagogical tool, and the ways in which detailed studies from many areas of life provide evidence of the situated nature of literacy.

Any theory deserves a method, and a social theory of literacy favours particular ways of doing research. One such method is the detailed examination of particular instances of social practices. Students can quickly learn to do research of this sort on their own. Its effects are many: students learn about specific practices; equally importantly they come to understand a social theory of literacy; and their research can increase knowledge about literacy practices. In my experience students have become excited and enthusiastic about the topic when they engage with it in this way.

This work can be located in broader conceptions of the importance of reflexivity and it draws together several distinct threads. In education, the importance of explicit reflection is emphasised both in Vygotskian approaches to learning as situated cognition (Vygotsky 1978; Barton 1994, pp. 132–4, 160); this is put into practice as reflective teaching and constructivist learning (as in Henderson 1992). Critical self-reflection is the basis of emancipatory adult education inspired by the work of Paulo Freire with his concept of conscientisation (Freire 1985). This is put into practice as critical pedagogy and links made with everyday life, for example where Ira Shor refers to 're-experiencing the ordinary' as a first step in critical education (Shor 1980, p. 93). Using self-reflection to link everyday practices and research methods can be seen as a development of qualitative research which emphasises the importance of reflexive methods (as in Schratz and Walker 1995), as well as contributing to more general debates about linking research and practice (e.g. Hamilton, Ivanič and Barton, 1992; Barton and Hamilton 1996). More broadly, awareness can be seen as the basis of human intelligence (Barton 1994, p. 49), and social theorists have identified this reflexivity as a characteristic of contemporary society crucial to constructions of identity (as in Giddens 1991).

Starting with students' own practices

Students often approach courses on literacy assuming that the topic is concerned with an autonomous skill which is just to do with education and with learning. Research is thought of as consisting solely of testing amounts or levels of literacy and examining what people cannot do. Students also come to classes in the expectation of studying the literacy of others and they do not expect to reflect upon their own practices. Unfortunately, this is particularly true of students in education: when working in education it is sometimes very difficult to realise that there are other literacies outside the classroom. It is also true of other students, who draw upon everyday media images of literacy as an autonomous skill.

In order to question students' initial assumptions, I usually begin courses by asking them questions such as the following:

- *Can you read and write music?*
- *Have you ever written to a politician? What was the outcome?*
- *What records do you keep of your life?*

Such questions work very well in stimulating a discussion, getting students to think about their own practices, getting beyond classroom literacies and getting them to question what literacy means. One form of this activity is given in Appendix 10.1.

I sometimes work with undergraduate students on Linguistics courses teaching them about literacy. I also work with adult education professionals on a Masters programme, or on short courses. In terms of my research I examine what people read and write in their day-to-day lives, researching everyday literacy practices. The questions posed to students are similar to questions we ask people in our research.

How we carried out research in the Literacy in the Community project

The Literacy in the Community project has been a detailed study of the role of literacy in the everyday lives of people in Lancaster, England, and been reported in Barton and Hamilton 1998 and elsewhere. Here I want to give an idea of the range of methods used in the study.

This was a funded project lasting several years. The research methods included a mixture of observing and talking to people, observing particular literacy events, and asking people to reflect on their practices. The central methodology of the whole study was in-depth interviews; these were complemented by observations, photography and the collection of documents and records. The study included a door-to-door survey in one neighbourhood of Lancaster and detailed case studies of people in twelve households in the neighbourhood. Alongside the case studies were thirty interviews of people in what we called access points for literacy, such as book-shops, libraries and advice centres. There were also interviews of twenty adults who had identified problems with their reading and writing and had been attending courses at the Adult College. More than a year after the main part of the study in a phase called the Collaborative Ethnography project we took back transcripts of interviews to ten of the people for further discussion.

In this research we were very conscious of the research methods utilised and have been explicit about the methodology. (See Barton and Hamilton 1998, Ch. 4.) At any point in the study the topic of interviews or observations was derived from earlier observations or interviews. The method was essentially cyclical, going back and forth between different methods of data collection. At some points it focused on individuals, at other times on the neighbourhood, on families and households, or on the practices of particular clubs and associations. The analyses developed during the study, alongside the data collection and the writing up.

Student projects

Whilst this range of methods is too disparate for student projects and the ethnographic research too extended, basic elements can be adapted for shorter projects. In a course taught by Anita Wilson and myself, entitled Literacy Studies, undergraduate and postgraduate students are asked to explore the literacy practices in any area of everyday life. They are given a brief outline of the steps involved in carrying out the research, as in Appendix 10.2 and summarised in Figure 10.1. They first have to identify a specific topic for the research, often a specific physical place, sometimes a particular activity. Some start with a specific text and then examine the practices associated with it. Others take a general domain and gradually

1. Identify domain or domains
2. Observe visual environment
3. Identify particular literacy events and document them
4. Identify texts and analyse practices around texts
5. Interview people about practices, sense making.

Figure 10.1 Some steps in researching literacy practices

make it more specific. The aim is to attend to detail. Having identified a topic, the students are encouraged to observe the visual environment, trying to look at it anew, with a researcher's distance, with an ethnographer's eyes, trying to see it as a stranger might. They are encouraged to take photographs and photography has often become central in the reports they make.

Step three is to focus on particular literacy events, documenting them. Regular repeated events in students' lives, such as shopping and travelling, often prove interesting in getting at the underlying practices. Unique and unusual events, such as planning a wedding, can also be revealing. Identifying the texts involved in the events is the next step, and observing how the texts are used; sometimes students are able to collect examples of texts, or photocopy or photograph them. Finally, in many cases they interview people about their practices, drawing on cultural knowledge and making sense of the observations.

In analysing what they have researched, students are encouraged to apply concepts used in a social theory of literacy (such as in Barton 1994, pp. 34–52); for example, they might identify particular roles people take, gender differences in participation in literacy events, the intertwining of different media, ways of learning new literacies. Sometimes they carry out background research, for example on the history of the practices they are studying, such as form filling or betting. Students have to provide short summaries, less than two pages, of their research findings to present to other students. Some continue with the projects and write their work up as assignments or as dissertations.

The topics chosen have been most imaginative; examples are given in Figure 10.2; where the lists provide glimpses of the everyday life of students. Sometimes they observe events they are very familiar with, such as a sport they participate in. Others venture out into new activities. Often they are carrying out original research, as there is no published work on the literacy practices of betting shops, women's rugby teams, or selling wallpaper.

The focus here is on how the students have carried out the projects and how the activity has acted as a way of introducing them to a new view of

Sport
Scoring in cricket
Attending a football match
Participating in a women's rugby team
The gymnast magazine
Sailing
Darts

Leisure
Betting shop
Fruit machines
Lottery
Bingo
Playing music
Ice climbing
Pub quiz
Disposable literacy in the pub
Fountain pen collecting as a hobby

Travel
Arranging a holiday
Brochures in the travel agents and at home
Road literacy
On buses
Train station literacy
On the train
Airport
Harbour literacy

Everyday life
Village life
Having a baby
Being arrested
Changing one's name
Comparison of self and parents
Comparison of self and grandparents
An 8-year-olds' Save the Birds club
In church
Tattoos
Wine literacy

In town
Dental surgery
Court trial
Shopping in supermarket
Fish and chip shop
Record store
Clothes store
Post office
Protesting against swimming pool closure

Working
Home decor store
Local newspaper office
Staff notice-board in the supermarket
Job search in the job centre

Student life
Practices of overseas students
Hall life
Message boards
Graffiti
Using the launderette
At the sports centre

Figure 10.2 Examples of topics of investigation of literacy practices

literacy, how reflexivity can be a pedagogic tool. The projects students have undertaken have also revealed much about the situated nature of literacy practices. In the seminars when they report back their findings we make links between the different studies, noticing, for example, similarities of places where people wait, or patterns in the different studies of supermarket practices; in this way we are carrying out research. Something could be said about each of these studies in terms of what we learned, both students and tutors, about literacy. I will provide just one example, that of the everyday practices of overseas students in Britain.

Literacy practices in a new country

A group of overseas students studied the new literacy practices they had encountered as students in Britain, concentrating on everyday literacies rather than their academic literacies. The investigation began as a result of an observation by one student that soon after he arrived in Britain he received a letter from Readers Digest which seemed to be informing him that he had won a million pounds. He was surprised both at the contents of the letter and at the fact that the company knew his address. In puzzling out the letter he had received he was struck by the way he was being incorporated into some everyday literacy practices which were new to him, but which, as he soon found out, were common to British people sorting through their mail.

The students pooled their experiences of arriving in Britain and they were surprised at the common patterns. These were all students who had been students in their own countries and who were used to speaking English; several were English teachers. In terms of language use, they found that they were now using English for different purposes; first their practices changed as they returned to the role and status of students; second, more everyday activities were now carried out in English. They also observed changes in their literacies. Here are some of the things they noticed about their everyday literacies:

1 Arriving on the campus, in many ways it was familiar – there are university campuses throughout the world – on the other hand, it was in a new unfamiliar culture and they needed to puzzle out how the culture works. Around the campus there are hundreds of notices attached to pillars, on walls, stuck on notice-boards. Initially the students had no idea what was significant and what was unimportant; they found they were reading every notice around campus, devouring them, while home students seemed to be able to pick out what was important and ignore the others.
2 In the department there are also many notices. One student recalled reading every notice along the corridors, soon after she had arrived, again not being able to discriminate the significant from the insignificant. She pored over the notices, trying to puzzle out how the department works, as if the meaning of the department somehow lay in the visual environment of notices and messages. Other students immediately recognised this phenomenon and recounted similar experiences.
3 In terms of using the computing facilities, many overseas students found that they used e-mail and the Internet much more for everyday

uses than home students. As well as straightforward e-mail contact with friends throughout the world, they kept in contact with their countries in several other ways. They might read Internet newspapers from home, browsing two or more papers in ways they had not previously, for example, or they participated in on-line debating societies or other discussion groups. They learned these new practices very quickly, often in informal ways, even if they had no prior experience with computers.

4 As an example of subtle differences in everyday activities, when shopping they felt they used the written word differently from British people. They spent more time reading labels in supermarkets for details such as food contents, partly because they were unfamiliar foods or packaging, sometimes for health reasons, and sometimes for religious reasons. Being in an unfamiliar culture made them more reliant on the available written information.

5 They were documenting their time in Britain, partly by collecting mementoes such as brochures from places they had visited. This even included keeping messages stuck to their doors, advertisements for events, or odd notes from friends which are usually treated as transient artefacts and thrown away. In their college rooms they created a sense of home, using literacy artefacts to transform their space, for example by making a display of post-cards they had received, and other mementoes.

In researching their own practices, students found it revealing about their own lives; they came to see the value of a social view of literacy, and all of us gained new insights into the role of literacy in people's lives. Student evaluations of the course were very positive, and they referred to the ways in which they had changed how they thought.

Photography as a pedagogic tool

A different example of how students can research literacy comes from an in-service professional development course for adult educators. A group of adult educators from Bangladesh participated in a course on how to research literacy. The course was based in Lancaster. It had various components, including: training and practice in interviewing about people's literacy histories; examples of ethnographic studies of literacy; and a practical introduction to the critical evaluation of texts. Here I will concentrate on one aspect of researching literacy practices. Near the beginning of the course, participants were given disposable cameras so that they could take pictures of literacy around the city and the campus. They spent an afternoon doing this in groups of four or five students; the photographs were then developed overnight and were available for the class the next morning. First, we just looked through the photographs;

the groups explained why they had taken the photos and what they had learned about literacy in Lancaster from them. As we had over a hundred representations of literacy, the photographs could then be the data for further research activities in the class; the students sorted, arranged, rearranged and classified them to make points about literacy, and we used them in class discussions of how literacy is socially situated, how it belongs to particular place.

The photographs became the bases of discussions about differences between literacy in Britain and Bangladesh, and the purpose of literacy programmes. To make one link between teaching and research, we also discussed how the students took different photos from the ones we had been taking in our research project and how the photos contribute a distinct view of the reading and writing in a British city. This brought up issues of being insiders and outsiders in research, and also insiders and outsiders when designing literacy programmes. To complete this phase of the course the students used the photos in posters they made about literacy. After the course the students took the photos away with them and utilised them in later reports and presentations associated with their work. These materials had a use beyond the classroom. (See also Barton *et al.* 1993; Hodge and Jones 1996 on using photographs in literacy research.)

Bringing these topics together

The various students who have researched literacy practices have then gone on to relate this work to the rest of their studies. The Linguistics students learned about the situated nature of literacy. Many of their other courses are concerned with the analysis of texts; by combining these perspectives they can see how a study of language needs to be a study of both texts and practices. Education students can relate this perspective on literacy to other work on reading and writing. In professional development such research can be a starting-point for developing and evaluating curriculum and materials (as, for example, in Rogers 1994; Hodge 1997). I find it useful for educators to keep in mind a simple triangle of their own practices, their students' practices and the society's practices. We can constantly move around the triangle making comparisons between these three sets of practices, and providing a context for the students' practices.

The examples given have been from my immediate experience; it is also possible for parents, for children, for teachers in classes to reflect upon their own practices. The main link between teaching and research is the fact that teaching about literacy is best done by getting people to do their own research, and that, at any level, researchers, teachers, parents, children, administrators can all become researchers of their own practices. (As a further example, Roz Ivanič and colleagues are exploring ways of getting children aged 10 to interview family members about home literacy practices as part of homework projects, as in Ormerod and Ivanič, Chapter 6 in this volume. See Barton and Hamilton 1996 for examples from Adult Education.) This work can go beyond much earlier work on teachers-as-researchers which is concerned primarily with the learning of education-defined literacies.

Carrying out research can be empowering for those carrying out the research. This is also true of the act of participating in research, of being a respondent or an informant in some research. As a graphic example of these effects (and of the possible relations of academic work and everyday life), one student got her father to read a chapter of the course text book so that he understood a social view of literacy and the two of them could co-research their different home literacy practices. She reported in her assignment on her renewed dialogue with her father and how they reflected upon similarities and differences in their lives. Returning to our funded study, in this research the people we interviewed at first thought we must be thinking of education when we said we were interested in reading and writing; it took some time for them to believe we valued their everyday literacies. In carrying out our research, we were getting people to reflect on a different theory of literacy. Both the researcher and the researched can learn more about literacy; similarly the teacher and the taught.

Acknowledgement

This chapter is based on a paper presented at the symposium, 'Literacy across Boundaries', BERA Annual conference, Lancaster, September 1996. I am grateful to the colleagues and students who have participated in these courses, especially Anita Wilson.

References

Barton, D. (1994) *Literacy: An Introduction to the Ecology of Written Language*, Oxford: Blackwell.

Barton, D. and Hamilton, M. (1996) 'Putting the New Literacies into Practice', in S. Fitzpatrick and J. Mace (eds) *Lifelong Literacies*, Manchester: Gatehouse Books, pp. 15–21.

Barton, D. and Hamilton, M. (1998) *Local Literacies: Reading and Writing in One Community*, London: Routledge.

Barton, D., Hamilton, M., Ivanič, R., Ormerod, F., Padmore, S., Pardoe S. and Rimmershaw, R. (1993) 'Photographing Literacy Practices', *Changing English* 1(1): 127–40.

Freire, P. (1985) *The Politics of Education: Culture, Power and Liberation*, London: Macmillan.

Giddens, A. (1991) *Modernity and Self-identity*, Oxford: Polity Press.

Hamilton, M., Ivanič, R. and Barton, D. (1992) 'Knowing Where We Are: Participatory Research and Adult Literacy', in J.-P. Hautecoeur (ed.) *Community Based Strategies for Literacy*, Hamburg: UNESCO.

Henderson, J.G. (1992) *Reflective Teaching: Becoming an Inquiring Educator,* New York, Macmillan.

Hodge, R. (1997) *Social Uses of Literacy: A Pilot Study of Existing Literacy Practices in Communities of South Dhading District Using Ethnographic and Other Qualitative Approaches,* ms, Community Literacy Project, Nepal.

Hodge, R. and Jones, K. (1996) 'Photography in Collaborative Research: Insider Outsider Images and Understandings of Multilingual Literacy Practices', *Lancaster University, Centre for Language in Social Life Working Paper 83.*

Rogers, A. (1994) 'Using Literacy: A New Approach to Post-literacy Materials', *ODA Occasional Paper on Education 10.*

Schratz, M. and Walker, R. (1995) *Research as Social Change: New Opportunities for Qualitative Research,* London: Routledge.

Shor, I. (1980) *Critical Teaching and Everyday Life,* Boston: South End Press.

Vygotsky, L.S. (1978) *Mind in Society,* Cambridge, MA: Harvard University Press.

Appendix 10.1: Questions on your literacy practices

Answer these questions for yourself, then ask them of some other people. Summarise your answers for each question; if you get good quotes from other people, make a note of them. Finally, ask yourself what is interesting, or problematic about each of the questions in terms of understanding what is meant by being literate.

1 a) Can you read and write music?
  b) When did you last write a map? Why?

2 a) Do you prefer to hand write or word process?
  b) Has your writing changed in the past year? How?

3 a) Have you ever written to a newspaper? What was the outcome?
  b) Have you ever written to a politician? What was the outcome?

4 How many different scripts do you know?

5 a) Do you do any writing for anyone else in your day-to-day life?
  b) Does anyone do any writing for you in your day-to-day life?
  c) What do you write collaboratively?

6 a) Has anyone made a family tree for your family? Who?
  b) What records do you keep of your life?
  c) Do you keep a diary?

7 a) Can you read train timetables?
  b) How do you find out what time trains leave?

8 a) Are you reading a novel?
  b) Have you written a novel? Would you like to write a novel?

Appendix 10.2: Literacy studies: notes on carrying out some research

In the seminar of week four you are going to plan a small piece of research on literacy practices, either individually or preferably in a group. You will then carry out the research in weeks five and six and report back briefly on it in week seven. As a rough guide, plan it between weeks four and five, carry it out between five and six, and analyse and brief write up between six and seven. Your group should meet each week – at least – preferably at your seminar time.

You can then stop there, or you can use the research you have done as the basis for an assignment (or even as the beginnings of a dissertation).

You can be imaginative in terms of *Topic*, and in terms of *Methods*.

Topic

You might research any area of everyday literacy, or work-place, or education. You might study a club you belong to, your family or relations, or what you see around you in Lancaster, or on the train or bus. In the past students have carried out studies of literacy associated with motorway driving, rock climbing in the Lake District; working in shops and other work-places; the intricacies of scoring in cricket. Other groups of students have gone round Lancaster with disposable cameras identifying everyday public literacies. You might study music, maths, media, computing, sketching . . .

One student researched betting shop literacy. He went into the betting shop and observed how packed with literacy it was. The walls are covered with it. He commented on the technology, the roles and the relationships; the reading the writing; and crucially noted that you cannot learn about betting shop literacy just by going into the betting shop; there were no instructions, it was assumed you knew, or you learned from friends, the student resorted to looking through the waste bin.

Methods

First, identify a domain or domains to focus the research on. Then there are several steps in literacy research:

- *Observing the visual environment of the chosen domain, maybe even taking photos.*
- *Focusing on particular literacy events and documenting them.*
- *Identifying texts and observing how the texts are used in particular literacy events; analysing the practices around the texts.*
- *Interviewing people about practices, how they make sense of them, their feelings and attitudes towards them.*

For your research you might do just one of the above steps.

Analysis

As you do your research you will need to look at literacy through the lens of a social view of literacy, applying some of the theoretical concepts you have been reading about to your particular area. You might note particular gender roles, networks of support, power relations, forms of control, how texts circulate and who has access to them, particular theories of what literacy is, domain specific practices, cross-cultural differences, public v. private literacies, the relation to visual literacy, etc., etc.

The write-up should be short, only between one and two pages, and should concentrate on your analysis. For example, it might be a set of headings, such as *Gender roles, Public and private, Definitions, Purposes, Identities, Visual and print literacy* – that is, your theoretical concepts, and what you found out about each. It can be in note form.

If you need some help, see either of us after the lecture, or at other times we are available (which we will tell you about at the week four seminar). The best way to contact us is actually by e-mail and you can ask us questions by e-mail.

The aims of this phase of the course are: to become reflective of literacy practices around you; to carry out a small piece of research; and to have some fun.

Be particular.

Look at detail.

Good Luck!

11

THE NEW LITERACY STUDIES

From 'socially situated' to the work of the social

James Paul Gee

The new literacy studies and the 'social turn'

Over the last several decades, in and across a wide variety of disciplines, there has been a massive 'social turn' away from a focus on individual behaviour (e.g. the behaviourism of the first half of the twentieth century) and individual minds (e.g. the cognitivism of the middle part of the century) toward a focus on social and cultural interaction. The New Literacy Studies (NLS) was one movement among a great many others that took part in this 'social turn' (see Barton 1994; Gee 1996; and Street 1995 for programmatic statements; see Heath 1983 and Street 1984 for seminal 'early' examples of the NLS). The NLS are based on the view that reading and writing only make sense when studied in the context of social and cultural (and we can add historical, political and economic) practices of which they are but a part. The NLS arose alongside a heady mix of other movements, some of which were incorporated into the NLS. These movements argued their own case for the importance of the 'social', each with their own take on what 'social' was to mean. I list fourteen of these movements below (NLS makes fifteen, and there are more). The order in which I list the areas below is entirely arbitrary:

1 *Ethnomethodology and conversational analysis*, and related work in *interactional sociolinguistics* (Heritage 1984; Goodwin and Heritage 1990; Schiffrin 1994, Ch. 4) has argued that social and institutional order is the product of the moment-by-moment intricacies of social and verbal interaction which produces and reproduces that order. 'Knowing' is a matter of 'knowing how to proceed' ('go on') in specific social interactions.
2 *Discursive psychology* (Edwards and Potter 1992; Harre and Stearns 1995) focuses on things like 'remembering' and 'emotions' not as 'mental'

and 'private' but as ways of talking that allow people to give 'accounts' of their memories and emotions, accounts that are negotiated in context and assembled as part and parcel of social interaction.

3 *The ethnography of speaking* (Gumperz 1982; Hymes 1974) has argued that language in use does not convey general and decontextualised meanings. Rather, participants in interaction use various lexical, structural, and prosodic 'cues', in speech or writing, to infer just what context (or part of a context) is relevant and how this context gives words meanings specific to it. The form and meaning of these 'contextualisation cues' differ across different cultures, even among people from different social groups speaking the same language.

4 *Sociohistorical psychology*, following Vygotsky and later Bakhtin (Wertsch 1985, 1991, 1998), has argued that the human mind is 'furnished' through a process of 'internalising' or 'appropriating' images, patterns and words from the social activities in which one has participated. Further, thinking is not 'private', but almost always mediated by 'cultural tools', that is, artefacts, symbols, tools, technologies, and forms of language that have been historically and culturally shaped to carry out certain functions and carry certain meanings (cultural tools have certain 'affordances', though people can transform them through using them in new settings).

5 Closely related work on *situated cognition* (Lave 1996; Lave and Wenger 1991; see, too, work in *activity theory*, Engestrom 1990; Leont'ev 1978), also with an allegiance to Vygotsky, has argued that knowledge and intelligence reside not solely in heads, but, rather, are distributed across the social practices (including language practices) and the various tools, technologies and semiotic systems that a given 'community of practice' uses in order to carry out its characteristic activities (e.g. part of a physicist's knowledge is embedded and distributed across his or her colleagues, social practices, tools, equipment, and texts). Knowing is a matter of being able to participate centrally in practice and learning is a matter of changing patterns of participation (with concomitant changes in identity).

6 *Cultural models theory* (D'Andrade and Strauss 1992; Holland and Quinn 1987), a social version of 'schema theory', has argued that people make sense of their experiences by applying largely tacit 'theories' or 'cultural models' to them. Cultural models, which need not be complete or logically consistent, are simplified and prototypical arguments, images, 'storylines', or metaphorical elaborations, shared within a culture or social group, that explain why and how things happen as they do and what they mean. These 'theories' (which are embedded not just in heads, but in social practices, texts, and other media) guide action, inform judgements of self and others, and shape ways of talking and writing.

7 *Cognitive linguistics* (Lakoff and Johnson 1980; Lakoff 1987; Ungerer and Schmid 1996) argues that all human languages are organised in terms of intricate, complex, intersecting, and overlapping systems of metaphors (and related figurative devices). These metaphors shape, in different ways in different cultures, how we interpret our experience and how we think about ourselves and the material, social, and cultural world. For example, in English we often think and talk about argument in ways shaped by how we talk about warfare ('I *defended* my argument and *destroyed* his case at the same time') or talk about minds as if they were enclosed spaces ('He just couldn't get it *into* his head').

8 *The new science and technology studies* (Latour 1987, 1991) has argued that scientific knowledge is rooted in scientists' day-to-day social practices and distributed across (and stored within) those practices and the characteristic spaces, tools, texts, symbols, and technologies that scientists use. Scientists' day-to-day practices are far more historically, technologically, socially and culturally conditioned than appears from the 'write up' of their results in books and journals. Scientists' knowledge is a matter of 'coordinating' and 'getting coordinated by' (in mind and body) colleagues, objects, nature, texts, technologies, symbols, language, and social and instrumental practices.

9 *Modern composition theory* (Bazerman 1989; Myers 1992; Swales 1990) has stressed the ways in which knowledge and meaning is situated within the characteristic talking, writing, acting, and interacting 'genres' (patterns) of disciplines and other specialised domains. These (historically changing) genres create both the conditions for and the limits to what can be said and done in the discipline at a given time and place.

10 Work on *connectionism* (Clark 1993; Gee 1992) in cognitive science has argued that humans do not primarily think and act on the basis of mental representations that are general rules or logical propositions. Rather, thinking and acting are a matter of using, and adapting to current circumstances, stored patterns or images of our past experiences. These patterns or images are shaped (edited) by the social, cultural, and personal contexts of those experiences.

11 The broad interdisciplinary field of *narrative studies* (Bruner 1986; Ricoeur 1984), which views narrative as the primary form of human understanding, has argued that people make sense of their experiences of other people and the world by emplotting them in terms of socially and culturally specific stories, stories which are supported by the social practices, rituals, texts, and other media representations of specific social groups and cultures. Narratives can, at times, e.g. in science, be transformed into and elaborated in other non-narrative genres.

12 Work on *evolutionary approaches to mind and behaviour* (Clark 1997; Dawkins 1982; Kauffman 1993) argues that human intelligence is not a

general and purely mental thing. Rather, our minds and bodies are the specific products of a long evolutionary process of mutual adaptation and shaping between ourselves and our material, social and cultural environments. Human intelligence resides in the 'fit' between these, and the proper unit of analysis is, therefore, 'persons and their material, social, cultural environments interacting through historical and social and interactional time'.

13 *Modern sociology* (Beck, Giddens and Lash 1994; Giddens 1984, 1987) has stressed the ways in which human thinking, acting and interaction are simultaneously structured by institutional forces and, in turn, give a specific order (structure, shape) to institutions such that it is impossible to say which comes first, institutions or the human social practices that continually enact and reproduce (and transform) them. Modern sociology has also stressed, the ways in which this reciprocal exchange between human interaction and human institutions is being transformed by global economic and demographic changes such that the nature of time, space, human relationships, and communities is being radically transformed.

14 Finally, a good deal of so-called '*post-structuralist*' and '*postmodernist*' work (e.g. Bakhtin 1984; Bourdieu [1979]/1984; Fairclough 1992; Foucault 1973, 1977), much of it earlier than the movements we have just discussed, has centred around the notion of 'discourses'. 'Discourses' are characteristic (socially and culturally formed, but historically changing) ways of talking and writing about, as well as acting with and towards people and things (ways which are circulated and sustained within various texts, artefacts, images, social practices, and institutions, as well as in moment-to-moment social interactions) such that certain perspectives and states of affairs come to be taken as 'normal' or 'natural' and others come to be taken as 'deviant' or 'marginal' (e.g. what counts as a 'normal' prisoner, hospital patient, or student, or a 'normal' prison, hospital, or school, at a given time and place).

Obviously, these movements, stemming from different disciplines, overlap at many points, and they have influenced each other in complex ways. While there are genuine disagreements among them, they are (including in work within the NLS) beginning to converge in various respects (e.g. John-Steiner, Panofsky and Smith 1994). It is not uncommon, in fact, to see citations to all or most of these movements in current work on sociocultural approaches to literacy and related aspects of education.

All these movements were, or have been used as, reactions against the behaviourism of the early part of the twentieth century and the 'cognitive revolution' of the 1960s and 1970s that replaced behaviourism, both of which privileged the individual mind. Cognitivism saw 'higher order thinking' and 'intelligence' as primarily the manipulation of 'information' ('facts') using general ('logical') rules and principles. Fact and 'logic', not affect, society and culture, were emphasised. For cognitivism, the digital computer stood as the great metaphor for what thought was: 'information processing' (and computers process information based on its form/structure, not its meaning). For 'social turn' movements 'networks' are a key metaphor: knowledge and meaning are seen as emerging from social practices or activities in which people, environments, tools, technologies, objects, words, acts, and symbols are all linked to ('networked' with) each other and dynamically interact with and on each other.

Is the 'social turn' politically progressive?

Many of us involved in the 'social turn' assumed that the movements that made it up were somehow inherently politically 'progressive'. That is, we assumed that focusing on the social would unmask the workings of hierarchy, power and social injustice, as well as create more humane, because less elitist and individualistic, institutions (e.g. schools) and communities. Many of us saw ourselves, too, as working in opposition to the fetishist profit motives of capitalism and in favour of seeing the significance of humans and their institutions in a much broader historical, social, cultural and political context than markets, profit and consumption.

I admit that, in the 1980s, when I began my own 'social turn' (away from generative linguistics), I saw the social turn in entirely politically progressive terms, though I was aware (and regretted) that some of its movements would not talk openly about politics (in part, I assumed, because it was thought that such talk would lessen the work's standing as 'science'). Imagine my surprise, then, to see how readily the 'social turn' was taken up by capitalism itself and that a so-called 'new capitalism' viewed many of the above 'social turn' movements in a quite positive light – in fact, financially supported some of them (Gee, Hull and Lankshear 1996).

The old capitalism was interested in the most efficient organisation of individuals as *individuals*. Knowledge and skills were broken into bits and pieces. Each individual, on a assembly line, for instance, did his or her bit or piece of the work process as an interchangeable cog in the machine, without knowing, or needing to know, the 'big picture'. Only the elite ('managers' and 'bosses') were supposed to be able to put the bits and pieces of the work process back together, otherwise their status and power (and claims to 'higher intelligence') might have been undermined by the perspectives and interests of the 'front line' workers.

In the old capitalism, it was dangerous to treat individuals as social beings with collective interests or to allow them to be so, because that might have further encouraged unionisation and collective organisation. Cultures were dangerous, too, because their specific ways and mores could stand in the way of the standard procedures and norms needed for large, secular, modern, rational, universal (that is, culturally transcendent) businesses. In the old capitalism, work was meant to have as little social, cultural, historical and political context as possible, much like knowledge and meaning in traditional psychology.

The new capitalism is the product of massive global and technological changes that have made competition global and hyper-intense. Under these conditions, businesses need to out-compete their competition by producing the highest quality product or service as quickly as possible at the lowest price. This means, in turn, no 'fat': no excess, no person, practice, or thing that does not directly 'add value' to the final service or product (Boyett and Conn 1992; Dobyns and Crawford-Mason 1991).

As more companies compete on this basis, across the globe, something else happens: products and services are less and less distinguishable based on cost or quality (you can get the best from overseas in a day by express mail), and more and more distinguishable by the 'knowledge work' that has gone into designing, producing and marketing them 'on time' and 'on demand' for just the right 'niche' in the market (Davidow and Malone 1992; Drucker 1993; Frank and Cook 1995; Imparato and Harari 1994).

The highest and most important form of knowledge and skill in the new capitalism is what I will call *sociotechnical designing*, that is: designing products and services so that they create or 'speak to' specific consumer identities and values (niches); designing better ways to organise the production and delivery of products and services; designing ways to shape consumer identities and values through advertising and marketing; and designing ways to transform products and markets based on consumer identities and values (Hamel and Prahalad 1994; Hammer and Champy 1993; Nonaka and Takeuchi 1995; Peters 1994a, b; Smith 1995). All this design work is heavily social and contextual and semiotic (that is, it often involves manipulating symbols of identity).

In turn, the highest and most important form of sociotechnical designing involves designing *new work-places* and *new workers*. New work-places are designed to leverage knowledge from workers' day-to-day practices. In the new capitalism, thanks to changing technology and the pace of innovation, the knowledge that 'front line' workers gain in ongoing practice as they flexibly adapt to new circumstances is more valuable than explicit knowledge based on theories and past practices, both of which go out of date too quickly.

Workers in the new capitalism are meant to continuously gain and apply new knowledge by understanding the whole work process in which they are involved, not just bits and pieces, and they are meant to proactively and continually transform and improve that work process through collaboration with others and with technology. With fewer workers, working longer and with less supervision, and amidst fast-paced change that often outstrips individual knowledge, new capitalist workers must work in teams (where workers supervise each other) that collaboratively and interactively design and redesign their work process with a full knowledge of and overlap with each other's functions, so that they can take over from each other when someone is missing (Lipnack and Stamps 1993; Peters 1994a; Senge 1991; Wiggenhorn 1990).

There are several essential paradoxes built into the new capitalism. New capitalist workers are supposed to know the whole work process with which they are involved. They are supposed to fully leverage their practical knowledge for the company. They are supposed to actively transform, improve, and adapt their work practices to fast paced changes in markets and technologies. What, then, is to prevent them from: (a) using their new found knowledge and status to critique the company, or, indeed, the new capitalism itself? and/or (b) walking off with their newly important knowledge (now that they, indeed, have something of their own to sell) and selling it to the highest bidder? Furthermore, (c) how is knowledge that is continually gained in practice, often tacit, and transformed quickly, going to get stored and passed on for the company's benefit (it won't do to just write manuals; they require explicit knowledge and, further, can go out of date before the ink is dry)?

These three paradoxes (a–c) are 'solved', in the new capitalism, by the sociotechnical device of a 'community of practice' (Peters 1994a, pp. 174ff; Nonaka and Takeuchi 1995; Schrage 1990; Smith 1995). Workers, on a rather egalitarian basis, engage in a 'whole integrated process' involving many functions (and roles) which they distribute among themselves and across their tools and technologies, but in overlapping and collaborative ways so that the practice can continue if the community is 'lesioned' by a person or tool gone missing. Further, since knowledge is distributed across multiple people, specific social practices, and various tools, technologies, and procedures – and is not stored in any one head – the problem of people 'walking' with their knowledge is, more or less, solved. The knowledge is *in* the community of practice which 'belongs' to the company, not in the individual.

Newcomers ('apprentices') are 'trained' by being scaffolded in 'joint practice' with those already adept at the practice (a very Vygotskian process), not (just) through overt instruction which cannot carry the full load of 'tacit knowledge in practice' and goes out of date. Everyone in the community of practice gains knowledge through immersion in the collaborative practice; knowledge that they may not be able to explicate in words, but which they can pass on through the socialisation of new members.

Within a community of practice all members pick up a variety of tacit and taken-for-granted values, norms, cultural models and narratives as part of their socialisation into the practice and their ongoing immersion in the practice. Tacitly accepting these values, norms, cultural models and narratives (in mind, action and embodied practice), and sharing them with others, is just what it means to be a *member* of the community of practice. This, by and large, solves the problem of critique.

The community of practice is continually transformed by being 'stressed' (a technical term in connectionism that applies to learning). They are 'stressed' through the acquisition of new ideas, new members, new technologies, and new social activities designed by sociotechnical engineers from either inside or outside the community of practice itself (often drawing on members' 'insider knowledge'). Such changes are adaptations to ongoing changes in technology or markets. When the company or the market changes sufficiently, the community of practice is disbanded and its members redistributed to other projects, other companies, or unemployment.

In this framework – a framework of 'communities of practice' based around 'projects' – individuals are seen as specific *trajectories* through all the projects and communities of practice of which they have been a part. An individual is seen, as well, as a *portfolio* of all the knowledge and skills achieved in this trajectory through 'project and practice space'; knowledge and skills which the individual can leverage, rearrange and transform for new projects and new communities of practice. I should point out that this is as true of 'front line' workers as it is of more elite 'symbol analysts' (Reich 1992).

Furthermore, in the new capitalism there is a continual emphasis on the flexible transformation (even creative 'destruction' or 'deconstruction') of people, practices, markets and institutions. There is an emphasis, as well, on crossing and destroying borders (divisions, departments) between people, practices, and institutions, because borders mitigate the integration of 'whole processes' and the flexible, but overlapping and collaborative distribution of knowledge and work (Hammer and Champy 1993; Lipnack and Stamps 1993). This flexible transformation of identities, practices and institutions, and its concomitant border-crossing, takes on a distinctly postmodern flavour in the new capitalism (Peters 1992). There is no use for old 'universal' fixed certainties (Bauman 1992). Differences of all sorts, including cultural differences (as long as the cultures have money and can consume) are celebrated since they simply allow communities of practice to be infused with diverse knowledge and skills (any of which might eventually become a novel source of change and value), as well as allowing for the creation of more market niches with their distinctive consumer identities.

I hope it is readily apparent that a great many of the themes in the 'social turn' movements I listed earlier are fully recruited in this rehearsal of the new capitalism and its paradoxes. The fact is that these social turn movements can easily be transformed into a theory and praxis for the new capitalism, fully subordinated to the goal of profit; though in the new capitalism it is profit with a 'human face' (i.e. empowered 'knowledge workers' working collaboratively to add 'value').

It should not have been surprising to me that these 'social turn' movements readily lent themselves to the goals of the new capitalism. It is one of the tenets of the NLS that *any* piece of language, any tool, technology, or social practice can take on quite different meanings (and values) in different contexts, and that no piece of language, no tool, technology, or social practice has a meaning (or value) outside of all contexts.

None the less, it *is* striking that the 'social turn' and the new capitalism's interest in sociotechnical designing of social practices arose at the same historical juncture (and, to take one example out of an entire process, the digital computer was debunked as a theory of mind by the 'social turn' movements just as new connectionist/networking computers offered the new capitalism an important new technology for integrating work processes and leveraging knowledge built up out of practice/experience). And, too, it has not hurt the new capitalism that the 'social turn' theories that undergird its practices are seen, in large part, as politically progressive (ironically, the Fordist theories that had undergirded the old capitalism were themselves originally seen as politically progressive, though they eventually came to be viewed as reactionary).

Before moving to the next section, let me anticipate a question the reader may be asking: What's so wrong with the 'new capitalism'? It sounds better than the old. What's wrong is this: the new capitalism, as Reich (1992) and Drucker (1993) and others have argued, leads to good, if risky, rewards for those who have sophisticated sociotechnical knowledge to sell (the people that Reich calls 'symbol analysts'). It leads to fairly meager financial rewards (though, perhaps, more control and meaning at work) for those who can work in sociotechnically designed environments by the canons of the new capitalist work teams – people Gee *et al.* 1996 call 'enchanted workers' (see Gee *et al.*, Chs. 4 and 5 for a detailed study of enchanted workers at work). However, a developed economy needs – and, in a 'lean and mean' environment can pay for – only so many symbol analysts and enchanted workers (Reich says about two-fifths of the population). Large numbers of less fortunate souls must be exploited (beyond even the exploitation of the enchanted workers) in order to make a company, region, or country 'hyper-competitive' in our global economy.

Thus, for large numbers of people in the developed world, and many more in the 'less developed' world, the new capitalism is leading to, at best, very poor pay and work conditions in 'service work', 'temporary work', 'brute work', the remaining backwater jobs of the old capitalist businesses, and multiple jobs that do not together add up to a living wage. These are the hordes who have no 'knowledge' that 'adds value' by new capitalist standards, hordes that, in fact, must work (if they can find work at all) at the lowest possible price in the highly competitive and global environment of the new capitalism, where businesses search the world for the cheapest labour.

At the same time, the new capitalism has created cultural and class-based affiliations among the wealthy across the globe while simultaneously undercutting feelings of 'co-citizenship' across class lines within local, regional and national communities. Reich has argued that it is harder and harder to know what would constitute an argument that 'symbol analysts' (who affiliate, both in real time and cyberspace, with other symbol analysts across the country and the world) bear any social responsibility toward their fellow less-advantaged citizens. More and more, such elites feel little affiliation and little 'co-citzenship' with such people. Drucker, himself a guru of the new capitalism, has argued, in turn, that social class in the future will be defined around 'knowledge', with a massive number of 'service workers' at the bottom of the new class system (and the unemployed out of it altogether). How such service workers are treated (disciplined?), he argues, will determine a large part of the social dynamics of society.

The new capitalism, in its demands on workers for 'total commitment' to the goals/vision of the business, constructs human worth and identity around 'knowledge' defined in terms of 'value added'. It breaks down the barrier between private and public life, demanding one's mind, body and soul for the business. For example, consider Boyett and Conn 1992, talking about 'Workplace 2000': 'A "cult of performance excellence" will engulf most businesses. Americans will be expected to buy in, join in, become a part of the company values and culture, or be forced out' (p. 3) or: 'What these "work hard, play hard" companies want is nothing less than total responsibility and over-the-edge loyalty . . . Employees are constantly on view and the line between work and play, the line between public and private becomes fuzzy' (p. 40).

However socially knowledge may be defined in the new capitalism, defining human worth in terms of 'value added' to a business process is wrong for all the same sorts of reasons that defining human worth in terms of simple capital and profits was wrong in the old capitalism. Even business gurus like Charles Handy know this: Handy (1994) has argued that it is imperative that we imagine notions of human worth, status, and community outside of financial rewards and markets even as he acknowledges the tendency of the new capitalism to co-opt all spheres of private and public life in the name of commitment to economic productivity.

Back to the New Literacy Studies

The NLS is based around the idea that reading, writing and meaning are always *situated* within specific social practices within specific Discourses (Gee 1996). As we have just seen, the new capitalism has surely 'bought' the idea that reading, writing, knowledge, work, meaning, and 'value' are inextricably embedded in the local, social, and material processes of work-sites, work practices and work groups. This is where the most valuable knowledge is embedded and distributed, and where sociotechnical discipline must be applied if 'value' is to be extracted and leveraged for the company's good.

Almost all the social turn movements I surveyed above came, at some point in their trajectories, to see that, in saying that meaning is situated in context, they were often appealing to a notion of 'context' that was too static. The fact is that words give meaning to contexts just as surely as contexts give meaning to words. Words and context are two mirrors facing each other, infinitely and simultaneously reflecting each other.

If they had not from the outset, sooner or later all the social turn movements came to argue that meaning and context are mutually constitutive of each other. A word or deed takes its meaning from a context which it, in turn, helps to create, given that it has that meaning. For example, certain sorts of utterances take on the meaning of 'sweet nothings' in the context of a romantic relationship, but the context of a romantic relationship is created (we know we are in such a context) by just such things as utterances like these having just such meanings. Or another example: the context of traditional formal schooling gives certain words and actions the meaning of 'test', but such words and actions with such a meaning are what, in turn, make formal schooling formal schooling.

What is often left out in discussions of the mutually constitutive nature of words and contexts is the person as agent who utters (writes) the words with (conscious and unconscious) personal, social, cultural, and political goals and purposes. Of course, in social turn theories, the person's deeds and body are part of the situation or context, but the person as an actor engaged in an effort to achieve purposes and goals is left out as an embarrassing residue of our pre-social days. Consider, for example, how many postmodernists talk about people ('subjects') not so much as authoring their words, but of their words authoring ('subject-ing') them (see, for example, Foucault 1972, pp. 95–6). The person disappears other than as historical and discursive construct.

Reflecting on the new capitalism over the last few years has made me want to move the idea of *work* (in the sense of human effort) to the centre of the New Literacy Studies. In particular, as a linguist, I am interested in a particular type of work to which I think language is particularly important, though never by itself, but always in tandem with deeds, interactions, other sorts of symbols, and ways of thinking and valuing. Let me, then, say something about the sort of human work I have in mind.

Situations (contexts) do not just exist. Situations are rarely static or uniform, they are actively created, sustained, negotiated, resisted, and transformed moment-by-moment through ongoing *work*. It is the nature of this work that should, I argue, become crucial to the New Literacy Studies.

This type of work I will call *enactive* and *recognition work.* Language is designed precisely to help us do just such work.

What do I mean by enactive work and recognition work? Think about the matter this way: out in the world exist materials out of which we continually make and remake our social worlds. The social arises when we humans relate (organise, coordinate) these materials together in a way that is recognisable to others. We attempt to get other people to recognise people and things as having certain meanings and values within certain configurations or relationships. Our attempts are what I mean by 'enactive work'. Other people's active efforts to accept or reject our attempts – to see or fail to see things 'our way' – are what I mean by 'recognition work'.

We attempt, through our words and deeds, to get others to recognise people, things, artefacts, symbols, tools, technologies, actions, interactions, times, places, and ways of speaking, listening, writing, reading, feeling, believing, thinking, and valuing as meaningful and valuable in certain ways. We attempt to make each of these meaningful and valuable in itself ('this is a scientist', 'this is a scientific instrument', 'this is objective information', etc.) and as a *configuration* of elements all related to each other in a specific and meaningful way ('this is a scientist at work with his/her lab assistants engaged in an experiment that will yield objective truth').

Of course, the individual elements in a configuration are meaningful and valuable only as they are related within that configuration. Our real enactive work is in creating and sustaining the configuration. This configuration here is a 'science experiment in a lab', this one 'a street gang looking for trouble', this one 'elementary school students demonstrating knowledge', this one 'a quality circle redesigning work', and so on and so forth through a never ending and ever changing list. Configurations change moment-by-moment unless energy is continually put into them to sustain them (and, of course, energy is often put into them to disrupt or transform them).

We can engage in enactive work from outside a configuration, e.g. a sociologist of science trying to get colleagues to view work in science labs as meaningful and valuable in ways quite different from how traditional historians of science have viewed such matters or how scientists view them when they are at work doing science or writing science. But we spend our lives always and also engaging in enactive work from inside the configurations we work in to get recognised in certain ways. We coordinate ourselves (in mind, body and soul) with the other elements in configurations (things, places, times, tools, symbols, other people, ways of acting, interacting, valuing, thinking, etc.) and, in turn, we get coordinated by them (Knorr Cetina 1992).

Getting 'in sync' with these other elements means not just controlling (coordinating) them, but adapting to (getting coordinated by) them. And this applies not just to people. It applies to things and symbols, as well: you can't just do anything you want with a hammer, for instance, and the hammer has certain affordances that make it easier to use in some ways than others. It is, for example, easier to get others to recognise you as engaged in adept carpentry if you use the hammer in some ways rather than others. Things and symbols are, in this sense, actors too. They work on us as we work on them (this is part of the point of Latour's 1987, 1991 actor-network theory and part of the point of Wertsch's 1985, 1991 Vygotskian-inspired ideas about the ways in which tools mediate human action and thinking).

The same set of people, words, deeds and things at the same time and place can be seen as different configurations (patterns) – what someone sees as a 'professor advising graduate student', someone else can see as 'male authority harassing female subordinate'. And a participant can attempt to change the meaning and value of a configuration in the midst of it. Think, for instance, of the many different ways we can attempt to get age and gender recognised within configurations, each in their own right and in relation to each other. Age and gender mean different things as and when we see them as part and parcel of different configurations of persons, deeds, words, settings, and things. And we can fight over – from without or within – what they are to mean within an emerging configuration of people, words, deeds, and things that await a name ('professor advising young graduate student', 'older male abusing his authority in regard to a younger, less powerful female').

We can say as well that any attempt to get the elements of a configuration and the configuration itself recognised in a certain way is an attempt to *pro-ject* these elements and this configuration into the world. Such work is, in this sense, always also a *project*, and a political one at that, since such configurations are the very stuff of our social relations, relations in which power and desire are always and everywhere at stake. Thus, one way we can analyse people, words and deeds is to ask what they seek to pro-ject into the world, what political projects they implicate.

To summarise my point then: it takes work to get a set of people, deeds, words, settings, and things recognised as a particular configuration with each of its members (e.g. age, gender, bullying tone of voice) recognised in a certain way. People inside and outside these configurations *work* to get specific configurations *recognised* (by themselves and others) as composed of just *these* actors, events, activities, practices, and Discourses, and not *those* – as recognised in *this* way and not *that*. It takes work to sustain such recognitions and to support or resist the work of others to unsettle such a recognition and transform it in various ways (think of all the efforts of the NLS themselves to get 'local literacies' recognised as 'literacy'). How the elements of these configurations are to be labelled, viewed or characterised, how configurations are to be 'carved up' into actors, events, activities, practices, and Discourses, is always 'up for grabs'. Actors, events, activities, practices, and Discourses do not exist in the world *except through* active work, work that is very often unstable and contested.

The new capitalism is engaged in quite overt enactive and recognition work using many of the same conceptual tools and theories used in some of the social turn movements. The important site of struggle with the new capitalism would be a battle over enactment and recognition work at the very sites where the new capitalism operates (though, for the most part, our battles have been in the university). It is ironic to meditate, in this regard, on the extremely low status of work on adult and workplace language and literacy in the US, and its absence from a good deal of work in the NLS.

The Lancaster School

I would argue that a focus on actors, events, activities, social practices, and Discourses as the 'achievements' of recognition and enactment work, with an overt focus on that work (including the researcher's), can help us take back our social theories from the new capitalism, while requiring us to own up to our own projects and engage with other people's – especially 'non-academic' people's – projects at a variety of levels.

I think that much of what I have said is at the heart of what the Lancaster group is up to, a group who might usefully be called 'the Lancaster School', since the group's work has become an internationally distinctive and distinguished approach within the NLS. For instance, Mary Hamilton's (Chapter 2, this volume) question about how central literacy has to be to an event for it to be called a 'literacy event' raises quite directly the issue of how 'written-language bits' are recruited into and integrated with 'other stuff' in meaningful configurations of words, deeds, objects, symbols, and ways of thinking, being and doing. Hamilton's question raises as well the issue of how people, both from within and without (e.g. we researchers), negotiate and contest over how to name and enact such configurations.

There is no answer to Hamilton's question. It is, in reality, a call for studying the ways in which people engage in enactive and recognition work, and what projects underlie and flow from such work. It is a call, too, for researchers to see their theories of such things as 'literacy events' as themselves instances of enactive and recognition work linked, tacitly or overtly, to their own projects.

The other chapters in this volume by the Lancaster group put on display a myriad elements (cattle, time, computers, televisions, science, prison cells, homework projects) entering and exiting configurations amidst the enactive and recognition work of diverse people with sometimes conflicting and sometimes linked interests, values and goals. In every case, there is a special focus on how the literacy bits work in relation to everything else. 'Literacy bits' are used almost like a radioactive isotope that allows bits and pieces of the whole configuration to be lit up, the better to find our way into the interlocking links among diverse elements that constitute the configuration. We can then study the human work it takes to get and keep these links forged, to destroy them, or to transform them. In every case, too, there is a focus on what is pro-jected out in the world and the effects this project has on people's lives and the implications it holds for issues of social justice.

The Lancaster School focuses on local situated literacies. 'Local' takes on, in their work, for me, a rather special meaning: the site at which people – in tandem with words, deeds, objects, tools, symbols, settings, times, and ways of being, doing, thinking, and valuing – work out their projects, as well as work on and rework the projects that flow at and to them from close and far.

References

Bakhtin, M. (1984) *Rabelais and his World*, Indiana: Indiana University Press.

Barton, D. (1994) *Literacy: An Introduction to the Ecology of Written Language*, Oxford: Blackwell.

Bauman, Z. (1992) *Intimations of Postmodernity*, London: Routledge.

Bazerman, C. (1989) *Shaping Written Knowledge*, Madison: University of Wisconsin Press.

Beck, U., Giddens, A. and Lash, S. (1994) *Reflexive Modernization: Politics, Traditions and Aesthetics in the Modern Social Order*, Stanford: Stanford University Press.

Bourdieu, P. ([1979]/1984) *Distinction: A Social Critique of the Judgement of Taste*, Cambridge, MA: Harvard University Press.

Boyett, J.H. and Conn, H.P. (1992) *Workplace 2000: The Revolution Reshaping Business*, New York: Plume/Penguin.

Bruner, J. (1986) *Actual Minds, Possible Worlds*, Cambridge, MA: Harvard University Press.

Clark, A. (1993) *Associative Engines: Connectionism, Concepts, and Representational Change*, Cambridge: Cambridge University Press.

Clark, A. (1997) *Being There: Putting Brain, Body, and World Together Again*, Cambridge, MA: MIT Press.

D'Andrade, R. and Strauss, C. (eds) (1992) *Human Motives and Cultural Models*, Cambridge: Cambridge University Press.

Davidow, W. and Malone, M. (1992) *The Virtual Corporation: Structuring and Revitalizing the Corporation for the 21st Century*, New York: Harper.

Dawkins, R. (1982) *The Extended Phenotype*, Oxford: W.H. Freeman.

Dobyns, L. and Crawford-Mason, C. (1991) *Quality or Else: The Revolution in World Business*, Boston: Houghton Mifflin.

Drucker, P. (1993) *Post-Capitalist Society*, New York: Harper.

Edwards, D. and Potter, J. (1992) *Discursive Psychology*, London: Sage.

Engestrom, Y. (1990) *Learning, Working and Imagining: Twelve Studies in Activity Theory*, Helsinki: Orienta-Konsultit.

Fairclough, N. (1992) *Discourse and Social Change*, Cambridge: Polity Press.

Frank, R.H. and Cook, P.J. (1995) *The Winner-Take-All Society: How More and More Americans Compete for Ever Fewer and Bigger Prizes, Encouraging Economic Waste, Income Inequality, and an Impoverished Cultural Life*, New York: The Free Press.

Foucault, M. (1972) *The Archaeology of Knowledge*, London: Tavistock.
Foucault, M. (1973) *The Birth of the Clinic: An Archaeology of Medical Perception*, New York: Vintage Books.
Foucault, M. (1977) *Discipline and Punish: The Birth of the Prison*, New York: Pantheon.
Gee, J.P. (1992) *The Social Mind: Language, Ideology, and Social Practice*, New York: Bergin & Garvey.
Gee, J.P. (1996) *Social Linguistics and Literacies: Ideology in Discourses*, 2nd edn, London: Taylor & Francis.
Gee, J.P., Hull, G. and Lankshear, C. (1996) *The New Work Order: Behind the Language of the New Capitalism*, Boulder, CO: Westview.
Giddens, A. (1984) *The Constitution of Society: Outline of the Theory of Structuration*, Cambridge: Polity Press.
Giddens, A. (1987) *Social Theory and Modern Sociology*, Stanford: Stanford University Press.
Goodwin, C. and Heritage, J. (1990) 'Conversation Analysis', *Annual Review of Anthropology* 19: 283–307.
Gumperz, J.J. (1982) *Discourse Strategies*, Cambridge: Cambridge University Press.
Hamel, G. and Prahalad, C.K. (1994) *Competing for the Future: Breakthrough Strategies for Seizing Control of your Industry and Creating the Markets of Tomorrow*, Boston: Harvard Business School Press.
Hammer, M. and Champy, J. (1993) *Reengineering the Corporation: A Manifesto for Business Revolution*, New York: Harper.
Handy, C. (1994) *The Age of Paradox*, Boston: Harvard Business School Press.
Harre, R. and Stearns, P. (eds) (1995) *Discursive Psychology in Practice*, London: Sage.
Heath, S.B. (1983) *Ways with Words: Language, Life, and Work in Communities and Classrooms*, Cambridge: Cambridge University Press.
Heritage, J. (1984) *Garfinkel and Ethnomethodology*, Oxford: Basil Blackwell.
Holland, D. and Quinn, N. (eds) (1987) *Cultural Models in Language and Thought*, Cambridge: Cambridge University Press.
Hymes, D. (1974) *Foundations of Sociolinguistics*, Philadelphia: University of Pennsylvania Press.
Imparato, N. and Harari, O. (1994) *Jumping the Curve: Innovation and Strategic Choice in an Age of Transition*, San Francisco: Jossey-Bass.
John-Steiner, V., Panofsky, C.P. and Smith, L.W. (eds) (1994) *Sociocultural Approaches to Language and Literacy: An Interactionist Perspective*, Cambridge: Cambridge University Press.
Kauffman, S. (1993) *The Origins of Order: Self-organization and Selection in Evolution*, New York: Oxford University Press.
Knorr Cetina, K. (1992) 'The Couch, the Cathedral, and the Laboratory: On the Relationship between Experiment and Laboratory in Science', in A. Pickering (ed.) *Science as Practice and Culture*, Chicago: University of Chicago Press, pp. 113–37.
Lakoff, G. (1987) *Women, Fire, and Dangerous Things*, Chicago: University of Chicago Press.
Lakoff, G. and Johnson, M. (1980) *Metaphors We Live By*, Chicago: University of Chicago Press.
Latour, B. (1987) *Science in Action*, Cambridge, MA: Harvard University Press.

LaTour, B. (1991) *We Have Never Been Modern*, Cambridge, MA: Harvard University Press.

Lave, J. (1996) 'Teaching, as Learning, in Practice', *Mind, Culture, and Activity* 3: 149–64.

Lave, J. and Wenger, E. (1991) *Situated Learning: Legitimate Peripheral Participation*, Cambridge: Cambridge University Press.

Leont'ev, A.N. (1978) *Activity, Consciousness, and Personality*, Englewood Cliffs, NJ: Prentice-Hall.

Lipnack, J. and Stamps, J. (1993) *The Team Net Factor: Bringing the Power of Boundary Crossing into the Heart of your Business*, Essex Junction, VT: Oliver Wright.

Myers, G. (1992) *Writing Biology: Texts in the Social Construction of Scientific Knowledge*, Madison: University of Wisconsin Press.

Nonaka, I. and Takeuchi, H. (1995) *The Knowledge-Creating Company: How Japanese Companies Create the Dynamics of Innovation*, New York: Oxford University Press.

Peters, T. (1992) *Liberation Management: Necessary Disorganization for the Nanosecond Nineties*, New York: Fawcett.

Peters, T. (1994a) *The Tom Peters Seminar: Crazy Times Call for Crazy Organizations*, New York: Vintage Books.

Peters, T. (1994b) *The Pursuit of Wow!: Every Person's Guide to Topsy-Turvy Times*, New York: Vintage Books.

Reich, R.B. (1992) *The Work of Nations*, New York: Vintage.

Ricoeur, P. (1984) *Time and Narrative*, Vol. 1., trans. by K. McLaughlin and D. Pellauer, Chicago: University of Chicago Press.

Schiffrin, D. (1994) *Approaches to Discourse*, Chicago: University of Chicago Press.

Schrage, M. (1990) *Shared Minds: The New Technologies of Collaboration*, New York: Random House.

Senge, P. (1991) *The Fifth Discipline: The Art and Practice of the Learning Organization*, New York: Doubleday.

Smith, H. (1995) *Rethinking America: A New Game Plan from the American Innovators: Schools, Business, People, Work*, New York: Random House.

Street, B. (1984) *Literacy in Theory and Practice*, Cambridge: Cambridge University Press.

Street, B. (1995) *Social Literacies: Critical Approaches to Literacy in Development, Ethnography and Education*, London: Longman.

Swales, J.M. (1990) *Genre Analysis: English in Academic and Research Settings*, Cambridge: Cambridge University Press.

Ungerer, F. and Schmid, H.-J. (1996) *An Introduction to Cognitive Linguistics*, London: Longman.

Wertsch, J.V. (1985) *Vygotsky and the Social Formation of Mind*, Cambridge, MA: Harvard University Press.

Wertsch, J.V. (1991) *Voices of the Mind: A Sociocultural Approach to Mediated Action*, Cambridge, MA: Harvard University Press.

Wertsch, J.V. (1998) *Mind as Action*, Oxford: Oxford University Press.

Wiggenhorn, W. (1990) 'Motorola U: When Training Becomes an Education', *Harvard Business Review* (July–August): 71–83.

12

THE NEW LITERACY STUDIES

Context, intertextuality and discourse

Janet Maybin

Introduction

In this chapter I draw together some theoretical and methodological threads from the various different studies of literacy represented within this book. These studies share common roots in the anthropological ethnographic tradition of documenting literacy activities in small communities, but also go beyond this tradition in their analysis of how the meanings of local events are linked to broader cultural institutions and practices. The New Literacy Studies researchers start by conceptualising literacy not in terms of skills and competencies, but as an integral part of social events and practices. This means that particular attention is given to people's use of oral language around texts, and to the ways in which the meaning and use of texts is culturally shaped. The notion of 'literacy events' highlights the mediation of texts through dialogue and social interaction, in the context of particular practices and settings (Heath 1983), and the conception of 'literacy practices' incorporates both events, and people's beliefs and understandings about them (Street 1995). The studies in this book explore and extend the analytical potential of these concepts, through a more detailed theorising of ideas about context and intertextuality, and about the role of language. They examine how language mediates people's interactions with texts, both at the local level in actual dialogues, and in terms of the broader discourses which shape local uses and meanings. I shall suggest that the taking on of more complex ideas about discourse and intertextuality in these studies of literacy enables the researchers to more clearly conceptualise the pivotal role of literacy practices in articulating the links between individual people's everyday experience, and wider social institutions and structures. It also enables them to explore issues of power, through examining the relationship between micro- and macro-level contexts.

As Jim Gee points out in Chapter 11, the New Literacy Studies is part of a broader movement within the social sciences, away from individual psychological and cognitive models, to focus on social and cultural aspects of language use, and on its constitutive role within social life. More specifically, the literacy studies in this collection reflect the influence of poststructuralist ideas about the discursive construction of knowledge and subjectivity (Foucault 1980, 1981), and about interdiscursivity (Bakhtin 1981, 1986; Volosinov 1986). At an analytic level the researchers are moving away from the conceptualisation of texts, contexts, individuals and communities as stable entities, towards more processual notions of text-mediated practices, of the articulation of links between different contexts in producing meaning, and of the ongoing negotiation of individual and community identity across different activities and contexts. At the same time as this poststructuralist turn, the studies also reflect social constructivist ideas about how individual activities are shaped and given meaning by the social and cultural contexts in which they occur, and also how these activities, in their turn, are constitutive of larger social structures and cultural processes. This suggests a dialectical relationship between structure and agency, and between micro- and macro-level contexts. Literacy events like writing up your school project, reversioning a prison canteen form, doing an exercise in a family literacy scheme, or filling in a form at the cattle auction, invoke broader cultural and historical patterns of literacy practices, and instantiate them, or subvert them, or comment on them in some way. These literacy events are also shaped by the aims and priorities of individual participants, and have important personal and practical consequences for the pupils, prisoners, parents and farmers in the examples above, for their sense of who they are, and for how they relate to the institutional imperatives that shape their lives. Thus literacy events are particularly rich in individual and social meaning, and the notion of literacy practices provides an important conceptual and methodological framework for looking at the interrelationships between the following three levels of analysis:

(a) individual activities, understandings and identities
(b) social events and the interactions they involve
(c) broader social and institutional structures.

Context and intertextuality

Whether in a home, classroom, prison, Catholic parish community or among Welsh hill farmers, the studies in this book focus at the local level, and on people's specific literacy activities as they go about their daily lives. As in most ethnographic work, the researchers use relatively unstructured methods: observation, interview and photography, and in their analyses they focus on uncovering the function and meaning of literacy for the participants themselves, within the particular social contexts from which reading and writing derive their meaning, before drawing broader patterns of meaning at a more abstract level. In the new literacy studies, researchers try to suspend judgement about what constitutes literacy for the people they are working with, until they can understand what it means for the people themselves, and For instance, in this volume Simon Pardoe (Chapter 9) argues for starting from students' own perspectives in an analysis of their successful and unsuccessful writing practices, and Anita Wilson (Chapter 4) stresses that prisoners' literacy practices have their own unique function within the prison institutional setting.

This emphasis on insider and contextualised meanings of literacy practices is related to the different ways of conceptualising context which have developed incrementally from Malinowski's argument (1923) that in order to understand language, we need to look at its 'context of situation'. This context helps to explain the precise practical and solid function of utterances and their situated meanings. Hymes' (1968, 1977) further developed ideas about the discursive layering of speech acts (utterances) within speech events, which are contextualized within speech situations in speech communities. Each 'layer' takes its meaning partly from its superordinate layers. More recently, poststructuralist ideas have led to an interest in how contexts are constructed and interrelated. The studies in this collection move from discussing the functional relationships between language and content to exploring more complex constitutive interrelationships. For instance, in Kathryn Jones' study (Chapter 5), Stan's conversation with the young farmer about the cattle movement form (Figure 5.3, p. 81) achieves both social and practical goals, as did the conversations that Malinowski recorded among the men organising their fishing activity on the Trobriand Islands. Stan's questioning of the farmer facilitates the practical task of selling cattle at the auction, and even the small talk at the beginning of the interaction 'How are you. Dreadful weather' has the important phatic function of creating an atmosphere of social ease within which the men can accomplish the bureaucratic business of booking in the cattle more pleasantly and efficiently. Malinowski argued that understanding the meaning of individual utterances in the Trobriand fishing conversations involved not just knowledge of the physical context, but also of local beliefs and practices connected with fishing. Similarly, within the context of the Welsh cattle auction, understanding the meaning of questions like 'Do you want the herd number or the other?' depends on insider knowledge about the numbering systems in herds and auctions. Hymes added to Malinowski's idea of the 'context of situation' a notion of different layers of context, which can be drawn on and combined to create meaning. An utterance from Jones' data, for example 'You're putting this last one first, are you?' (a 'speech act') has a particular meaning within the context of the interaction around the animal movement form (the speech event), which in its turn takes meaning from the context of the cattle auction (the speech situation), and from language practices both in the local speech community and in the wider agricultural bureaucratic order. Jones shows how the language of the interaction functions both within the immediate context to book the animals in for sale, and also to embed this local literacy event within the wider context of the agricultural bureaucratic order.

To take a second example of this kind of contextual layering, in Anita Wilson's study (Chapter 4), when the young prisoner rejects the prison shoes which have been 'customised' into Adidas trainers for him by a prison officer drawing two stripes on them (see p. 58), and says he wants Nikes (the 'speech act'), the meaning of this refusal draws on the argument between himself and prison staff about regulation footware (the 'speech event'), the context of readmission to prison after a visit to court (the 'speech situation'), and also broader shared understandings within the prison (the speech community), about roles and rules and how far they can be bent or stretched. The symbolic meaning attached to Adidas as opposed to Nike trainers in turn draws on wider community meanings beyond the prison. In this example, the relationship between these different contextual layers of meaning is actually the crux of the argument. Wilson stresses the importance for the prisoners of incorporating aspects of the 'outside' into their life inside the prison through personalised uses of literacy. However, a crucial aspect of this incorporation is that it is within the prisoners' own personal control and choice, and is frequently oppositional to institutional regulations. In rejecting the 'Adidas' trainers, the young prisoner is refusing to go along with the prison staff's reappropiation of the cultural evaluation of different kinds of trainers from the outside world into the impersonal institutional world of prison regulations, even though the staff themselves are breaking prison rules about defacing property to do this. Wilson's argument suggests that the prisoner's own defacement of his shoes would have had quite a different meaning if it could have helped him to create a personally meaningful environment within the impersonal structures of the prison. A further issue here is whether the drawing of two stripes on the shoes actually counts as 'literacy'. The stripes are certainly 'read' by the prisoners, and for Wilson this event has links with prisoners' other informal and often subversive uses of literacy. It does raise the question, however, about the boundaries of the concepts of 'texts' and 'literacy'.

For both Jones and Wilson, the ways in which links between different contexts are established and articulated are a central focus of their analysis, and they extend this analysis through taking on a Foucauldian concept of discourse, as I shall discuss in more detail below. Before doing that, I want to look at how two other studies in the book use ideas about context in exploring the relationship between literacy events and literacy practices, and the intercontextual references within practices themselves. In her analysis of media photographs, Mary Hamilton (Chapter 2) lists the main components of the literacy events documented in the photographs as 'Participants, Settings, Artefacts and Activities' (Table 2.1, p. 17), echoing Hymes' 1968 list of the significant components of speech acts as: Setting, Participants, Ends (goals), Act sequence (the order and content of the message), Key (tone, manner), Instrumentalities (channel), Norms of interaction and Genres ('SPEAKING'). Hamilton suggests that the various components of the literacy events invoke different aspects of underlying social practice. For example, in addition to the visible participants who are interacting with the text in a newspaper photograph, there are also the invisible participants who were involved in the text's production, circulation and regulation. These invisible participants are associated with particular collections of belief systems, value judgements and relations of production, and all these also have a bearing on how the texts are used, and what they mean. In a Bakhtinian sense, the reproduction and framing of images sets up intertextual relationships and potential meanings in a similar way to the connotations of genres and registers that are invoked by the reproduction of a particular voice. Hamilton suggests that this kind of tracking back from different components in the photographic image to the related, inferred, elements of participants, settings, artefacts and activities is one way in which photographs of literacy events can be used to explore the more abstracted notions of literacy practices.The fact that photographs of these events have been selected and reproduced within the media adds another layer of meaning in the sense that they are seen to be socially salient, sometimes an important aspect of public ritual and display.

In her analysis of the media photographs, Hamilton also noticed that these images contained texts which, although not directly central to the main event featured, were nevertheless an important aspect of its semiotic context. For instance, in a photograph of people in a shop buying lottery tickets, there was a public notice telling people where to queue, labels on the shelves of sweets and chocolate, and on the goods themselves, and the shop assistant was wearing an overall bearing the name of the shop. Although texts such as these may not be explicitly referred to by the participants, Hamilton argues that they may still invoke practices which are salient, as a kind of invisible regulatory influence on the current event. In this sense when people put on a shop staff overall, or obey a public notice, they become incorporated into a range of social practices in which they are not necessarily actively engaged, but which impact on their current activities and interactions, and on their sense of who they are (shop employee, good citizen, and so on), with particular notions of compulsion and choice.

For Hamilton, images of literacy events include traces of literacy practices, and for Roz Ivanič and Fiona Ormerod (Chapter 6) these kinds of traces are also recoverable from literacy artefacts. Their study focuses on the literacy practices that are involved for children aged 9 to 11, in producing home-made projects on topics of their choice. Ivanič and Ormerod used these pieces of work and interviews with the children as the basis for their analysis. They found that the physical characteristics of these projects not only carry traces of decisions about the linguistic, visual and material representation of subject matter, but also constitute evidence of different kinds of literacy practices, appropriated by the children from a range of contexts. Explicit links are being made, not just between texts, but also between social practices. The children know that their own productions are not destined for the public book trade, but they are claiming connections between, say, their own written-up project on 'Bats' (see p. 84), and the volumes on natural history in the school library and the local book shop. The practices of natural history research, publishing and marketing are appropriated and reframed by the child working on his project at the kitchen table at home, within a classroom-generated and pedagogically motivated task. Through their analysis of these references between different texts, contexts and practices, Ivanič and Ormerod deconstruct the notions of participants, setting, artefact and activity, in a similar way to Hamilton in her work on photographs. For instance, although the participant in this case is ostensibly the child writing his project on bats, hidden participants include all the people who provide help with the task and – although not their focus in this study – other hidden participants such as the naturalist whose writing the child reversions and the photographer whose work he copies and sticks in. In addition, the way the children produce and package their work reflects an anticipation of the different ways in which they expect it may be read by, for example, teacher, family and other pupils. Ivanič and Ormerod's analysis would suggest that the meanings of literacy practices are in part constructed interdiscursively, through conscious or unconscious choices about the the expression of intertextual and intercontextual connections.

Discourses and interdiscursivity

I want to turn now to look more specifically at how studies in this collection have developed ideas about the importance of oral language in the mediation of texts within literacy events, through taking on poststructuralist Foucauldian notions of discourse. These suggest that the language people use at a local level inserts them into discursive patternings associated with wider social institutions (for instance 'Adult Further Education', or 'The European agricultural bureaucratic order'), and that these wider patternings encode particular conceptions of truth, knowledge, power and subjectivity. The articulation of these discourses at a local level therefore provides a key linkage with broader social structures. In addition, because discourses carry particular potentials for the positioning of individuals and their subjectivity, their articulation in local activities is also tied up with negotiations and struggles around people's sense of their own identity.

The relationship of local language interactions to broader discourses is illustrated particularly clearly in Kathryn Jones' study (Chapter 5). The talk around the completion of the animal movement form, where Stan reads the questions, interprets them and negotiates the answers with the farmer and then writes on the form, reinterprets the bureaucratic discourse through informal local talk. Thus Stan, as the mediator of distant impersonal regulations within a local context, fulfils Giddens' (1990) 'face-work commitment' in representing the bureaucratic order in an acceptable way to the individuals in a small community. The bilingual context, where the informal daily 'agos ati' (see p. 85) discourse of the local community is in Welsh, and the discourse of agricultural bureaucracy is in English, reveals this process of negotiation particularly clearly. The translation of the distant bureaucratic/impersonal into the local/ personal is the focus of Jones' analysis, and although she does not describe the characteristics of these discourses in any more detail, they are doubtless organised around rather different conceptions of what counts as significant knowledge, and construct different kinds of identities and social relationships for the participants. Jones argues that the literacy activity within the booking in process is therefore a key nodal point for the interpenetration of two contexts: the local farming community in north-east Wales, and the wider European agricultural community. These contexts are discursively represented and constructed within the talk around the form. In this way the literacy practices involved in booking the cattle into the auction are regulated by, and also partly constitutive of, broader structures of social organisation and control.

While Jones documents the mediation of one discourse within another, around a specific literacy event, Kathy Pitt in Chapter 7 shows that intersecting discourses may themselves be multiple and conflicting. Pitt studied four 30-minute training videos which were produced by the British Basic Skills Agency 'To increase knowledge and understanding of constructive approaches to Family Literacy' (Basic Skills Agency 1995). These videos include scenes of activities from family literacy courses showing parents (mainly mothers) working together on literacy activities in a classroom, and also reading with their children at home. Pitt analyses the discourses drawn on in these two different contexts of home and school, which the family literacy course aims to bring together. In the adult activities, she suggests that the dominant discourse is that of education. The teacher initiates all literacy events, and parents are positioned generally as fairly passive 'pupils', talking of their own writing in terms of how it will be evaluated by the teacher. There are traces of a more informal, egalitarian Adult

Basic Education ethos (the coffee mugs on the table, and references to the negotiation of individual work plans and course content with parents). The video also refers to the kind of accreditation scheme that is part of a new colonising discourse in Adult Basic Education which prioritises the economic function of literacy, and sets up standardised core curricula. There are thus three different, and in some senses competing, discourses being drawn on in the scenes of adult group learning: those of education, of traditional Adult Basic Education and of the accreditation scheme. These discourses have different conceptions of learning and reading, and contrasting positionings for parents and teachers, for example parent as active exploratory learner versus parent as receiver of specific skills training; teacher as facilitator versus teacher as transmitter of knowledge and accreditation gate keeper. Pitt sees the positioning of parents as pupils as particularly significant, as part of the securing of their committment to a system within which they may previously have been marginalised.

In the parts of the videos representing parents working with children at home, Pitt again found that a particular kind of classroom discourse was dominant, in spite of the superficial home backdrop. Parents shown working with their children focused on the mechanics of reading rather than on stimulating the child's imagination, or on making sense of the world (p. 115–16). However, parents also spoke of the excitement of being encouraged to make books and games, and of the pleasure from starting new practices like reading to their children at bed-time (p. 117). Pitt suggests that again there is an uneasy mixture of rather different discourses represented in the examples: a rather narrowly conceived educational discourse within which reading is seen as a matter of learning decoding skills, and an alternative discourse which emphasises enjoyment and creativity. These discourses conceptualise the process of teaching and learning in contrasting ways (the transmission of hierarchical skills versus facilitating experiences of real books and discovery), and involve different kinds of relationship between parent and child. They also encode different models of what counts as literacy, and as its most important functions. Thus the activities between parents and children at home, as well as those of parents in the classroom, draw on different and conflicting discourses about reading, learning and pedagogic relationships. Contrary to the Basic Skills Agency's claim that family literacy courses provide a 'foundation for reading and writing that can last a lifetime' (Basic Skills Agency 1995), Pitt suggests that the ways in which these parents are inserted into the discourses would not suggest that they are being prepared for the creative and problem solving initiatives of the New Work Order of the future. Rather, she argues, the positioning of the parents within discourses in the scenes on the videos suggest that family literacy intervention programmes are part of the internalisation of the discipline process whereby mothering practices beneficial to the state become 'pedagogic norms within the mother's own desires and fantasies' (Rose 1989, p. 196, quoted by Pitt in Chapter 7, p. 120).

Jones and Pitt both use an analysis of the discourses invoked in literacy events to show how individuals are inserted, through local activities, into broader regulating discourses. The language interactions around texts have an immediate function in accomplishing bureaucratic or educational tasks, but they also serve to induct the individual into the discourses of wider social structures, which have specific consequences for people's positioning in relation to particular kinds of knowledge, their social relationships and their sense of identity. In both these studies the individuals concerned appear fairly compliant. In contrast, Anita Wilson's discussion of literacy in prisons (Chapter 4) suggests a much more active and resistant role for the prisoners in their articulation of interdiscursive links between the literacies and discourses of the outside world and the official Literacy of prison. Wilson argues that prisoners draw on both inside and outside discourses to create a 'mushfake community', a 'third space' which is Bhaba's (1994, p. 38) 'precondition for the articulation of cultural difference' (see p. 65). Prisoners draw on outside social practices to generate their own literacies in decorating private space, setting up storage systems for private letters, and swinging newspapers and notes between cells. They also appropriate and subvert the official prison Literacy through 'reversioning' institutional texts like the canteen order form. Wilson suggests that the writer of the 'I am transvestite' letter (Figure 4.1, p. 65) is using his knowledge of the discourses both of the prison and the outside world, and understands the place of both official Literacy and informal literacies, in relation to his current environment. She argues that this kind of creative use of literacy, and the drawing on and manipulation of different discourses, is vital if prisoners are to retain a sense of personal worth and identity, against the depersonalising institutional forces of the prison.

The prisoners in Wilson's study use literacy to transform their own context, from an impersonal institution into a personal community, with more congenial possibilities for individual positioning and relationships. Two other studies in this volume look at how engaging in particular literacy practices can bring people who in other ways lead rather separate lives, into a single specialised discourse community. In Tusting's study, this is a Catholic parish community, which is also in its turn part of the world-wide discourse community of practising Catholics, and in de Pourbaix's research, a virtual community of students using a computer conference at a Canadian university. In both these cases, literacy practices create a new discursive context, which has both social and personal consequences.

In her study of the Catholic parish (Chapter 3), Karin Tusting shows how the community's religious activities are synchronised through the distribution and reading of the parish newsletter, so that community identity is forged partly through people doing the same thing at the same time. Not only does the newletter carry the dates and times of public activities like regular and special masses, meetings and fund raising events, but it also specifies times for private prayer, in relation to everyday activities. For example, it indicates the prayers to say while preparing breakfast, going to work, and so on. Thus when people across the parish are praying at home, many other parish members are simultaneously doing the same thing. The newsletter also includes a 'thought for the day', so that not only the times for private prayer, but also their spiritual focus, are shared and synchronised across the community. The content and timing of prayers is also given for special days within the international Catholic calendar, for example 'World day of prayer for vocations', has a suitable prayer printed on the front of the newsletter (see Figures 3.1 and 3.2, pp. 52 and 53). The taking on of these prayers and their timing provides a vehicle for the construction and expression of each individual member's identity as a Catholic, as well as strengthening and consolidating their sense of belonging to a community of fellow worshippers, both at a local and international level. At a more profound level, the community itself is discursively constructed through synchronised activities like the simultaneous though separate acts of private prayer.

While Tusting shows how relationships between the individual and the social, and between local and international contexts are mediated through the Catholic parish newletter, in Renata de Pourbaix's study of computer conferencing at a Canadian university (Chapter 8) we see how students from very disparate backgrounds in terms of language, ethnicity, out of course interests and proposed field of study are brought together in a virtual community which generates its own distinctive identity and practices. As students following a 12-week preparatory course on English as a Second Language for Academic Purposes, their eventual aim is to gain access to the discourse communities of their chosen academic disciplines. In this sense, the conferencing is a ladder into academic literacy, and de Pourbaix traces how students negotiate and internalise the netiquette (p. 138) practices involved in discussing each other's work and ideas within the conference, and then move on towards a greater confidence in their own individual academic identities. This shift is particularly visible in the way participants redesigned their 'signature' (in one case seven times, see pp. 142–4), from the standard form of name, university name and e-mail address, to new versions that included additional information relating to their academic and non-academic identity, and which reflected the overlapping communities to which they belonged. As the students became more confident in computer literacy practices, and in their bids for membership of specific academic discipline communities, they changed their signatures again, to foreground their identity as members of the specific faculties of their degree programme. De Pourbaix comments on the speed at which, within the virtual community, practices emerged, and were altered and adapted.

De Pourbaix shows how the rapid changes in these computer literacy practices are related to students' own aims and changing identity. The electronic conferencing community is a transient one, bringing students from diverse community backgrounds together for just twelve weeks, as part of their induction into other academic communities. Although it facilitates communication across the boundaries of time and space, the community itself has a time-limited function, in contrast, for example, to the community of practising Catholics, which has a history stretching back for hundreds of years, creating additional layers of contextual meaning around contemporary events. However, in both de Pourbaix's and Tusting's studies, literacy events create discourse communities, inducting participants into new contexts.

Conclusion

These New Literacy Studies are part of a continuing argument about the importance of theorising literacy as social and cultural practice, rather than in terms of decontextualised skills and competencies. The studies in this volume have common theoretical and methodological threads in their focus on literacy events and literacy practices, within an anthropological ethnographic tradition of studying the social and cultural aspects of people's uses of literacy in small communities. However, they extend their analysis beyond the local context of these communities, to explore how the meaning of specific literacy events relates to broader social structures and processes. While in many ways the studies provide a continuation of Malinowski's exploration of the 'context of situation' and of Hymes' work on the layering of different contexts within language use to create meaning, they also draw on social constructivist ideas about the relationships between micro and macro contexts, and poststructuralist ideas about intertextuality and discourse, which enable them to deconstruct events and practices, and develop their analysis of the meanings of literacy.

Within the work reported in this volume there is a shift of attention away from events and practices as stable categories, on to the processes which are involved in the mediation of texts through language, and the implications of these processes for the participants involved. The researchers show how literacy events are part of a continual construction and negotiation of identity for people in different kinds of groups and communities, from academic electronic conferences to Catholic parishes, family literacy schemes and prisons. While conceptions of power remain limited within the frameworks of ethnographic thick description, by taking on a Foucauldian notion of discourse, the researchers are able to show how people's subjectivity is shaped through their insertion, via local events, into the broader institutional discourses of, for example, education, agricultural bureaucracy, or the Catholic church. Thus institutional power is diffused throughout the social order, so that it 'reaches into the very grain of individuals, touches their bodies and inserts itself into their actions and attitudes, their discourses, learning processes and everyday lives' (Foucault 1980, p. 39). This insertion is not straightforward, and the intersection of discourses can provide the potential for individual manipulation, as is shown in the case of the prisoners. While the studies in this volume focus mainly on a contemporary analysis of discourses and practices, some authors begin to examine issues of time and change, for example in the formation of student and Catholic identities. The historical construction of discourses and practices is obviously another important aspect of the layering of context in producing meaning, and suggests possibilities for further research.

The researchers in this volume are particularly interested in theorising the precise ways in which local literacy events both reflect and contribute to the constitution of broader social structures. Again, they use the concept of discourse to show how literacy events provide nodal points where there is a dialectic translation of micro-level knowledge, relationships and subjectivity, into macro-level regimes of truth, structural positioning and identity. In addition to micro–macro relationships, literacy events, with their concentrated semiotic potential from the layering of language acting on language, set up semiotic relationships with other texts and events. The researchers explore this through their analysis of intertextuality, which shows how literacy artefacts and images invoke social practices from a range of different social contexts, and how these are drawn on and combined within a specific literacy event. Meaning is thus created partly through the articulation of particular intercontextual choices, for example by children within project work, students designing their virtual signatures, or prisoners in creating their 'third space'. This analysis of the intertextual constitution of meaning, together with the theorisation of how people are inserted, via literacy events, into broader discourses, takes the new literacy studies forwards, with a stronger conceptualisation of power, and of the relationships between micro- and macro-level contexts.

The analyses here would suggest that literacy practices, like languages, are 'heteroglot from top to bottom' (Bakhtin 1981, p. 291), so that we need a term beyond intertextuality, intercontextuality or interdiscursivity to capture the sense in which social practice itself is made up of the articulation of a complex web of interrelated meanings. While processes of interdiscursivity and discursive hybridity have been identified as important indicators of social change (Fairclough 1992, 1996), the research reported in this book shows that the articulation of different discourses is centrally and dynamically interwoven in people's everyday literacy activities. In this sense literacy events represent the instantiation of an unstable, contested ideological world within everyday verbal exchange, and these studies analyse some of the complex processes through which individual identity, social relationships and institutional structures are instantiated and negotiated through what people actually say and do with texts.

References

Bakhtin, M. (1981) 'Discourse in the Novel', in *The Dialogic Imagination*, Austin: University of Texas Press.

Bakhtin, M. (1986) *Speech Genres and Other Late Essays*, eds Caryl Emerson and Michael Holquist, Austin: University of Texas Press.

Basic Skills Agency (1995) *Developing Family Literacy*, London: Basic Skills Unit.

Bhaba, H.K. (1994) *The Location of Culture*, London: Routledge.

Fairclough, N. (1992) *Discourse and Social Change*, Cambridge: Polity Press.

Fairclough, N. (1996) 'Border Crossings: Discourse and Social Change in Contemporary Societies', in H. Coleman and L. Cameron (eds) *Change and Language*, Clevedon: BAAL in association with Multilingual Matters, pp. 3–17.

Foucault, M. (1980) *Power/Knowledge: Selected Interviews and Other Writings 1972–9*, ed. Colin Gordan, London: Harvester Press.

Foucault, M. (1981) 'The Order of Discourse', in R. Young (ed.) *Untying the Text: A Post-structuralist Reader*, London: Routledge & Kegan Paul.

Giddens, A. (1990) *The Consequences of Modernity*, Cambridge: Polity Press.

Heath, S.B. (1983) *Ways with Words*, Cambridge: Cambridge University Press.

Hymes, D. (1968) 'The Ethnography of Speaking', in J. Fishman (ed.) *Readings on the Sociology of Language*, The Hague: Mouton, pp. 99–139.

Hymes, D. (1977) *Foundations in Sociolinguistics: An Ethnographic Approach*, London: Tavistock.

Malinowski, B. (1923) 'The Problem of Meaning in Primitive Languages', in C.K. Ogden and M.A. Richards, *The Meaning of Meaning*, London: Kegan Paul, Trench, Trubner.

Rose, N. (1989) *Governing the Soul: The Shaping of the Private Self*, London: Routledge.

Street (1995) *Social Literacies: Critical Approaches to Literacy in Development, Ethnography and Education*, London: Longman.

Volosinov, V.N. (1986) *Marxism and the Philosophy of Language*, trans. by L. Matejka and I. R. Titunik, Cambridge, MA: Harvard University Press.

13

NEW LITERACY STUDIES AT THE INTERCHANGE

Karin Tusting, Roz Ivanič and Anita Wilson

As the writers of this chapter we feel strongly that the reader should not see it as either a postscript which we have merely tacked on or a post-mortem on something which has finished. Neither is it merely an addition or an aside to the individual chapters. Rather we would like it to be seen as a means by which to express the collective voice of those who are re-presented here and hope that the comments we articulate will be carried forward into the work of others. We have written this final piece not as any form of closure, but as more of an interchange which we came to via a number of routes and left by others, having gone round in a number of thought-provoking circles! We invite the reader to do the same, and feel that the themes which we discuss in this chapter may provide sign-posts to a number of fundamentally important avenues along which to truly expand the New Literacy Studies.

The time we spent together preparing this chapter involved collecting the thoughts of a gathering which brought together Lancaster Literacy Research Group members and colleagues from a variety of other research environments. The notion of 'expanding' the New Literacy Studies not only drew us together through a common wish to look at theory and practice in new and exciting ways but also allowed us the opportunity to 're-diversify' and develop new variations on the themes we were already exploring. Through discussion informed by all the papers, interesting links, themes and angles on literacy of which we might not previously have been aware began to emerge. This not only drew the work presented in this volume together in unexpected ways but inspired us to look again at it in the light of the emerging themes. In this chapter we are attempting to include the main themes from these fruitful discussions which produced ideas ripe for development in future research in the New Literacy Studies.

The thematic diversity was almost overwhelming and we have tried to pull out – in order to pull together – those issues which people found of

particular interest. These themes were not imposed in advance but grew out of our discussions and were made explicit as foci for discussion as they became apparent. We gathered together all observations and listened to the tape-recordings of the group discussions before we began to write this interchange. When we studied these themes retrospectively we found that they were all present and significant in various ways or at various times and to greater or lesser extents in the discussions. As a way of giving some sense of direction we are sign-posting themes as they occur in the text by placing them in bold type. We hope that this approach will serve as a useful means by which to open up both the notion of the pervasiveness of the themes and the myriad ways in which the reader can re-create them. What follows is a collective voice, pitched at two levels – one: the voice of those who wrote this chapter, and the other: the represented voice of all the contributors.

In addition to making unexpected links between our various projects, we found that the themes could be applied specifically to aspects of methodology. The theme of **presence and absence** was a broad and pervasive one, one aspect of which was the inclusion of ourselves, as researchers, as present in many of the issues we addressed. We were adventurous, not only in our approach to the initial theme of the book – Expanding the New Literacy Studies – but also as we reflected on our existing practices, theories and approaches through self-appraisal and critique. This allowed us to take a fresh look at our existing presence as researchers: not only at what we research or at the way we do it, but also at other aspects which had remained implicit rather than explicit parts of our work.

Acknowledging issues around **social responsibility** in our work involved looking at ourselves and this promoted a defence of some aspects of our work and a critique of others. We felt that in our own work we need to retain our focus on qualitative work, on ethnography and the heterogeneity of small-scale research as a balance against the autonomy of grand narratives. But we also accepted that we have a sense of social responsibility to those we research alongside – an issue which figured strongly in discussion – and we felt that we should take our theories forward, seeking to bring them in from the margins at which we often work. 'Working between the cracks' is no longer sufficient; we often found ourselves questioning who the theories were written for, who they were about and who would benefit from them.

These thoughts tied in to notions of **change** and we addressed the continuing need to challenge and change public perceptions of literacy. We addressed issues of globalisation, localisation and improvisation under the theme of change, not only in the spaces where literacies are at work – as we discuss later – but in the changing roles of all those involved in the research process, noting that change could be facilitated by individual and group effort. We also highlighted a developmental change in the shifting definitions and foci of literacy studies over a period of time.

We felt that we should be braver – making our attacks on **power structures** more explicit – particularly with reference to institutional literacies. There is a need to work out how different literacies are situated in different social spaces within institutions and show how literacy practices contribute to the (re)production of existing structures. The inclusion of a symmetrical approach (as introduced in Simon Pardoe's study, Chapter 9) was felt to be a way forward as a means by which to redress the imbalance of power in relation to the people we studied with. Instantiations of **symmetry** appeared in unexpected and exciting ways. Seemingly incommensurable research sites found a common theme and it was noted that symmetry could be mobilised as a vehicle by which to help theorise the relation of research and practice in Adult Basic Education. Discussing the ways by which to redress the inequity of dominant power structures, acknowledging the changing environment of literacy studies and taking our theories forward all required that we look again at the spaces in which we worked and the spaces we needed to find.

Other themes emerged as tools for refining New Literacy Studies theory and for pushing forward research in the field. We discussed how to **theorise texts and practices in an integrated way** in order to develop new analytical frameworks for future studies of situated literacy. Here we attempt to sketch out the ways in which these concepts are being defined and used in the New Literacy Studies, to share our explorations of possible alternative definitions, and to show the connections which we have been making between them.

The term **practices** is central in a New Literacy Studies approach to literacy. The term is used in two ways:

(a) To refer to observable, collectable and/or documentable specific ethnographic detail of situated literacy events, involving real people, relationships, purposes, actions, places, times, circumstances, feelings, tools and resources.

The term 'practices' in this sense often *contrasts with, and hence complements* the term 'texts', since it refers to those other aspects of literacy which go beyond the text itself.

(b) To refer to culturally recognisable patterns of behaviour, which can be generalised from the observation of specifics.

The term 'practices' in this sense often *includes* 'textual practices': the culturally recognisable patterns for constructing texts.

The process of recognising 'literacy practices' in sense (b) involves identifying the values, beliefs and power relations which sustain them (see David Barton's study, Chapter 10). The term 'practices' is particularly powerful in the New Literacy Studies because it makes the connection between ethnographic detail and theory. However, it is potentially confusing, because it is often used in the two senses indiscriminately. There was some feeling that it should be reserved for the second.

Several types of literacy practices can be identified: two important ones are, first, the social practices which give written language its purposes, in which the production and use of written texts is embedded; and second, the technological, interpersonal, cognitive and textual practices which are associated with the production and use of written texts. Practices therefore involve many processes; viewed in this way, texts become quite a small element of an account of practices: just the outcomes of writing-for-a-social-purpose, and the sources which are read-for-a-social-purpose. And language within texts plays an even smaller role: just one part of the material, visual and linguistic meaning-carrying whole. On the one hand, it is important to recognise this embeddedness of texts and 'keep them in their place'. On the other hand, it is important not to forget that 'textual practices' (material, visual and linguistic) are worthy of attention alongside all the other sorts of practices which are relevant to the study of situated literacies – an integration which is illustrated particularly by Kathy Pitt's study, in Chapter 7.

Two meanings of **embedding** were opened up in our discussions in relation to literacy. Firstly there is the fundamental observation of the New Literacy Studies that a text and the literacy-related behaviour associated with it are always embedded in a social practice – as referred to above. This meaning of embedding is linked to the question of the **boundaries** of the term literacy events. Raised explicitly in Mary Hamilton's chapter (Chapter 2), it is also a more generally salient question: how central does literacy have to be to an event for it to be called a 'literacy' event? There are some social practices in which literacy is relatively constitutive of the practice: for example, the social practices of letter writing or newspaper reading would not exist without literacy. In other arenas, literacy can be ancillary, playing little or no role in some social practices: for example, it does not play a big role in parking a car. Sometimes literacy can even 'disappear' when you're very familiar with a social practice. But foregrounding it can be a political act; to continue the previous example, when a parking attendant issues a fine for illegal parking, literacy is foregrounded, both in the parking ticket itself and in the notices posted on the street which state the parking regulations.

The second meaning of embedding in relation to literacy is the way in which written language embeds everyday, lived experience into abstract, bureaucratic reality, a reality in which people are dispensable and interchangeable (see Kathryn Jones's study, in Chapter 5). One of the most important roles of literacy is the transcendence of **time**; making a record of something locally present in order that it may be reconstructed/ remembered/drawn on in the future when the event itself will be absent. Local historicity – the materially, visually, temporally present – is inscribed into a future, non-material, abstract, probably virtual bureaucratic order. One of the means by which literacy transforms time and regulates change, making the temporary permanent, and the concrete abstract, is through the use of bureaucratic language and literacy. Legislation shapes bureaucratic texts which are invariably written and hence can perform this function of 'embedding' the local in the global.

Practices in the sense of culturally recognisable patterns of behaviour often co-occur in recognisable configurations – Gee calls these configurations of ways of being, doing, reacting, using space, thinking, and using language **Discourses**. For example, working in isolation at a desk, using a computer and unlined paper, producing texts with high lexical density, few social actors, little or no reference to emotions and senses, and producing uniform lines of typed black text without graphics are a configuration of literacy practices associated with a traditional academic Discourse. People contribute towards sustaining one Discourse rather than another by entering into the practices associated with it. Contributors recognised the concept of Discourses as a way of theorising diverse aspects of their data in a coherent way. Discourses constitute and are constituted by social realities, social relations and social identities, and different Discourses do so in different ways.

It therefore became apparent that there are several types of **relationships between texts, literacy and social practices**, which we suggest are worth elaborating on in future literacy research: texts are always motivated by social practices; textual practices are a sub-set of literacy practices in general, and are necessary but not sufficient to the formation of Discourses; and the visual and material aspects of texts are traces of some of the practices which produced them (as Fiona Ormerod and Roz Ivanič discuss in Chapter 6).

Questions of **presence and absence**, as has already been mentioned, underlie many of the issues raised. This was most evident in Mary Hamilton's study (Chapter 2) where a distinction was made between **visible and invisible** elements of a literacy event. This distinction is by no means a clear one. First, what is 'visible' and 'invisible' in a literacy event is to a large extent determined by the observer's pre-existing framework and knowledge of Discourses involved. The same visual phenomenon – for example, 'a businessman reading a newspaper' – could be interpreted very differently by someone from a culture where 'man in suit' does not signify 'businessman' and 'black and white collection of loose pages' does not signify 'newspaper'. The newspaper is present in a **material** sense, but that which makes it mean 'newspaper' is not. This knowledge of cultural practices is 'present' in the event, but in a very different way; we can posit this knowledge on the part of those engaged in the event, but cannot point to it or touch it in the same way as we can a newspaper. Presence and absence are therefore not binary opposites, nor even a continuum of possibilities, but overarching terms for some very different phenomena. What is 'there' and in what way it is 'there' – what practices and events consist of – is becoming a much more complex question than the paradigm examples of a literacy event, 'someone writing a letter' for example, might lead us to imagine.

So, there is a material present – things that can be touched. There is a visual present – things that can be seen. Both of these presences are only given meaning through pre-existing observers' frameworks. But there is another distinction between **visible and invisible** that becomes salient in chapters dealing with 'hidden' literacies. Anita Wilson's discussion of third-space theory (Chapter 4) makes us aware that some literacies, while very visual and visible in the sense that they are material and can be directly observed, are not in a space defined by the system as producing 'permitted' literacies and are therefore made 'officially' invisible. While the events are visible to those engaged in them, and can become visible to representatives of the system, 'official' invisibility is necessary to escape punishment and to maintain the practices over time. In the third space of the title, members both of the dominant system – the prison – and of the dominated – the prisoners – collude in negotiating the relative visibility and invisibility of particular practices and events. The same event might be made visible – and therefore punishable – or invisible in different contexts, on different days, with different people. The negotiation of the visibility or invisibility of subversive literacy events is more complex than simply whether something can or cannot be seen. This negotiation differs from one context to another.

The awareness of the different layers and possibilities of presences and absences has implications for **the theorisation of literacy practices and literacy events**. Only literacy events ever 'happen' in reality, that is to say come to presence directly. However these events are seen as instantiating practices (at least by literacy researchers with a particular pre-existing theoretical framework!). And some aspects of these practices are never made material in literacy events; practices also consist of attitudes to and beliefs about literacy. So a distinction can be made between the tangible, material present and those aspects posited to be part of the people involved. Within this, some aspects of practice can be brought to presence in consciousness – such as explicit beliefs about different literacies – and therefore investigated by the researcher through interviews or diaries. However, other aspects may be purely unconscious, built up through experience over long periods of time, as an accumulation of past events and experiences which is not open to direct reflection. These 'absent' aspects can only be brought to presence through extrapolating theory from observation. What does this imply for our theorisation of practices?

We also discussed the **relationships among literacies**. Different literacies have meaning and relevance only in terms of their relationships with other literacies and cultures. The meaning of any present event is constructed with relation to what it is not, to other things that are known to exist within the same system, knowledge of which is one of the things which makes up people's cultural frameworks. These absences are what give the presences meaning; while they are absent in the material sense, they are brought to presence through their role in meaning-making.

It is in terms of different literacies' relationships with each other that some are legitimated and others not. These relationships have been constructed over time, and are in a state of continual evolution. However some literacies gain power and dominance through the relationships appearing to be fixed and stable. People's **roles and identities** also play an important part in legitimating particular literacies. Literacies are partially legitimated through the statuses and roles of people engaged in them. Roles and identities change according to where people are and what activities they are engaged in, and legitimated literacies change with them.

This **legitimation** is a constantly evolving process which relies on being seen as permanent and constant for its force. Literacies rely on being seen as 'always' or 'naturally' dominant to be legitimised. One of the important ways in which the New Literacy Studies could continue to counter the hegemonic dominance of particular literacies and institutions is to focus on change, on the temporal and cultural specificity and contingency of particular literacy practices within particular institutions. One of the critical tasks of the New Literacy Studies is to make visible, or to bring to presence, the process-based and therefore challengeable nature of the dominance of particular literacies.

The question of what a **domain** consists of and whether or not it is a useful concept was also raised. Often 'domain' can be defined in rather static terms; the frequently-used examples of work-place, home and school focus on site as a definer of domain. However aspects other than space – for example, time – can also define domains. Anita Wilson's chapter (Chapter 4) emphasised the fact that at one site there may be several competing spaces within which different literacies are practised and differently legitimated. At any one site there may be many different Discourses and competing epistemologies, making the definition of a 'domain' in practice rather more difficult than it might initially seem.

The term **space** is sometimes used interchangeably with the term 'site' to refer to actual, physical environments, or to refer to smaller parts of sites. Practices and text-types associated with different domains can vary from space to space, and can be intermixed within a single space. Space in this sense is a very concrete concept, part of the object of ethnographic study. But the term 'space' can also be used metaphorically, for example in referring to 'mental spaces' and 'social spaces'. Looking at space from a slightly different perspective, the way in which a physical space is treated is in itself a social practice, and hence also an element in a Discourse (as we mentioned in the discussion of the term 'Discourses'). For example, a classroom is a space which figures differently in different Discourses: in one Discourse it may act as a boundary, neatly divided into further, isolated spaces for each learner; in a different pedagogic Discourse it may act as an open resource, with constant movement from one such space to another, and learners moving freely around it.

Change also became a significant topic of discussion. Linking with the concept of **time**, a thread raised in Karin Tusting's chapter (Chapter 3) and running through many of our discussions, it became evident that change and time in literacy practices can often be overlooked because both are particularly difficult to document. Neither change nor time are visible, or present in a tangible way. A photograph cannot show change or time. However both are important concepts to make part of our theoretical framework. Without an understanding of change and time, it would be impossible to see the evolution of dominant literacy practices, the development of literacies within wider social and cultural change (James Paul Gee's 'new work order' for example), or the changes in people's lives relating to new literacy practices.

The environments within which we research are constantly changing and this is something of which we must be aware. The rapid change in literacy practices we are experiencing through the advance of computer technology calls for the expansion of the New Literacy Studies to deal with the virtual dimension. This requires rethinking our concepts of space, time, visuality, materiality, presence and absence. We can take Renata de Pourbaix's study (Chapter 8) as a concrete example of changes in literacy practices linked to social and cultural – in this case, technological – change. In this chapter a virtual community is created which is present in a very different way from a community in real time and space, but clearly still very much exists, with its own relationships, practices and legitimate and illegitimate literacies. This virtual environment is mediated by literacy, but a literacy which is very differently present from the paradigm concept of 'words on paper'. Only materially present as a hard disk somewhere, it can be called up at any time and at any place throughout the world with an Internet-linked computer.

The aim of writing this interchange has been to take the reader along some of the routes we travelled while compiling the chapters for this book and in the discussions which led to it. We see it as a beginning, rather than as an ending, and encourage everyone who joined us on the interchange to carry on travelling, either by taking the routes we have sign-posted here or by finding new routes and directions of their own.

INDEX

Printed in the United States
44653LVS00001B/271-300

9 780415 206716